LONG ROAD TO THE COTTAGE

Norman Prescott

LONG ROAD TO THE COTTAGE

BY THE SAME AUTHOR

'A BOY FROM GLASGOW STREET'

NORMAN PASCOE

© Norman Pascoe, 2015

Published by Easter Morn Publishing

www.nowty999@gmail.com

A CIP catalogue record for this book is available from the British Library.

ISBN 978-0-9929563-3-2 (Paperback)
ISBN 978-0-9929563-4-9 (epub)
ISBN 978-0-9929563-5-6 (mobi)

Book layout and cover design by Clare Brayshaw

Prepared and printed by:

York Publishing Services Ltd
64 Hallfield Road
Layerthorpe
York YO31 7ZQ

Tel: 01904 431213

Website: www.yps-publishing.co.uk

PROLOGUE

This book the second and last of my autobiography, is my life after meeting the most caring and wonderful woman a man could ever meet. My lovely five step children, grandchildren and great grandchildren whom became the heart of my world for the last nearly forty years. The different exciting jobs and characters I met along my journey will hopefully interest my readers, give them a good laugh and entertaining read. I never dreamt all those years ago as a boy in Glasgow Street that so many adventures and unique people would enter my life. From meeting a good mate down the sewers, also a great friend Richard, an author and a Lord on safari in far off Kenya. Possibly my biggest surprise was finding out my friend and ex crew mate on our trawler, being arrested as a spy for trying to sell a top secret item to the Russian Embassy for $4.8 million dollars.

A donation from each book will go to our village Duddon Inshore Rescue boat just like my first book "A Boy from Glasgow Street."

ACKNOWLEDGEMENTS

A great big thank you goes to my beautiful wife Pauline for all her support and love over the years, and to Duncan and the professional team at YPS. Not forgetting the support of all the Askam villagers and local people who bought my first book. The first edition soon sold out and this necessitated a second printing, this was amazing. I have needed to change some names; I do not want to embarrass anyone in any way. All the mistakes I apologise unreservedly for. My favourite teacher from school got in touch after reading "A Boy from Glasgow Street" saying how proud of me he was. Thank you Geoff Gibbons that meant the world to me, you were truly an inspiration to me and many other school children!

The money from my first book was used to upgrade some much needed equipment for our village inshore lifeboat; our boat is totally funded by our local supporters since 1969. Our local Evening Mail and Westmorland Gazette have given us some free publicity; FAFB website donated a year's free advertising, a big thank you Dave, and not forgetting Cormac editor of Fishing News. Kevin from Radio Cumbria did a fantastic daily radio show called 'My Life' with me telling my story of growing up in 59 Glasgow Street in the 1950's, the result was the book sales shot up.

CONTENTS

CHAPTER ONE

LONG ROAD TO THE COTTAGE

The boat heeled over as a fierce gust of wind roared in over the estuary causing the petite brown haired girl to grasp the rail with one hand, and tighten her grip on the trawl warp with the other. "For God's sake don't let go of that rope" I shouted above the wind. Knocking the engine out of gear I rushed to help her as the boat became beam on to tide and wind, her side decks dipping dangerously under the waves. The orange mesh of the trawl appeared nearing the surface, as we both heaved with all our strength to pull in the heavy net. The cod end of the net floated high in the water full of large cod thrashing and flapping, trying to find a way out to freedom. "That is some catch of fish" I said "The problem is can we manage to get the net aboard in this weather."

The girl turned her head toward me saying calmly "No problem Norm between us we will manage!" Pauline my wife never ceased to amaze, she genuinely loved every minute of her time spent crewing for me on my trawler. I told everyone she was the best deckhand I ever had by far. We eventually dragged the ropes and net aboard, emptied the cod end of its mass of sea life dredged up from several hours of trawling in the shallow water of Ulverston channel in Morecambe bay. Pauline discarded her bright orange waterproofs, and after hanging them up behind the wheelhouse door, proceeded to steer the boat with deft occasional adjustments towards the distant white painted Walney Island lighthouse. I looked down at the seething mass of sea life flapping and writhing in the fish pound, the variety never ceased to fill me with wonder. Huge cod, skate, whiting, and plaice with bright red spots so bright they looked like they had just been painted on. Colourful sea anemones, cuttlefish, starfish, seaweed, crabs and a large blue lobster which told me my net had passed over some rough ground, I knew we had been extremely lucky to have got away without ripping our trawl net.

A hand holding a mug of tea appeared out of the wheelhouse door, closely followed by a huge slice of Pauline's homemade meat pie. "Grab this Norm and have a rest before you start gutting the fish, or would you prefer if I did that and you steered the boat?" Not for the first time did I realise I had won life's lottery falling in love with this very special woman. My sister Jean had introduced me to her friend Pauline in the Harbour pub one night, and I was immediately attracted to her warmth and lovely smile. We made a date for the following Saturday. To my sister and Pauline's annoyance I cancelled the date when told Pauline was divorced, was thirteen years older than me and was the proud mother of five children!

After the biggest telling off I have ever had from my sister about breaking my promise about the date, and letting a lovely lady down, a new date was arranged. On the next date, I of course turned up and to my surprise got on like a house on fire, arranging to meet Pauline's children the next weekend. Driving to Askam village to meet my new girl friend's children I was understandably nervous wondering if I was taking a step too far. Parking at the back of a row of terraced houses similar to Glasgow Street where I lived, I spotted the backyard door open. I stood looking in amazement at the sight of thirty or so large salmon spread out on a canvas sheet and a young lad looking up with surprise at my sudden appearance.

"Bloody hell who are you?" the young boy said, looking surprised.

I laughed and said "Relax, it is not the Fisheries men, your secret is safe with me, where the hell did you get all those salmon from?"

"First who are you?" he asked, looking at me suspiciously.

"My name is Norm and I am here to see your mum, you must be Tony she has told me what a good fisherman you are."

"I caught them netting in the estuary this morning and am just going round the village to sell them for my pocket money, I will see you later maybe." A lad after my own heart I thought, not sitting on his backside he is out earning his own money, full marks to him. Pauline opened the door with a big smile and giving me a hug invited me inside, where three delightful pretty girls were waiting to shake my hand. Eldest was Elaine, Marian and then Susan, Raymond or Tammy to everyone who knew him was introduced to me later.

Pauline and I had a walk along the lovely Askam shoreline getting to know each other and talking about our families. I was beginning to fall in love for the first time in my life but envisaged many difficulties to overcome in the future. Pauline invited me in for tea, not surprisingly it was fresh salmon cooked to perfection, what else would it be? After tea we had a couple of drinks in one of the village pubs, and walking her home afterwards Pauline's youngest child Susan invited me in for supper. The lights had been dimmed in the lounge, and a coffee table adorned with a white cloth had a single candle lit. On the table the girls had put sandwiches and cream crackers out for us. To say I was touched is an understatement, what a lovely thought. Driving the nine miles back to my house in Glasgow Street in the shipbuilding town of Barrow that night, I could feel that my life was going to change dramatically forever.

Two weeks after meeting Pauline to her surprise I asked her to marry me and passed over an engagement ring. "Do you need time to think about it love," I said, knowing it had been two years since her divorce.

She looked me straight in the eyes and said "Yes I would love to marry you, but I must tell you that my children can be an handful, also the age gap could become an issue, so would not blame you if you preferred to just stay friends".

My reply was I love her and so must love her children as well, knowing the age gap was an issue and the five children in the equation was probably going to make the relationship fail. "I said talk is cheap we will have to prove to everyone who doubts us, that over time we can make it work". We celebrated our engagement with a bottle of wine from the village shop, cakes and pop for the kids. Truth was I was financially embarrassed after borrowing the money from my best mate to buy the ring and needed a lucrative boat charter to make me solvent again. I lost count of the people who enjoyed telling me I was mad and heading for disaster, fair enough the odds were stacked against us, but love finds a way. My lovely sister Jean was over the moon for one and my parents said that I must be barmy; dad mentioned that he had dropped me on my head when I was a baby!

CHAPTER TWO

THE BARGE

Lucky or what! Just when you need a break fate takes a hand, I had a phone call from a guy who owned a plant hire business, and I was to meet him at the Majestic hotel to discuss a charter for my boat Silver Spray. This was a hell of a contract to tow a huge barge being assembled in the Graving dock at Barrow, (now part of The Dock Museum) into Walney channel and northwards to Scarf Hole where the barge would anchor, and over several tides an effluent discharge pipe from British Cellophane factory was to be laid under the sands and into a deep hole in the middle of the channel. The barge was to carry a huge tracked crane, with different types of grabs, portable cabins and tons of equipment. I told the contractor that due to the size and weight of the barge I would have to hire at least three other small boats for the tow up channel. "No problem Norm I will leave it all up to you the boating side of the job." I was told to meet the contractor in Barrow graving dock at high water where the barge would be ready to leave in two weeks time.

The due day arrived, and on a perfect calm day my four boats were tied alongside the bull nose quay at Ferry beach, the skippers adjusting tow ropes and taking the piss out of each other but mostly me. Judd the skipper of the Empress shouted to me "Norm who ordered those five boats coming through the Jubilee Bridge they look like the Roa Island lad's, we don't need them for God's sake!

The five rival boats rafted alongside us and everybody started talking at once. It seemed like the contractor had edged his bets and overbooked. The contractor looked at this small armada of boats and a load of angry men and said "Sort it out among yourselves I am only paying for one squad and not two!

There were ten men from Roa Island and eight men on the Ferry Beach boats and all getting aggressive by the minute. I said to the rival boat's leader that the job was on our patch, and it was my living, all his men had jobs to go to. Next minute someone threw a punch, all hell broke loose. Next thing the rival gang threw off the mooring ropes and headed back down channel, shouting obscenities and threats. "That's settled lads, now we can start work at last" I said.

Judd said "You can get stuffed Norm you could not organise a piss up in a brewery, I am going home." Followed by the other boat's crews leaving me and my buddy Brian all alone. A red faced angry contractor stormed up to me shouting,

"What the hell is going on Norm, where are the other boats? I said get rid of one squad not the whole bloody fleet!

"I am going now, it is entirely all your fault that everyone got up early this morning and are going home with no wages" I said.

"You cannot let me down Norm I have thirty men on a loaded barge in the Graving dock and the tide starting to ebb; I am up the creek without a paddle! Get your lads back and I will pay double what you asked for originally.

I weighed up that I could get one more boat, George the skipper was still aboard and I waved him back over. With the promise of double the charter rate George was happy, and the contractor was willing to pay the Ferry Beach lads the money they had lost by going home. This kept me on good terms with my local boat men, the Roa Island men would just have to live with it. The tide flowed north for two hours after high water so all we had to do was let the tide do the work, and we could almost drift down with it. I informed the barge skipper by radio when to let go his anchor. Using the tidal flow, George towing with the Barracuda and me on the barge's stern, we eventually reached the allotted position much to the contractor's amazement, achieving the task with only two small boats. I was promised more work on this particular job and a survey contract as well so things were looking up. George did a grand job and I promised him the job of towing the barge back on completion. When I got back to

Ferry Beach I was greeted by some very aggressive friends wondering why I had agreed to do the job without them. Their frowns soon left when I paid them in cash for not even having to do the job. All's well that ends well!

CHAPTER THREE

MARRIED LIFE

Now that we were engaged Pauline asked me to move into her terraced house in Askam village, where gradually we all got used to each other's little ways. What a learning curve it was for me, the eldest child was only six years younger than me so I did not know whether to act like a friend or a step parent. Mistakes I made by the dozen over the next few months and all because of me feeling like a fish out of water. Looking back over the years I realised slowly that there is no right or wrong way, everyone is different and even if I was their biological parent, mistakes would still be made. The youngest two children were still at school and the others started full time working. I was very lucky to have joined such a close knit family, and I could see how much all the children adored their mother, how respectful and good mannered they all were. Any problems were caused by my inexperience and not any of the children.

Over the coming years we all grew even closer when I realised that I had to earn my step children's respect by actions and not just words. Quite soon after I moved in permanently we set a date to get married. We lost count of the people, including family who advised us not to take the marriage commitment, and doubt closed in on some of these occasions. Pauline and I took on board all this so called well intentioned advice, and decided to go with our hearts and not our heads. It was a good job we did, being still together after nearly forty years and still just as much in love, the family grown from five step children to ten grandchildren, and six great grand children. The children were excited about our forth coming wedding, but first our eldest daughter Elaine and her fiancé Chris were to be married in our local beautiful church. The ancient building sat on a steep hill overlooking the village with breath taking views over our beautiful Duddon estuary and the Lakeland Mountains. The reception was held in quite a posh venue in Barrow and very well attended; Elaine looking stunning dressed in a lovely white dress. Our wedding in contrast was going to be a very low key affair due to our lack of funds. Only a very few close family were invited to the registry office and afterwards a town centre pub where a meal was laid on upstairs. I was still supporting my aged parents in Glasgow Street, and dropping in regularly to check and pay the final demand bills that my mother still stashed behind the clock on the mantel piece. Mother still could not run a house budget even for two people and had become so used to me paying for everything. I would call in on a freezing cold day to see the coal bunker empty and those two sitting in a freezing house, I could not just walk away. A quick drive to the coal yard for a bag of coal, and a sack of kindling wood to put them on with, also pay for ten bags of coal to be delivered sometime later in the week. Throwing a chainsaw into the back of my land rover I drove along the tide line of Walney Island, cutting up all the tree trunks washed up after the last storms had deposited them ashore. When I could not fit any more logs in my vehicle, I stacked the logs in dad's backyard so he could supplement the coal, thus saving me money. Dad was highly delighted with this and I felt good being appreciated, being the last to leave home I felt responsible for them, and all my siblings were married with small children, they did not have any money to spare. When I was not out fishing because of bad weather I placed an advert in the local paper to remove house hold rubbish, and sacks of logs to be delivered locally. To my amazement I received quite a few enquiries and realized I might have a chance of keeping two houses going after all, especially when the fishing was poor.

Pauline was working at Glaxo in Ulverston in the catering department, evenings we both spent decorating mum's house to brighten the place up for them. It was Pauline's idea she was so kind hearted always thinking about other people. The day of the wedding arrived, a beautiful morning in May and I was extremely nervous, in fact I felt the same way when I was summoned for an interview with the Inland Revenue manager a month earlier. My best man Brian (from my trawler days) turned up at Glasgow Street with six mates, for a pre- wedding drink at ten in the morning. Dad declined to come to the wedding so nipped to the corner shop for some more beers. The wedding was not booked until after lunch, so Brian decided that we should move nearer to the Registry Office which was quite near the Theatre bar in the Barrow town centre. The gin and tonics flowed and the hours passed, my nerves had gone and I clean forgot that I was even going to be married. I had never been so drunk before or since, the bar owner sent out for more bottles of gin, we had cleaned out all his stock. The bar owner asked who it was that was getting married, and on being told it was the little fellow slumped in the chair with the terrible voice, singing "I'm getting married in the morning ding dong the bell's are going to chime!" He proceeded to force black scalding coffee down my throat, which instantly raised huge blisters on my lips. "You are a bloody idiot mate! It is going to be a wedding day disaster; no sane woman would marry a man who turned up in your state," he pointed out.

My eldest stepson Tammy who was with us said "He's right Norm, my mum's going to kill you." My other stepson Tony asked if it was all right to miss the wedding ceremony he needed to catch the tide, the salmon were in the estuary, and he would come to the party in the Wellington pub in Dalton later that night. "Some best man you turned out to be Brian, I thought you were supposed to be looking after me!" I mumbled through hugely swelling lips.

"Bloody hell Norm you look like 'John Merrick' the elephant man, if I was you I would do a runner, the wedding photographer may as well bugger off home!" I said there would be no wedding photographer we could not afford it. Before the discussions turned into a fight the barman herded us all out of the door and in the direction we needed to go, saying he did not expect to see us again, even though Pauline had booked his pub for the after wedding reception.

Through a drunken haze I spotted the guests waiting outside the Registry Office in Duke Street, there seemed to be a lot more than were officially invited, and that was me seeing double being taken into account. I spotted Pauline and bridesmaid sister Jean glaring at me, and I thought if looks could kill.

"Have you been drinking Norm?" Pauline hissed.

"I am so ashamed of you Norm!" Jean hissed.

"Only had one to steady my nerves love, honest," I said.

I was literally saved by the lady registrar telling Pauline that she was ready for us and would the guests file in and take a seat.

Pauline glared at me and said "What has happened to your face it has all swelled up; you need to go to hospital, what on earth happened to you?" I will explain later, I managed to mumble through lips that felt like two balloons. Managing to stay upright unaided was an achievement for me, and to the Registrar's credit, I only had to repeat my vows three times before she was satisfied that all was legal. It may have been my imagination, but I had the distinct impression that everyone in the room, including Pauline were mentally calculating how this could be the shortest wedding in history. Outside the designated wedding photographer, who happened to be our Jean's husband, was told to not take any close up pictures of the bride and groom. In fact he was told by Pauline to keep moving away further and further from us, that is why there are no close ups of our wedding day.

So we all started to walk to the nearby Theatre Bar for our reception. Pauline was asking me, "Why has all these people turned up and are now following us to the pub, you did tell them the meal was just for thirty and I counted sixty including the children?"

"Don't worry love, I will sort it with the landlord, I was sure that all my family and friends had been told the arrangements, but maybe not! The landlord's first words were, "Bloody hell Norm has the wedding gone ahead? I am utterly amazed. Everything is ready upstairs for thirty people but a bloody coach party as just turned up!"

"That's not a coach party it is all the people that were not supposed to be here, can you set some more places and I mean quick, my new wife looks as if she is going to take her children and drive off any moment now!"

To the landlords credit he played a blinder, saying "Best I can do at short notice Norm, is ham and eggs for the adults, fish fingers and chips for the kids, followed by ice cream."

I could have hugged the man.

Catching Pauline, the kids and my sister Jean just about to drive off, I shouted that I had sorted everything out and it was all right to come back inside. Peace restored at last we all settled down to enjoy the dinner, me thinking how the hell I was going to find the money for the extra meals. The speeches seemed to go down well, even Pauline said I bought the house down with my very witty, off the cuff speech; it must have been the alcohol inspired me. I solved the problem of paying the landlord, Brian the best man settled up. The night do went well in the Wellington pub in Dalton, the place was packed with well wishers and everyone seemed to have a great night. I apologised to my new wife and family, promising that I would never ever get into a state like that again. This vow I did keep for nearly forty years, putting my bad behaviour down to wedding and step children nerves. Pauline had the good grace to give me one last chance and I took it.

Mind you Pauline's two boys could be a handful at times; I left my old beat up fish van on the grass outside of her house and drove off for the day in Pauline's mini car. When I came to drive mine the petrol tank was always empty. I spent hours under my vehicle looking for the source of petrol leak, but to no avail, it became an unsolvable mystery. That is until twenty years later when my stepson Tony admitted to hot wiring my van, and the gang used it to race along Askam beach having a whale of a time. Another time we came home early to find a Transit van hurtling along the beach, our Tony forty feet in the air on a parachute and harness, tethered by a long rope, and his brother Tammy and best mate Rip Kirkby driving. They were just as wild as the Glasgow Street boys, never a dull moment in our village! It was no small wonder that I felt at home in Askam!

Our Tony was a lot like me always bringing home rabbits, ducks and fish for his family, like me he was always outdoors, sometimes big brother Tammy went along with him. Tammy went into rugby and played for Askam rugby league for many years, Tony did occasionally but like me fishing was his passion. Eventually he like me became a successful skipper/owner of his own fishing boat.

The first birthday I had whilst moving in with Pauline was a great surprise for me. Walking into the house at teatime after coming home from fishing, all the kid's were sat around the table, on which sat the first birthday cake I had ever had, complete with candles, homemade cakes as well. With the candles lit and my new family singing happy birthday I had a massive lump in my throat.

CHAPTER FOUR

WORKING ON THE RAILWAY

It was lovely living with Pauline's children in the little terraced house, but it would be nice to have more space we all agreed. A large three storied terraced house and empty drapers shop became available in the main street in Askam. An added bonus being a large two story extension was added on the back of the house as well. Pauline was working full time at Glaxo in Ulverston and hoped to open up the shop as a high class fruit and vegetable establishment.

We put Pauline's house on the market and the deal was the owner of the shop took our house in part exchange, so contracts were exchanged very quickly. The children were over the moon about the move and everyone helped on the big day. This house in Duke Street seemed absolutely enormous after our small terraced house, and we all lost track of each other in all the various rooms.

My various small enterprises were not paying very well; I was switching from trawling and selling fish, cutting up trees in Barrow cemetery that had been blown down in gales and delivering to my log clients. My advert in the local paper for household rubbish collection was sometimes a feast or a famine. The variety of request were amazing, from taking van loads of rubble to the tip to removing a very large piano from a posh house. This job nearly killed my assistant Harry (a very strong pensioner) and me. The posh lady insisted that the piano had come through the front door several years ago. We were very doubtful about that claim, and spent several hours busting our balls trying to manoeuvre the dam piano through the doors without scratching her newly painted and decorated lounge. Of course with hindsight we should have just walked away from the job in the first place. Harry drenched in sweat, the veins in his neck bulging with strain said "The bloody piano must have come through a patio door and since then must have been blocked up!" The posh lady assured us that it had come through the front door, and we had taken on the job so must see it through to the bitter end. She was right about seeing the job to its conclusion we were stuck in the final doorway and could not go back if we had wanted to. Well with a lot of cursing and swear words we finally got the piano halfway out of the front door, ahead of us were five steep steps leading down onto the driveway. We were both drenched in sweat, every bone in my body was aching, but only a short distance to go was the open back of my van. The lady said we could keep the pristine "Steinway" piano, and she would pay us a bonus for removing her troublesome piano without causing any damage to her paintwork. Now we had been struggling with this bastard piano for three hours now, and Harry was about to lose his temper big style.

The only consolation to all our grief I could see was the price we would receive after selling this beautiful piano to some lucky pianist in Barrow, and in the next few days hopefully. Just when our piano was balanced on the top step ready for one last effort, a top of the range Jaguar car pulled alongside my tatty old van. A distinguished looking man in a suit shouted up to the posh lady. "How clever of these chaps to get this piano out of the front door without having to cut the legs off it, it came through the old patio doors before we had it bricked up, when we bought it for our little Quentin all those years ago!"

Harry's eyes bulged, his face was bright red, and he then pushed me to one side and with a great heave pushed the piano down the flight of stairs in a fit of pure madness! With a crash and a bang the highly polished piano screeched its way down the concrete steps, shedding and scratching the varnished woodwork. "That's what I think of that bloody piano Norm this lady has just taken the piss out of us!" Harry spat out.

Driving to the municipal tip the dead piano in several pieces rattling around in the back of my van, I said to Harry through gritted teeth, "Well thank you very much we have spent all afternoon nearly killing ourselves, and my only consolation was the thought of me getting a good price for that bleeding piano, to compensate us somewhat for all the aggro we have had, you idiot!"

This rubbish removal could be lucrative on occasions; I knew a rich landlord who hired me the odd time to clear out houses after his tenants had done a runner, usually owing him lots of money in back rent. This terraced house in a rough area of Barrow looked neglected, and on opening the front door a mound of letters and circulars knee deep greeted us. "Bloody hell Harry nobody has been in this house for a while," I said. Walking into the kitchen the smell hit us, food was rotting on the table, and mugs of coffee had green scum floating on top. In the lounge a dead budgie lay feet up in its cage dying of starvation no doubt. Harry said "This is creepy Norm like the 'Mary Celeste' let's take a look upstairs we might find some answers."

The bedrooms had clothes strewn everywhere, a brand new pair of rigger boots were next to the bed, lucky for Harry the right size for him. On the bedside table was an opened letter summoning this guy to the magistrate's court in connection with drug dealing and other criminal activities? It seemed that he was a young South African citizen, and we worked out from other letters lying around, that he worked as a contractor welding new oil rigs at Barrow docks. We certainly had no sympathy for this creep and realised he must have skipped the country, and a warrant for his arrest must now be in force, hence his hasty departure. The cruel swine could have given the budgie to a neighbour before leaving.

Harry said "That settles it, our orders are everything in this house is for the rubbish dump so pick out anything of value Norm and we will split it!" We spent a happy couple of hours searching the house thoroughly from top to bottom, finding small stashes of drugs and money. The drugs we flushed down the toilet and the money we split between us. The fugitives work clothes were new and Harry picked some new shirts and I found a nice pair of expensive binoculars. It took several trips to the tip to dispose of stained mattresses and bedding, any decent furniture Harry gave to some needy pensioners he knew.

The waste of space that had once lived in the house, his belongings gave a bit of happiness to a few old people and a few weeks' wages for us. The house we left completely scrubbed out and clean, ready for the decorators to get the place ready for new tenants. The landlord was so pleased with our work that he insisted on giving us a small bonus. Harry had the last word about this job saying, "Every cloud has a silver lining Norm!"

My wages were becoming more and more erratic and it was getting harder to be self employed. My friend's dad worked for British Rail, he suggested that I got a proper job now that I had responsibilities, saying you might even like it Norm. In those days if you knew the right people you could walk into most jobs even if you were unskilled or semi skilled, especially in Vickers shipyard. Harry my mate got me my first and last job in the shipyard as a red leader (painter), this entailed going for an interview with Harry's friend the Head Foreman painter. It was just a formality, he asked me if I could stand heights, and that was all, I couldn't but hoped I was painting inside the ship, in a cabin perhaps. He told me to report for work Monday morning. My family had bets on how long I would last in Vickers, dad and most of my siblings guessed from one day to a full week. My lovely sister Jean, who knew me better than anyone, said I would be home at lunch time and promptly started getting the wagers in. Monday morning arrived and I did the slow walk from Glasgow Street after leaving my car there, over the High Level Bridge towards one of the several gated entrances, just as the seven twenty five shipyard buzzer sounded. The next buzzer was the seven thirty last chance to get through the gates. I had a knapsack over my shoulder with flask and sandwiches, Pauline had prepared for me earlier. "Never thought I would live to see the day you walked into Vickers Norm I am amazed!" she said.

Looking around at the sea of faces crowding around me, it suddenly dawned on me that everyone looked pissed off. The last buzzer was just about to stop and the Vickers security guards started to shut the huge gates, I knew that I could not work here, I had made a mistake. Turning around I quickly walked back through the gates taking the guards by surprise, "You won't get back in now son, one shouted."

"That's all right I said, it is not a problem." I was back in my home ten minutes later, giving everyone a good laugh.

So everyone thought now I was married it would be the same scenario working on the railway. This time it was different I had more responsibilities and needed the money, it was wintertime and I had not been able to fish for six weeks so was desperate. The first morning I was told to report to my foreman whose headquarters was at the side of the main railway line, this was where all our tools were stored in a small brick built shed. We were to be based here near Salthouse Bridge for the time I was employed as a plate layer. We parked our cars on the main road and climbed up the high banking to our work shed, in the shed was a large wood table and assorted wooden chairs. The foreman introduced me to the four other men I was to work with, showing me where the shed key was hidden and the first man in had to light the coal fire. "First job son after lighting the fire is put the bloody kettle on and mine is three sugars!" said my new boss.

They seemed a grand bunch of friendly lads I thought but certainly in no hurry to start work. I finished my tea and asked "when we were going to start work?"

"You're a keen little sod" one of the lad's said "we will have to keep an eye on you!" My boss looked out of the window and told me to go outside and tell him if it was raining. "Just the odd spot of rain boss nothing to worry about," I said.

"I will be the judge of that not you son, when it rains we cabin up and get the playing cards out. Right you lads get your money on the table, and let play commence." This set the pattern for the next few weeks, on the rare sunny day we would walk the tracks and do a little maintenance work. Sometimes the train driver would report part of a stretch of railway line would require lifting. This entailed us dragging the stone ballast away from the wooden sleepers, and then forcing small stones under the sleepers to lift and firm them up using the edges of our spades. Whilst doing the work on the line we would put out warning detonators on the rails a quarter of a mile away to warn of any approaching trains hurtling our way. A necessary precaution as several railway workers learned to their cost, being lax about safety was a definite no, even with warning detonators placed in a howling gale of wind you might not hear them going off. We usually took turns to keep a visual watch as well.

When we had several days of wet weather it really got me down stuck in the cabin all day playing cards, always losing did not help and the basic pay was poor. The boss said to me one day "Norm the only way to make money on this job is to work every evening and weekends to boost your wages that is why we take it easy during the day, I know you are bored."

"I was bored out of my skull and understood the other lads taking it easy during the day, but then one morning when everyone was cabined up, I asked the boss if I could walk the railway tracks leading into the docks. Carrying a spanner with a spiked end and a sledge hammer, I inspected the tracks and headed to my favourite place, Barrow docks. On route I tightened up the fishplates with my spanner, this was before all the tracks were welded together, and the sleepers mostly timber. Any steel clips that had sprung out I hammered them back into place, all in all having a really good time. Before long I was walking the tracks that led to the graving dock and past Low Road garage. I had a wander into the graving dock and saw a huge shoal of mullet entering the open entrance on the flood tide. I had a flash of inspiration and ran to see my friend Nicky the full time fisherman at Ferry Beach, luckily he was in his shed. "Nicky get your net into the big punt there is a huge shoal of mullet just swimming into the Graving dock, if we hurry we can block them in," I said gasping for breath.

"Now young fellah it is not that easy with mullet, they are a very clever fish, and seeing how keen you are about it, I think me and thee shall give it a try."

Pulling a zinc bath with a net stacked and ready to fish, down the stone steps alongside his boatshed, we both lifted the heavy bath tub into Nick's heavy wooden punt. I started to row us the two hundred yards to the entrance to the dock.

"Quietly now Norm, sound carries and the minute the shoal suspects danger they will all head for the exit like scalded cats."

I held the punt in the entrance whilst Nick got the net tied to the left hand side, and then he told me to gently row across the opening, paying out the deep net as we moved toward the opposite side. Gleefully I patted Nick on the back saying, "That was perfect Nick, the bottom of the lead weighted net was on the seabed, and the top of the net with cork floats on, was straight across the entrance. The shoal is trapped with nowhere to go it is impossible for any to escape Nick! What a team."

"Firstly Norm I don't hold with crowing about victory until the last fish is inside my shed, packed neatly into fish boxes. Secondly, we need to block any gaps down the sides of the Graving dock where they could slip around; I told you before they are clever fish are mullet."

Realising how premature I had been, we set to and plugged up all the gaps we could find, it was now high water so the tide would soon begin to drop. The sun was shining, the sky was blue and the birds were singing their little hearts out. Nick had tied the punt to the stone steps of the dock entrance and we sat together fascinated, our feet dangling over the quayside parapet, watching the antics of our trapped mullet shoal.

"I must ask you Norm, why were you carrying a heavy hammer and a huge spanner when you burst into my shed?"

"I am working for British Rail Nick, inspecting the dock railway lines and just happened to spot the mullet swimming into the graving dock."

"Are you not bothered about getting into trouble Norm?" Nick said laughing.

"Actually when I go back to our store shed this afternoon Nick I am giving my notice in, the job is definitely not for me, married or not, I will look for another job."

Nick pointed down to the net, it was like watching sheep, the lead mullet would nose up to the headline of the net and gently try to push through, then back away and try another place. The thousand odd other fish patiently waited to see what the scout fish did, no panic at all yet. Then a remarkable thing happened, the scout fish managed to find a couple of mesh missing halfway down the deep net that Nick and me had not spotted. The single fish gently manoeuvred his large body through to freedom, the rest one by one, unhurried and fearless waited their turn for freedom.

"Quick!" I shouted let's get into the punt and row over and try and stop them Nick, they are all going to escape."

"By the time we row over to the centre of the net and lift it to mend those missing meshes, the mullet will be gone, we had our chance and the fish won on this occasion," said Nick.

The mullet were heading through the small hole at great speed now and I realised my friend was right, and he had warned me from the start it would not be easy.

"The bright side is that we have both had a nice afternoon outdoors and in the sunshine Norm, better than being stuck inside a factory, would you agree?"

After helping to pack away the net in the boat shed, Nick asked if I would leave the heavy hammer for him, no point in carrying it two miles on your back on a hot afternoon like this Norm, and you're leaving the job anyway!

My foreman and his gang of merry men were still playing cards when I eventually opened the shed door. "Had a nice walk Norm? A lovely day for it son, put your feet up and pour yourself a mug of tea, soon be home time. We are coming back after tea greasing and oiling points and such like, are you joining us son?"

"Sorry boss I am not coming back ever, no offence but I cannot do this routine every day, even though you are all a great set of workmates." I shook hands with them all and did not look back, and left them all playing pontoon. They had not moved out of the hut all day even though it turned out to be a lovely day after all. Fair do's they would be working again after their tea but this way of life was certainly not for me, and I hate playing card games!

CHAPTER FIVE

WORKING DOWN THE SEWERS

Never in my wildest dreams could I ever imagine that I would be wading through three feet deep of human excrement in order to release a blockage in the sewer. The smell was appalling, my eyes were watering, and I vomited my breakfast into the gaseous mess at my feet. My new workmate and friend laughed and said "Don't worry Norm you will soon get used to it, everyone hates it at first, but we have good days, honest!"

A few days earlier the interview had gone well I thought, this was for a job on the water board and I was told to wait outside the office for ten minutes. Then the pretty secretary asked me to come back inside. The manager said the vacancy for a fresh water operator had been taken, but they could give me the other job available which was on the sewerage side. The upside to this job was if I worked on the fresh water side I would need a very strict medical, and several injections. If I chose the sewerage side I would not need any injections at all, and could start tomorrow.

"That is strange I would have thought it should be the other way round, anyway I needed the job, we had just decided to make a going concern out of the huge empty shop we now owned. Pauline had thought long and hard about what kind of shop would pay in our small village. She finally picked high class fruit and vegetables, hoping to create a living for herself. Rigging the shop out with shelves and display cabinets, weighing scales, cash till etc., all this was going to cost lots of money. Hence the desperation to earn quickly, bit ironic really, the man who loved to work in the fresh air was going down the sewers that is what responsibility does for you!

Monday morning I reported to Hindpool Road headquarters, where a posh talking boss informed me that I was not to visit the fresh water lads mess room under any circumstances, due to contamination issues, and it would cause a strike. He passed me two pairs of overalls, two jackets, a set of rain gear, telling me we worked in any weather conditions, wellingtons, waders, gloves etc. I remarked it was like Christmas day for me. The boss man said "Don't worry Norm you will need everything, believe me. Get in my van I will drive you down to your sewerage depot where you will report every day in future. Your mess room is also there, and all the sewerage lads and your vehicles are kept in one place."

When we got to our depot a large sign said 'Salthouse Sewerage Depot', I was shown a locker to store my gear in, the place smelt quite ripe, a sickly sweet smell seemed to pervade the air. No vehicles were around they must have been out doing their rounds. My boss got into his van, radioed his call sign and called up a man named Jim, asking him where he was, and informed him that he would be dropping me off forthwith. A five minute drive to an address in Barrow, and I saw my new work mate, he was pulling and shoving with all his might at a set of drain rods that led into a sewer. After a brief introduction my boss drove off.

Jim had a kind, intelligent looking face, was a couple of years older than me and I knew him and me were going to get on like a house on fire. He told me that we would nearly always work together, and be the quick response team to deal with any household drain and sewer blockages that occurred in the Barrow and rural area. Strangely he was interested in what my wife had packed me for my lunch, nosey bugger I thought. Jim told me that most of the equipment in our Transit van would be adequate to deal with most blockages, and we had a huge heavy duty sludge tanker with a high pressure hose attached, for major industrial sewer blockages to radio, if needed. "What are we doing now Jim?" I asked.

"Jim said the blockage is fixed now, nip into the house and tell the lady to fill her bath with cold water, when it is full pull the plug out and the water will flush out the sewer pipe. Got that Norm? And tell her to put the kettle on, mines two sugars". The young lass seemed relieved when told she could use her toilet again, but not happy when told that the blockage was caused by the many used condoms, and we suggested tactfully she put them in the dustbin in future. I mentioned to Jim about what he had said about the condoms, it must have been very embarrassing for her. "That is because, before we told her what the blockage was caused by, she told me her husband was in the navy and had not been home for eight months!"

Jim told me to undo each rod has he pulled the long length of joined up rods out of the manhole, and wipe the excrement off using my gloved hand so it fell into the open man hole. That made cleaning up easier afterwards, and then I had to fill buckets with water to swill it around the area after putting the manhole top back on. A gallon of industrial disinfectant liberally sloshed about made the air smell sweeter. I could not drink my tea so Jim drank it, waste not want not, I suppose. The lady gave us a five pound tip, which Jim gratefully put in his pocket, he had unblocked it before I had arrived, so said he would share in future, that is of course if you turn up tomorrow, the last two new starters only lasted one day.

Getting in the front of our Transit van having stowed away the shitty drain rods, I said "Jim it stinks in this vehicle how can you get used to this mate?"

"Look Norm if you give the job a week I guarantee that you will stick it and come to enjoy working with me, we will have some laughs." We drove back to the sewer depot to have our lunch and meet our other workmates. Our first job was getting out the hosepipe to hose the drain rods off, our gloves and wellington boots. Then the other various teams turned up, some were involved in repairing deep sewers that had collapsed, some repaired household drains, and the big sludge tanker team had a cushy job. It looked like I had the best of the jobs; being mobile and quick response we had more freedom than the other teams, and as Jim explained harder for the boss to find us. Jim introduced me to the sewer brigade, a right hard bunch of men who filed into the mess room with their pack ups and flasks. Bloody hell the place stank and I did not think I would be able to turn up tomorrow, on the plus side I liked my new mate Jim, and he was a good laugh, I envisaged never a dull moment with him.

"What have you got in your lunch box Norm?" Jim asked again. Lifting the lid off my Tupperware box, I saw that Pauline had given me a real treat expecting me to be doing heavy manual labouring. Two huge prawn buns, two huge pieces of homemade fruit cake, crisps and several

Mars bars filled the large box to capacity. The other men were all smiling at me and I soon sussed out why, they knew that until my senses got used to the smell, I would not be eating my lunch. Jim gleefully passed around my lunch saying, "I like your Pauline already Norm, she sure looks after you, she's a right treasure, after a week your appetite will be normal. That's why you have to take home an empty lunch box or she won't pack as much next time. Trust me Norm I know what I am talking about."

My lunch certainly made me popular with the work mates, I was glad I did not have jam or cheese sandwiches on my first day, it broke the ice. The afternoon went well; Jim just drove around Barrow showing me where we had to check every week to see that all the sewers were running free. Also I was going home with a good feed of mushrooms we picked in a water board field later in the day. Jim was right it was not all about human poo, and a few perks he had sussed out seemed interesting. I was required to go on a weekly rota for twenty four hour call outs for sewer blockages which could entail Christmas day and New Years day at double time pay. Going home at the end of my first day I walked in the front door. A great deal of shouting met me, consisting of "Jesus! What the hell is that smell has something died?" The kids shouted "please do not come in, we are all having our tea," Pauline fetched me a dressing gown and told me to throw all my clothes into the washing machine, then suggested a shower.

"You will not be going back tomorrow will you Norm? The children are right, you do smell something terrible, and it must have been a horrible experience."

The plus side is I like my new work mate, the money is good and weekends are free if I am not on call out rota. I think I will give it a week like Jim suggested. I did not tell Pauline about the possibility of contacting Weil's disease, a common danger to all sewerage workers, caught off rat's urine and untreatable in those days, and various other horrible possibilities. In the near future that would become my greatest fear, rats love sewer pipes and I would meet many. Jim would turn out to become a true and loyal trusted friend; I was privileged to work with him.

CHAPTER SIX

PAULINE'S FRUIT & VEGETABLE SHOP

Every night after work and weekends, we all mucked in helping my brother in law to construct all the shelving and counters needed to store the bulky fruit and vegetables on display. He used to be in the building trade so was very handy, and what a cracking job he made of transforming a huge empty space into a gleaming shop. The shop was double fronted with the doorway in the middle, and the shop front was Victorian in style. I scraped the very many paint layers off and painted the window frames a bright blue, to finish off; Pauline's name was painted in large letters above the door. We were both excited and worried at the same time; Pauline had left a good job in Glaxo to start this new venture, and she was worried whether any customers would walk through the doors at all. I said "Not to worry love, if no customers turn up the fruit and vegetables will not be wasted with the size of our family."

Monday morning our wholesalers delivery van turned up with one sack of potatoes, a box each of apples, oranges, pears, grapes literally one box of everything needed. The shop was so large it all fitted in one window and looked nothing in that space. I had taken the day off from work to help and console Pauline in the unlikely event of having no customers, it really was an unknown quantity, and I felt worried for her being disappointed. Pauline had made us both a nice green apron, so we both looked the part of green grocers at least.

"Oh Norm, I have had you spend so much money on my dream, what if it was just indulgence on my part, and we will be laughing stocks in the village?"

"We will do all right I have every faith in you, and you will succeed I am sure of that," I said, fingers crossed behind my back. The shop door bell rang and in walked our very first customer; he nearly got crushed in our eagerness to serve him.

"Good morning" Pauline said, giving him her brightest smile, "What can I get you, it is all fresh in this morning.

"I don't want to buy anything; I just want to know what time the post office opens?" the man said.

Poor Pauline what a letdown, shortly after, our first genuine customer walked into the shop, we both happily practiced weighing apples and suchlike on our old fashioned scales. Pauline said to the delighted customer, "You can have this order for free, to celebrate being our first customer."

Irony being, the bugger never returned to our shop ever again!

The floodgates opened, the villagers piled in, everything sold out very quickly, much to Pauline's delight. I was kept busy driving back and forth all day to the wholesalers in Barrow to stock up. Pauline decided from the onset to only stock grade one fruit and vegetables, it was much more expensive, but the villagers demanded quality at all times. That night after the children had been fed and watered; we went downstairs into the shop and surveyed the empty shelves and boxes. "Bloody hell Pauline, it looks as if a swarm of locust have been in our shop, I cannot believe it. You were certainly justified with having the courage to pack in a good job to follow a dream, well done!"

Crying with relief my lovely wife said, "We have a partnership Norm and will always do all right, if we stick together."

Pauline put a much larger order into the wholesalers that night, and early the next morning before I left for work, it was duly delivered. She even had me polishing each individual red apple until they gleamed. I phoned home at lunchtimes, and Pauline would get me to pick up stock on my way home from work, that she needed quickly. The shop really took off in our village, and Pauline needed to take on a lovely girl called Tina to work part time. A real asset she turned out to be, honest, hardworking and a good laugh. Each day trade increased more, and customers kept asking for items we did not stock. We made the decision to expand into cooked meats, frozen food, in fact everything we could think of. We invested in display cabinets, freezers, and bacon slicer, an ice cream cabinet, even new electronic scales.

We had a visit one day from a salesman representing a big firm similar to the 'Spar' shop chain. This nice man persuaded us to become part of the 'Wavy Line' group; they came and fitted out our humble shop with wall to wall modern shelving and equipment. A huge articulated truck crammed to the brim with cases of every possible grocery a modern shop would sell, from huge cheese wheels to ham and beef cooked joints ready for slicing. The lorry blocked up half the street all night whilst a team worked fitting the shelves and another team unloaded the hundreds of cases of various goods. To say we were overwhelmed would be an understatement; we kept thinking what have we signed up for, we must be mad our shop would never be the same again. The couple who owned a 'Wavy Line' shop in Barrow were fantastic, Stan and Delia that ran a thriving store gave up their valuable time to help us get our new shop organised ready for opening the next morning. I was worried about the huge cost involved in paying for all this equipment and stock, wondering how we would manage to pay for it all. I need not have worried the lovely people of Askam village supported us and we tried to give a good service, we made it a shop to be proud of, with help from our family and friends, kept it going from strength to strength.

My stepchildren seemed to enjoy all the new found space in the huge house, compared to their last one, and it kept us all fit running up and down all the stairs. I was working all day long on the Water Board, and every night in our shop, stocking shelves and doing jobs for Pauline. I was getting worried about mum and dad, when we called to see them at weekend at Glasgow Street they did not look well, their coal bunker was empty and the red final demands were stacked behind the usual place, the clock on the mantelpiece. Pauline said to me "It is obvious to me how worried you are about your parents Norm, I have a suggestion."

Pauline's idea amazed me; her plan was to convert the bottom floor of our rear extension into a cosy flat with fitted bathroom. In all it would be bedroom, bathroom, lounge and kitchenette. The major building work to be done by my talented brother in law Charlie again. We could do all the decorating ourselves and the final touches to make it homely. They had lived in Glasgow Street for so many years I could not envisage their wanting to move. Also would it be wise to have my step children and elderly parents, plus a very busy shop to run?

Pauline said "If your mum and dad agree to the move, we would have peace of mind knowing they were safe and warm with us, and their pensions they could keep and live free of any bills."

I knew my dad thought the world of Pauline, but my mother was always difficult to live with and could be very hard work. Pauline said we could put dads name down for an allotment in the village and that may give him a new lease of life. Reluctantly I agreed to see them at the weekend and ask them their opinion. I took coal and some of Pauline's homemade pies and cakes with me. After some small talk and after dad had eaten a very large meat pie, I hesitantly broached the subject of them moving to Askam to live permanently with my new family. Quicker than a rat running up a drainpipe, dad said "Yes how soon can we move in with you?" I told dad to discuss all the details with mum, but his answer was still yes, and as soon as possible. The flat was finished it seems in no time, and we moved my mum and dad into a newly built and tastefully decorated new home. Pauline arranged for dad to have his dream village allotment, my new friends on the sewerage department donated all the wood for his potting shed, all the fencing to replace the old, and even all the spades, tools etc. He needed to find nothing, and was highly delighted with all the donations that appeared, and the project seemed to give them both a new lease of life. When dropping off some fencing post acquired (I didn't ask where from) we saw my mum digging like a navvy with a spade nearly as big as her. Dad made his shed really cosy with comfy seats, cupboards for his seeds, waterproofs and wellington boots, he only had to mention what he needed once and it magically appeared. So watching him and mum sat in the warm shed drinking tea and smoking, Pauline and I thought that we had done the right thing by them.

Mind you life was not all perfect when you had a mother like mine to keep you on your toes. The shop was getting so busy that Pauline had a long row of teacups lined up behind the counter, all gone cold with having no time to drink it or her Tina hers. Mother kept playing hell "Saying you should stop and have a rest you girls, look at all this tea I have made you, gone cold." She started to clean all the cups in the shop.

Then a lady rushed into the shop saying that huge clouds of dense black smoke was pouring out of mum's lounge window, "I have phoned the fire brigade "she shouted. Just at that moment Jim and me were delivering some planks of wood for dad's allotment, and passing the end of our street saw the black smoke belching out of mum's flat. "Bloody hell your house is well on fire Norm, let's make sure your parents are not in there!" Jim shouted.

Dashing into the back door under the smoke, I could see quickly into all the rooms making sure nobody was in, and then rushed out again coughing and retching. Dalton fire brigade turned up then, one of the part time firemen was Charlie, my brother in law who had done all the renovations on the shop and flat. Luckily I could tell them there was nobody in danger and they could deal with the fire straight away. My brother in law carried a melted chip pan outside, "This is the cause of the fire Norm, your mum must have forgotten all about it, pity you have just spent a small fortune on creating your parents a lovely home." The main thing is nobody was hurt and the damage did not spread to any other part of the house, it could have been much worse. We all mucked in and ripped off all the wallpaper, took all the furniture and curtains, cooker and bedding to the local tip. We repainted and degreased everywhere and bought new stuff, obviously we were all peed off with mum but accidents happen. I phoned the insurance company and they said basically that it was too much of a coincidence that the fire started so soon after we had renovated the flat, so would be sending their assessor to check the damage and it could be a week at least. I said "So you expect me to wait a week before doing any renovation, with two elderly people living there? And with me starting on the work so soon, my insurance policy may be void?"

"That about sums it up adequately sir" the snotty bitch said.

"Stick your insurance then, I will cancel my policy and join a superior firm in the future, goodbye."

There was certainly no dull moments living in our new house, the shop was either filled with customers or constant streams of visiting friends of my step children, climbing up the stairs. The shop was taking over our lives, even after closing time we had to visit wholesalers, and restock all our shelves at night. The shop was so successful beyond all our expectations, and hard work equals success, everyday's shop takings were higher than the last day. Meanwhile Jim and I travelled around the district like the cape crusaders, unblocking drains, inspecting deep sewers and having a good laugh, most of the time. Sometimes our supervisor turned up to make sure we were doing a good job, or to make sure we were where we said we were on the vehicles radio. One morning he radioed us to meet him at a location in town, Jim said "This is a deep sewer Norm and the shaft leading down to the bottom is very narrow, I wonder what the hell he wants us to do?"

I had a bad feeling about this job and thought the supervisor did not seem to like me very much. We pulled up behind his van in the middle of the road, he had a few traffic cones spread around a manhole cover, which looked as if it had not been disturbed for years. "Right men what I want you to do is lift off the manhole cover, and then Norm is going down the shaft to the bottom, getting down on his knees look up the sewer pipe shining his torch and tell me what he sees, he will be checking to see a pipe as not dropped or broken, of course he will have on a harness with a safety line tied on."

This was in the time when safety was getting better, and stricter rules were coming in, new gas alarms were soon to arrive. Our old equipment was gradually being replaced; the sewers were very dangerous and deadly gasses could be lying anywhere. Sometimes we would hear about a sewer worker in another area contracting Weils disease from contact with rat's urine. The heavy cast iron cover had not been off for many years, and took Jim and myself a solid hour to loosen off and finally lift onto the roadside. The sweat was running off us, and both of us were getting short tempered with our supervisor, thinking was this exercise really necessary. "Jesus" Jim said "Look at the size of those bloody huge spiders!"

Now we have all seen big spiders, but these were enormous and scuttled about all around the old brickwork in the shaft, the many iron steps leading downwards were covered in a mass of cobwebs. By the light of my torch I could see that there was little room at the bottom of the shaft to crouch and peer into the sewer pipe, my face would be very near the sewer pipe entrance. What if I came face to face with a large rat and did not have the space to get out of its way, I have seen the ferocity of rats when cornered, and I have been cursed with a surfeit of imagination, which was not good for working down manholes. I must confess that I was frightened and Jim could see this in my eyes. Jim said "You stay up here Norm and lower me down on the safety line."

"You won't Jim, I have already told Norman he was doing this sewer check, and if he cannot do it, well there are plenty on the dole who can," said the boss.

I took my time getting kitted out hoping the boss would get fed up of standing around, and bugger off back to his nice warm office, and leave us in peace. No chance of that, he was looking forward to me meeting a rat, and enjoy seeing me freak out. Slowly I climbed down to the bottom, swatting the spiders on steroids, away from my face. At the bottom I practically had to put my legs in the air, and my face right up close to the sewer pipe and gritting my teeth hold the torch so I could see down the length of the pipe. I heard Jim shouting down the shaft "The chances of a rat being there now is remote Norm, all the noise we have made will have frightened them away, give it a quick look and get yourself back up here."

It is sods law, the torch illuminated the tunnel, and not six inches in front of my face, was the huge head of a rat staring at me and momentarily being dazzled by my torch beam. In shock I twisted my head away from the pipe, smashing my face into the iron rung of the ladder, my safety helmet took most of the blow but my nose was cut on the rung. I swear that the rat was the size of a cat; it bounded onto my chest and ran down the other pipe. I literally wet my pants, shouting up to my mate "Did you see the size of that beast, the chances were remote you said Jim, you burke!" Jim helped to pull me up to the surface and assisted me in removing my harness. "Where's the boss I wanted a word with him," I said.

"He's shot off back to the office, he thought it was best he disappear Norm, and I told him he was being very wise!"

Jim got out the medical box and did a good job on my nose bleed, and other scrapes sustained in getting out of the rat's way. Jim admitted the spiders, and my rat, were the biggest he had ever seen in twenty years of sewer work, and he was glad it was me down there and not him. I bored him to tears for a while telling how the rats whiskers were so long, they were touching each side of the sewer pipe. Jim said "When you calm down the boss wants a report on what you saw."

"What about the size of the rat?" I said.

"No you idiot the state of the sewer pipes."

You never knew where you would be sent on your next call; it could be a Chinese restaurant, fish and chip shop, any street, road or house in the district, a huge variety of destinations. Sometimes, just sometimes it could turn out to be a nightmare for me. The radio crackled into action, a voice from control said "Control to Lima 5, are you receiving me, over!"

Jim said "Here we go again, no peace for the wicked Norm, this is the fourth call out today, and I think the boss has heard about us picking mushrooms!" The call out was to a bad blockage at the slaughter house, my nightmare scenario had arrived, the message also said our supervisor was waiting there for us. Jim said "You are suddenly quiet Norm; it is a bit weird when you go silent, and you usually can talk a leg off a donkey!"

"You know I cannot go into a slaughter house Jim, it upsets me even to hear the sheep and cattle in the pens outside."

"This is part of your job Norm and I cannot see how you can duck out of it, especially with a supervisor that is not very fond of you, waiting at the abattoir."

We pulled up behind our boss's vehicle and he strolled over towards us, saying, "Jim I have been inside, it looks like the drain is blocked with the usual blood and gore, get Norm to use the drain rods to try and unblock it, if that does not work, call out the big sludge machine, got that?"

He looked at me and said "What are you waiting for Norm, get your arse into gear, and I mean now!"

I could hear the sounds of animals in the abattoir and it upset me then, and I was still sitting in the vehicle. I looked him in the eye and said "I cannot go inside boss, sorry,"

"Then pick your cards up at the office on your way home," he said.

Just at that moment the boss's radio broke in with a message for him to go to the depot immediately, "Jim make sure he goes in and does the job or he goes, you got that?" he said flouncing off into the sunset.

"Stay in the vehicle Norm I will sort the blockage out, I have been here before and it does not bother me, back in ten minutes you watch," said Jim.

True to his word, Jim and his set of drain rods were soon back and throwing them into our van. Driving away Jim radioed the boss that I had gone in and completed the job myself and everything was all right.

Jim said to me "I cannot understand you Norm, you used to be a full time trawler man you must have gutted thousands of fish in your career; I thought you would not be squeamish about sheep or cows being slaughtered?"

"It is hard to explain Jim I even felt sorry for gutting the fish, but I loved being a fisherman and the adventures I had, but killing warm blooded animals is too much to bear, a step too far and I am quite prepared to leave the water board over this principal."

Jim replied "No need to worry Norm, we might not need to visit an abattoir again for twelve months, and do not forget to bring an extra couple of Pauline's delicious prawn buns in for my lunch tomorrow, I think you owe me!"

The following week I owed him yet again when we had a call from an irate lady who lived alone in the town centre, seemingly there was a huge rat in her backyard and she was hysterical. Pulling up at her address Jim shouted to me to grab a shovel, "To bury it with Jim?"

"No you dick, to bloody kill it!" he said.

"You do not mind if I stay here Jim, I really do not want to see you kill a rat," I said.

"You really try my bloody patience sometimes Norm," he said, and off he went with the shovel. The sound of banging and clattering could be heard for a few minutes coming from the ladies backyard and a loud squeal, then Jim with a big grin on his face, walked to our van carrying a rat by the tail, and it was the size of a tom cat.

"Bloody hell Norm, no wonder that lady was hysterical this rat is a fat bastard, and the tenner tip she gave me will buy me a few pints tonight. A couple of my usual prawn buns tomorrow if you please Norm, I do not think I could afford not to have you as a mate, I love working with you."

I bought a vintage trawler called 'Jane' a little cracker owned by a great mate called Jack, he was the lovely man mentioned in my first book who had helped us a hell of a lot on our tug Melanie Jane. My new boat was at a small boat club alongside Walney Channel, she was all painted up except the bottom needed anti fouling to stop weed and barnacles growing, and Jack Dewhurst had a good reputation for keeping all his boats in tip top condition. She was laid up on the high water mark on legs, so it was a perfect time to do this laborious chore. The next tide where she would float was in two days time. Today was Monday and I was at work, my workmate solved the problem as usual.

"Tomorrow bring your paint and brushes and it just so happens I can put the boatyard down for sewer outfall inspections, it has not been done for years anyway. Two of us will soon have the bottom anti fouled in no time, and if anybody wants to know why the water board van is parked here we can give a genuine reason. Simple eh Norm!" said Jim.

Once again my friend came to my rescue; we checked the sewer outfalls and quickly got the boat painted. Two days later Jim fetched my boarding dinghy down in the back of our van, I rowed aboard at high tide, cast off all the mooring ropes and headed into the middle of the fast flowing channel. Radioing Jubilee Bridge I asked the bridge master for a lift. Shortly after the lights and barriers came down, all traffic and pedestrians were stopped from crossing over the span. The huge spans of the bridge started to lift, many heads appeared looking to see what kind of ship was coming through and holding them up. No doubt disappointed to see such a little ship causing so much disruption to them. In those days the bridge was manned two hours before high water until two hours after high water, every tide, seven days a week. A fire engine had to be sent across the bridge onto Walney Island from Barrow each time in case the bridge got stuck in the open position, this happened more often than you would think. It was a very necessary safety precaution in case of a fire on the Island. When a break down did happen people would curse us and say the bridge should be permanently closed to boating traffic. Nowadays you have to give plenty of notice if you need to have a bridge lift. Giving the lads on the bridge a wave as the tide swilled my new boat through the centre of the wooden dolphins on either side. When a small fleet of fishing trawlers worked out of Barrow's Ferry Beach we used to drop a basket of prime fish off for the bridge operators, as a thank you for being quick to get the traffic stopped, and us through fast in order to get ourselves home after several days away at sea. Mooring my boat up at Ferry Beach I rowed ashore to see my pal waiting with the van.

"Hurry up Norm we have a call out, it is that young mother that has the little boy who always stuffs his teddy bear down the loo and flushes it away, the loo is blocked again. At least we will have a brew and a piece of homemade fruit cake. She is lovely that lass, her ex husband must be brain dead to leave a lady like her."

Jim never said the drain fault was the house holder unless the boss was there on site. He always said it was the water board responsibility, to save passing the blockage and call out charge onto the house holder, which we should have done. Unless of course the owner of the house was rude to us and then we just told them it was on their property and should call a plumber out, the water board in those days were not responsible on private property unless they shared drains with a neighbouring property.

CHAPTER SEVEN

I LOVE PARIS IN THE SPRING TIME

The months rolled by, and Jim and I were kept busy on call outs and having a good laugh together, even Christmas day we were called out to drains blocked and overflowing, but the week after I was off. Plenty of tips from relieved house holders and drinks were shoved into our hands. The shop was very busy selling toys and boxes of chocolates by the ton, Pauline's dad bless him, dressed as Father Christmas and handed out glasses of wine to the adult customers with chocolates for the kiddies. The shop was doing a roaring trade, and we were all completely wrecked on Christmas Eve. Pauline spent all that night with me cleaning up the debris in the shop and preparing four sacks of brussel sprouts that had been overstocked, for the freezer later, we both could not abide waste. The revellers passing the shop window must have thought we were mad, working at that hour. We had to put all the kid's presents under the lovely Xmas tree we had in our huge lounge. We had sold out of real Xmas trees a few days before, but had kept a good one for ourselves. The shop was closed for a full week and we were looking forward to spending time with the children and my mum and dad. It was strange to have a full week after Xmas off, with no grafting or ordering stock for the shop.

The shop became busier than ever, our best friend's decided to get married, for both it was the second time. The wedding was lovely, but the bombshell was they both wanted us to go to Paris on honeymoon with them for a long weekend. Pauline was really close to her friend of many years and I wanted her to go, she deserved a little rest from the shop for a few days. I told her to go because I had no holidays left from my job. The three of them persuaded me to phone into work to say I was sick, which I did, I am easily led! Thinking that my boss would call around my house to check up on me, I told everybody to say to my boss if he called, that I was in bed sick. I had a little foreboding about this, but set off for Paris from Askam village train station one sunny morning whistling 'I love Paris in the springtime.' I must admit it seemed a little strange to be going on somebody else's honeymoon, but what the hell we were going to enjoy every minute. In those days you travelled by train to London, and then Dover, the trip across the English Channel on an old cross channel ferry was a bit rough due to a big swell rolling in, lots of passengers were violently seasick. We then boarded a train straight through to magical Paris, my second visit. Our small, but cheap and spotless hotel was in the centre of the city, most of the sights we could walk to. We did all the usual visiting the Arc de Triomphe, Eiffel Tower, several palaces and Notre Dame Cathedral. We bought freshly roasted chickens, bottles of red wine and had a picnic on the riverbank of the Seine, it seemed like heaven, and that Pauline and me were on honeymoon also. Our last honeymoon being short of money was spending two days at the port of Heysham in a lovely cottage, which was thanks to our daughter Elaine's inlaws. The time was going so quickly and happily, that when I phoned home to check up on the kids and shop, I received some disappointing news. This was the third time we had phoned home in two days and we were expecting similar news, as before. It rang for ages which was strange, the house was usually busting at the seams with people. Somebody finally picked up and I recognised my young nephew's voice, he was visiting with my sister Jean. "Hold on a minute mum needs to speak to you Uncle Norm."

"Hi Norm are you having a lovely time?" Jean said.

"Paris is wonderful and it has been sunny weather every day, how is everything at home Jean, all my step children all right, mum not set fire to the house?"

"Well do you want the good news first or the bad news Norm?" she said.

Oh dear I had a premonition about this honeymoon with our friends, "Give me the good news first Jean."

"The good news is the weather here has been foul, wet and very windy," she said. "The bad news is you are sacked! I am so sorry your boss came hammering on the door about an hour ago, he asked where you were, and our Graham said you were on holiday in Paris. Your boss said to Graham, would he not mind giving you a message when you phoned home, and the message was you are sacked. The strange thing was he was laughing after he said it, did he not like you Norm?"

Dam! Our Jean was the only person I forgot to tell about my cover story, if anybody visited or phoned from work. Not to worry I reassured her, I was thinking it was about time I went to work full time in our shop, and it was getting too busy for Pauline to manage with just part time help.

I missed working with my mate Jim, he had been a cracking workmate to me and we had many a good laugh, he was one of the best, but it was now time to move on. We expanded the shop to sell even more lines; I opened a fishmongers section for fresh fish and smoked fish. The girls who worked in the village K shoe factory kept us going buying small tubs of prawns and prawn filled baps, every lunch time. Twice a week, I would get up at four o'clock in the morning to drive down the motorway to Fleetwood fish market. I loved to buy fresh fish, boxes of prawns, Manx kippers and smoked haddock; it bought back happy memories of when I was a trawler man working out of Fleetwood harbour. The favourite fish my customers liked were the huge cod I bought off the big Fleetwood Icelandic trawlers, when returning home from trips of three weeks duration. Often I would spot Mandy, the Fleetwood hooker I wrote about in my last book 'A Boy from Glasgow Street' coming down the gangplanks of various ships berthed in the docks, her huge arms clasped around the waist of a swarthy looking seaman. She was real character and I would never forget her in a hurry.

With my van stacked to the roof with fish, I headed back up the motorway as fast as I could, to commence filleting my huge cod and be ready for the morning trade. The other downside of being a fishmonger was the sudden delivery of several boxes of plaice at ten o'clock at night, at the back door, so fresh they were still flapping.

"Some fish here for you Norm, we have just got ashore and do not have enough to send on to Fleetwood market, so pay up with cash and we will get away home to our beds, it has been a long day."

That is all I needed at the end of the day, several hundred plaice to fillet before I could even think of my bed. Telling the fisherman that I did not want his fish, and that I was tired myself, he dumped his boxes of fish on the pavement and drove off in the direction of Barrow. His parting words were, "Don't worry about the money now, pay me next time you see me, cheerio Norm!"

I could hardly stagger up the stairs in the early hours of the morning, every muscle in my body was aching, everyone else was tucked up in bed, for they all had work in the morning. Any cod or other whitefish left over at the end of the day were made into fishcakes, and put in our freezer cabinet by Pauline. On bonfire night she also made her own toffee apples and treacle toffee, which sold very fast indeed. To keep our business viable and profitable, we found you could not rest on your laurels, but had to continually think of new lines to stock, in order to keep the customers interested. We started to stock large sacks of potatoes and deliver them to the surrounding estates, even buying Pauline a small van to deliver orders to the farms and hamlets locally. We had to keep giving a personal, special service to offset the buying power of the supermarkets nine miles away. It really annoyed me when a customer came into our shop and complained that our carrots were three pence a pound dearer than Asda's, his wallet bulging with notes and a brand new car, parked in front of our shop. Pauline used to usher me into the store room just as I was going to blow a fuse! "The customer's are always right" she would say to me, "even if you think they are miserable, we would lose a good few customers Norm, if I did not keep my eyes on you".

Pauline asked me to buy a new potato scraping machine for the shop; we had queues of people inside and outside the shop and sold them by the sack load. The only snag was when we were all busy serving customers I would forget the potato scraper was switched on with a full load of new potatoes in, on emptying it the potatoes were reduced to the size of marbles, oh dear!

Working hard in the shop one wet and windy day, I was preparing a large order of prawn baps for the girls in our village shoe factory. I saw this harassed young couple enter the shop with two young children in tow. After the usual good morning, and what can we do for you pleasantries, the young lady sounding as if she was from Yorkshire said, "Can you give us two weeks of good weather it has been raining every day nonstop, it is no fun stuck in a caravan with two bored children, I think that I am going out of my mind!"

Her husband piped up and said "Since we bought the caravan two years ago we have not had one decent stay in it, we seem to have a lot of bad weather days here in Askam."

His wife said "If somebody gave me any offer at the moment I would rip their arm off, I am that fed up with it, and we have just paid another years site fee's, that was a big mistake."

Now this family really were depressed with the weather, and had their dreams shattered with the caravan. I asked them where the caravan was sited. It was nearly unused, four berths; site fee's paid and was obviously not wanted anymore.

"How much do you want for it then?" I asked mainly out of curiosity.

"How much have you got in the till?" she said.

Actually the morning had been very busy, but not busy enough to buy a four berth caravan I knew. I counted out the notes and it was about two hundred and fifty pounds only. She took one look at the money and said "Have you any more cash in the house?"

I had not anymore money and told her so, "That will have to do, "she said. Taking the money she scribbled out a receipt and said they will go back to the caravan straightaway, pack up their car and drop the caravan keys back in the shop in an hour, and they all left our shop.

Two customers had been watching this weird transaction occurring in amazement. One said you have just been done Norm, you will not see them again, it must have been the easiest two hundred and fifty pounds they have ever had!

Cue for Pauline to enter the shop, the customers said with glee, "Your Norm has just lost his marbles Pauline, he has bought a fictitious caravan for all the money in your till, and they have drove off promising to drop the keys into your shop, it was like taking candy from a baby, wait till I tell my Roger about this!" and left laughing.

Pauline dashed to the till and saw it was empty of notes, she said "Norm this tells me not to let you alone in my shop, you are too trusting, this reminds me of simple Jack of the Beanstalk fame, whose mother sent him to market with their precious cow that he exchanged for worthless beans! You can get on the phone to the police!"

"No need for that love I trust her to come back, you will see mark my words".

Three hours of strained silence followed, our customers must have thought that we had some kind of domestic problem. The lady did eventually drop off the caravan keys, Pauline apologised profusely and we had got a bargain.

Most people that are married and work full time together, say they could not get on working together each and every day. Hand on heart I can honestly say we loved working together in our shop, we got on really well and appreciated that all our hard work was paying dividends working as a team. The down side to our shop was never having any time off together, when not actually open we stocked shelves, collected stock from the wholesalers in Barrow and further afield, and when people saw the light on at night knocked on the door for bread or milk for their husband's pack up the next day. Our health began to suffer with the increasing hard work, and with trade increasing every week, I developed nose bleeds and both of us had constant back pain. I also had a yearning to have an outdoor job again, so reluctantly Pauline agreed to put the business up for sale. The children had lives of their own and were independent, so we could downsize the house. We missed the laughs with Tina and our Marion working part time in the shop with us.

Not surprisingly the business sold quickly and we bought a house on Walney Island that had a huge half acre garden at the rear. We inherited the sheds, and chicken coops, all in all a smallholding which would keep my parents busy to their hearts content. The new house was ample size for my parents, and anybody who wanted to move back in the future. I really wanted to go back to sea but could not find a suitable fishing boat, so in the meantime I visited the job centre. Now in my early job seeking days you signed on as unemployed, then had to sit in a booth with a person who interviewed you, and gave you some of the choices on offer that day, that were deemed suitable for your education and experience. Some of these staff were just plain arrogant and seemed to look down their noses at you, most of the others had really good people skills and understood that sometimes you became unemployed due to circumstances beyond your control. I remember when I was a share fishermen working out of Barrow and Fleetwood, when we were stormbound in harbour and not able to fish, the Fleetwood lads went to the Labour exchange and signed each weekday for bad weather and received the equivalent daily unemployment benefit. It was explained to me and my two crew, that we were entitled to it whether in Fleetwood or Barrow. So we signed on in Fleetwood and received our money. Then we tried this when stormbound in Barrow, we were shown the door and thrown out unceremoniously. So we asked to see the manager in his office, and he explained that Barrow was not a real fishing port like Fleetwood and so if we wanted to get the same benefits as those fishermen, we should all go and live in Fleetwood. To me this was grossly unfair and against the rules, we persevered and eventually the manager admitted they were breaking the law and agreed to pay us. Unfortunately this made us a little unpopular with a few of the staff in the Labour Exchange, because at this time there were three other boats fishing from Barrow and about twelve men tramping in at various parts of the day ruining the staffs routine. We had a special counter to sign at and segregated from all the other poor unemployed people who were standing in long queues, some of the staff thought it was their personal cash they were handing out.

It came to a head one day; I was on my own stood at the counter to sign on for my daily bad weather signing, you were allowed to call in any time of day before closing time. This was certainly a bone of contention with some of the staff. Unfortunately for her she was about to give the crowd of claimants a bloody good laugh at her expense. The haughty cow said to me "Why are you not out fishing today Mr Pascoe? "Because it is blowing a gale out at sea and I value my life," I said. She looked out of the window, the sun was shining, and the sky was perfect blue, not a cloud in the sky. In a loud voice so that all the people waiting in the other queues could hear she said, " Come now Mr Pascoe it is a lovely day I cannot let you sign for bad weather, you should be out fishing in my opinion."

"So you are telling me I should be out fishing and not cluttering up your Labour Exchange." I said, becoming a little annoyed.

"Yes that is correct Mr Pascoe," she answered with a self satisfied smug look on her face, convinced she had at last, got one over on me and of course my fellow fishermen. A few of the crews had turned up by now, and were wondering what the problem was. Then I had an idea, I asked the clerk to look out of her window and I went outside. I stood outside her window wearing my peaked skipper's hat; the hat blew off my head straight away, sailing high into the sky. In Duke Street it was like a wind tunnel, when I arrived back at the desk, she said in a quiet voice, "What took you so long Mr Pascoe?" "I did not catch up to my hat until the Town Hall!" I said in a loud voice. The place erupted in laughter, the red faced clerk slammed my paper onto the counter and I signed. My last words to her were "Just because the sun is shining and blue skies, does not mean the Irish Sea is calm, the shipping forecast is severe gale nine imminent. Believe me madam all the fishermen would prefer to be at sea trawling than visiting this dreary place, and have to look at your miserable face!"

The weather forecasting in those days was definitely not as efficient as now, what with dedicated weather satellites, weather buoys stationed out to sea, computers and faxes etc. We only had Liverpool coastguard and the shipping forecast on our radio receivers. We had a running joke that for weeks the forecast for the North Irish Sea where we were trawling was force 3 to force 4; every day at sea it was howling, and barely safe to fish. We had to tow downwind with the high waves rolling up our stern, the deck was constantly awash and a basket of high value Dover sole was washed overboard.

Cries of "I wish the bloody man from the weather centre was out here knee deep in water and trying to keep his feet on this rolling pig of a boat, experiencing his force 4 wind, force 4 my arse!"

CHAPTER EIGHT

THESE KIDS ARE RUNNING WILD MISTER

I was impressed the first time I needed to seek out the services of a modern Job Centre, in stark contrast to the old Labour Exchange. The place was brightly lit, warm, and above all, cheerful. Lists of various jobs were on boards, all clearly labelled with the qualifications each required, and in their different types of trade. I wanted to go back to sea and was having difficulty selling my small fishing boat that I used for fishing with just Pauline as crew. I was thinking that winter was looming and any job would do to tide me over Christmas. At the interview desk a lovely young girl gave me a lovely smile, took down my details and suggested that I gave a thought to an outdoor job that might just appeal to me.

"Actually Mr Pascoe, the lady holding interviews is in our office upstairs packing up and heading home to Kendal, she has been interviewing for three days now and not found anybody suitable, I have a feeling you might be in luck."

I was thinking she might be bloody desperate by now, the job she had on offer must be rubbish.

The lovely clerk put the phone down and said in a breezy voice, "You're in luck Mr Pascoe she was just about to leave for home, up the stairs the door on the right, and good luck!"

The lady was desperate; she was standing in the doorway waiting for me.

I saw that she was about sixty years old and spoke with a lovely cultured voice.

"Good afternoon Mr Pascoe, please take a seat and I will tell you all about the job I have to offer you. The post is a Supervisors position and you will need a clean driving licence, it involves taking eight or more young unemployed school leavers to outward bound schools, village halls, working for the National Trust etc. to paint and decorate inside and outside various buildings. Indeed a rich variety of different skills will be required, the area covered is all of South Lakes and you will be reporting to our office in Kendal. All the youths will be from the Barrow wards and are unskilled and unemployed, their contracts are for six months, and your contract is twelve months, renewable as funding is allowed, or available. The wages for the youths is low and yours will be quite generous, I will be honest with you it is just to show that the government is doing something for the school leavers that have no qualifications."

"So the scheme is basically 'Job Creation' cheap labour and makes the youth unemployment figures look better. Just when the kids are getting the hang of working and learning new skills, it is time for them to go back on the dole after a mere six months," I said.

"That is correct Norman but the plus side is the youths are going to have a reason to get out of bed in a morning, see some lovely countryside and just maybe you might make a difference to them. The job is yours if you want it and I have a feeling you will enjoy the challenge, what is your answer?"

"I am not sure that this is the right decision but my answer is yes" I said.

Her face lit up, and after a few days interviewing in Barrow I could understand why I bet she could not wait to drive back to Kendal. I was summoned to the Kendal office to answer any questions that I may have, such as is it really necessary to pick eight youths up in Barrow, and then travel to Ambleside or over Kirkstone Pass. After a long journey sitting on a wooden bench in the back of a Sherpa van with no windows, and expecting to actually have any time to work, after having their one hour lunch break. The back of the van filled with work clothes, tools, paint, paint brushes, their bags containing flask and sandwiches left no room to even stretch out. I was assured that this was happening everywhere, and teams of youths were being ferried about in hire vehicles attempting to work on various jobs all over Cumbria. Apparently there was no youth unemployment in the Kendal area, hence me bringing the poor lads all the way from Barrow each day. I caught the train to Maryport to pick up my hire van and drove it home ready to start work the next day, wondering what I had taken on. Of course health and safety nowadays would not allow this type of situation to happen. The first eight children on my list to pick up were all supposed to meet me outside the public library, at eight in the morning. One tall blue haired, ring in the nose Punk Rocker was waiting for me, nobody else. I introduced myself and he said his name was Mike. At least he had brought a bag with him; he opened the passenger side door, threw in his bait bag and let out a loud fart.

"Better out than in," he said. "Just to let you know this is where I will be sitting for the next six months, that is the only reason I turned up first, the others can sit in the back!"

"Now listen to me I give the orders around here I am your supervisor, you lads can have a rota to take turns sitting in front, and two can sit on that seat, not just one!"

"We can sit here all day, and at going home time, there will still only be the two of us. Tomorrow I will not be here you will have to pick me up at my house just like the others, you have a lot to learn Norm."

"All right Mike why are the others not here, you seem to know more than me what is going on."

"Simple Norm we have been forced to take this job, or lose our meagre dole money, if we come to work for forty hours we do not receive much more, so if you expect us all to walk from different areas of Barrow to meet you here at eight in the morning, maybe in the pouring rain you can get stuffed. Have you got an address for each of them, I suggest we hurry up and call before they all bugger off back to bed."

Taking my list he directed me to the nearest house and got out and hammered on the front door. The door was opened by a huge lady with a moustache, she glared at me saying "You must be an idle sod our 'Sprout' has been waiting since eight; he was just about to go back to bed, Sprout get your arse out here now, it is another slave labour scheme, don't you be doing too much!"

I realised why the lad was called Sprout he was tiny and wore glasses that had the thickest of lenses not unlike jam jar bottoms, Mike said something to him and let him in the back door. Next house visited I could see a young lad looking out of the front window; he came out smoking a cigarette and had a beaming smile.

"Hi boss another slave labourer for you to exploit, my name is Ben" he said and jumped into the back of the van.

I was beginning to wonder exactly why nobody else had taken this job on, the young lads all seemed resentful. Eventually I had picked up all eight from their homes, and all lived in deprived areas of Barrow, and I should know being brought up in a similar area. Only half had a packed lunch and refused to go and get something, even when I offered to wait for them. I pulled into a lay-by and introduced myself, explaining that the first day was in Kendal kitting them all out with work clothing at a builder's warehouse. I asked them to call me Norm and was told what to call them, there was Mike. Ben, Sprout, Lurch was a huge soft hearted lad and chronically clumsy, and Ginger, Rocky, Spiv and last but not least Kevin. If I had known what the future held, maybe it would have been wise to capitulate there and then. Mike the punk rocker was the real supervisor, all the lads seemed to be in thrall to him, I tried to invite another of the lads to sit in the front with us, but all refused. I only had to pull into a lay-by once more on the seemingly long road to Kendal, and this was to break up a fight in the back, and try to restore some sort of order.

At the stores in Kendal I learned another lesson the hard way; I should have taken them in two at a time. It was chaos, the lads not being served were wandering around looking suspiciously like shoplifters, and the store man was going red in the face becoming very flustered. Each boy received boiler suit, gloves, steel toe capped work boots, waterproof leggings and jacket. The boys seemed delighted with the free goods supplied, the first time they had smiled all morning. When they all were fully equipped, they made a dash for the exit and found me blocking the door. I made them line up back at the counter and empty their pockets, to the store man's surprise a heap of small tools began to pile up, screw drivers, paint scrapers, torches, you name it and it was there.

"Bloody hell!" said the store man "That is amazing, so much stuff nicked in so little time."

I explained that it was my first day with the lads and they were testing me out, and would he let me deal with them without calling the police. The kind man said that if I left them outside in future, that would suffice, and I needed a bloody medal to take this job on. After the lads had apologized and thanked the man for not grassing them to the police they filed out. Our next stop was our office to introduce myself to the area manager and pick up lots of paperwork, mileage forms, discipline forms and instructions of where our first job was. The back of my vehicle was filling up with tools and equipment, several gallon of paint etc. etc. I explained that it was not healthy for all these youths to be cramped into the back of a smelly old van, unsafe with all the tools, stepladders etc. for such long road journeys. He just told me to chill out, all the other teams had to put up with it in the county, this was government job creation policy and everyone in the office including him had been unemployed before starting on this scheme. This would never be tolerated nowadays from any perspective, it was totally against health and safety, and indeed there were serious injuries happened on several occasions in different parts of the county. Not all the supervisors were fit and suitable to do this demanding type of work, and I saw myself that staff was picked just to fill the numbers needed, with little or no checks made. These were somebody's precious children, the scheme was very flawed, and a vast amount of money was wasted. After Job Creation the 'STEM' scheme which stood for short, term, employment measures, came into being, basically another job creation effort. I quickly realised that my new job could turn out to be a poisoned chalice.

The next morning I picked up the boys expecting to see them suitably attired in their new work gear, some of them had sold items already, and these I sent off to retrieve the various items back, on pain of taking the cost from their meagre wages. The time was now nearly midday and I was getting a little disillusioned with my new job. Finally leaving Barrow we set off for our first assignment on my list of various projects. My assistant supervisor the punk rocker asked where we were bound, and I replied that it was a remote lane on the other side of the Lakeland village called Ambleside.

"What may I ask is our assignment at this remote location?" said punk rocker.

He could be very articulate and nobody's fool this lad. "We have a few miles of National Trust metal railings to paint, they have not been touched since first put in place in Victorian times," I said.

" Bloody boring, repetitive, soul destroying work, that nobody over the years could be arsed to do until some bright spark in an overheated office thought of us!" said punk rocker.

A chorus of voices from the back shouted in unison "You can go and stuff yourself Norm; we are staying in the van until home time."

All I could say was to wait until we saw the actual job and then have a talk about it, we would be there shortly. Pulling up at a very short lay-by, we all piled out of the vehicle and looked in amazement at the row of rusty railings disappearing miles ahead until the next bend in the road. A National Trust van pulled up and a posh looking man in a suit got out, in a lovely cultured voice said, "Where the hell have you been, I was told by your office to meet you here at nine this morning, it is now one thirty, five times I have driven up this road looking for you, if this is an example of how you are going to be every day, you may as well bugger off back to where you came from!"

Being already threatened with mutiny by my team of boys, I was feeling rather peed off, and said "You cheeky sod, do you know how hard it is to motivate these boys, who have all been out of work since leaving school. All you are doing is supplying the paint for this task, the labour is free, you ought to be bloody grateful, and my lads can see the bloody railings have not been touched for donkey's years!" I told all the boys to get into the van, turned to the posh guy saying "I am with the boys on this one stick the job up your arse, we are going home."

Never have I seen a guy back track like this man did, in a conciliatory tone he whined, "Now hold on gentlemen I think we have started on the wrong footing, may we start afresh with an apology from me, and all shake hands?"

The boys were tickled pink; they piled out of the van and probably for the first time in their short lives shook hands with somebody, particularly with a National Trust officer. Peace was restored and I was still in employment. The officer who we will call Kevin explained in more detail how we were expected to renovate the metal railings.

First stage was removing the years of accumulated rust, using a wire brush, apply a coat of grey primer, second coat a brown coloured paint. The final coat was black. So every yard of rail was required to be attended to four times manually over a distance of several miles, which would be extremely boring and repetitive work for young people to do over several weeks. How to keep them motivated I had yet to discover, how to get them started at all? If I spread the full team out in a line, wire brushing and priming it might seem that progress was being made, at least in this remote place no shop lifting could occur, or could it? The upside to our task was that we were working in a particularly beautiful part of the Lake District and getting paid for it. In a show of hands all the boys said they had not ever been out of the town of Barrow before, and did not seem at all impressed with the lovely scenery. The warden said the boys could go into the woods on either side of the lane, and collect windfall branches to cut up for firewood and take home for anybody with a log fire. We had Bushman saws in our tool collection, so thought that when the boys were fed up they could let off steam sawing branches into logs. This idea came back to bite me on the bum later. By the time the boys were organised after their lunch of butties, crisps and fags, we had one hour left to actually make a start on our Forth Bridge project.

The National Trust were not daft, all their railings painted and the woodland cleaned up at the same time, a good deal for them all round. So over the next couple of weeks I did my best to achieve some progress on the railings, surprisingly most of the boys turned up each day. It was good job overalls were provided, the boys were slap happy using the paint, more ended up on their clothes and faces than on the railings. When they started to get bored, I sent two out with the bow saws to cut up fallen branches in the woods. They filled bags with neatly sawn logs to take home for their parents to burn on the fire. I was amazed at how many sacks of logs we squeezed into the back of our van. On the way home one afternoon I needed to call in at my father in law's who lived in the market town of Ulverston. Introducing him to all the boys he shook their hands and told them what a good job they were doing, and hoped that they would get full time employment soon. Punk rocker said "Do you have a coal fire Mr Sill?"

"I do as a matter of fact, why do you ask?"

Punk rocker ordered the boys in the back to carry all the sacks of logs into the pensioner's coal shed. Tickled pink my father in law Ben got out some money to pay the boys for the wood, Punk rocker said no way are we taking money from an old man, then jumped into the van. Ben thanked them all profusely and put a ten pound note in my hand, "Buy the boys some cakes tomorrow Norm, what a grand bunch they are, you can learn something from them as well!"

My father in law was one of life's gentlemen, kind, honest and cared about the community. He had worked for the same firm for fifty years as a foreman, working long after the official retirement age. I thought the world of Ben and his lovely wife Emily and he treated me like a son.

When the weather was hot I drove the boys to a nearby river, and they could either have a swim or sunbathe on the bank. The boys were heartily sick of painting railings and I did not blame them, so was I. The most annoying thing was what the steady stream of walkers going by invariably said, "You lucky lads, fancy getting paid to work outside in this beautiful place, the sun shining, we have travelled all the way from, America, Australia, Japan, New Zealand etc", well you get the drift!

At first the boys told them they ought to be here wire brushing on a cold, windy day, doing a boring job for the equivalent of peanuts, but soon became fed up with talking and just ignored the cheerful global tourist. Packing up all our gear at the end of the day was hard work, paint brushes to clean, lids to be put back on the gallon tins of paint. I had to ban Lurch from putting paint lids on, his method was to place on lid, then stamp on it with a large boot, the lid would buckle and his boot embedded into the tin, paint shooting out everywhere, he was one large clumsy sod! We started to finish working even earlier to try and clean the lads up, and make them a little more presentable before taking them home to Barrow.

CHAPTER NINE

YOU LITTLE CRETINS

Of course the honey moon stage was soon over, it happened one lovely sunny afternoon. I was supervising the gang working on the railings and heard raised voices coming from the direction of the woods. I recognised Kevin's voice, the warden, calling somebody 'cretins', then Kevin appeared with two of my wood cutting team. His face was bright red and he was obviously very angry about something. He walked to my van and slung two bushman saws into the back. "The bloody kids have been cutting the trees down for their firewood, which is criminal damage, I am going to bring in the police, these lad's are a bad lot from Barrow and need teaching a lesson!"

Punk rocker nipped to fetch Kevin a cup of tea; it needed all my powers of persuasion to convince him that the boys were doing an excellent job and deserved another chance. If the police were bought in they would never have a chance of gainful employment with a criminal record. Eventually tempers cooled down and after we promised to cut no more logs, calm once again prevailed. I could not help liking my team, the more we worked together the fonder I became. My wife unpacking my lunch box that night let out an almighty scream, the boys had found a huge toad and placed it inside of the box on a bed of lettuce leaves. Pauline did eventually get the joke after the initial shock, "Little sods your boys Norm" she said, "And you can take Mister Toad back to the Lakes tomorrow, and mind I do not want to see him again."

Every night afterwards I saw her opening my lunch box ever so carefully, I said to the lad's good joke but once is enough. One more week and the task was complete to the National Trust standards. It had been a marathon boring, repetitive project and everyone was glad to see the back of it. Kevin took us all to a pretty country pub, and treated us to the boys first bar snacks, including a half pint of beer. The boys were over the moon about it and I thought we were becoming a good team. The next Monday morning, we headed towards Kendal to find out where our new assignment would be, hoping it did not involve metal railings that would cause another mutiny. I thought it strange when phoning my office in Kendal, they asked me to bring all the boys into their office to see the top manager. All sorts of reasons why came into my head, had the National Trust decided to prosecute, did an overseas visitor to our shores feel insulted by the boys? After all I could not watch them closely all the time, when they were spread out along different lengths of railings. We were asked into the nicely appointed office and told to sit down and relax, tea and coffee, chocolate biscuits were offered. This does not look like a bollocking I thought, everyone is being very friendly.

"My star team welcome," the top man said, "I have here a glowing letter of praise from the National Trust informing me of the brilliant job done on their Victorian railings. Furthermore they realise what a thankless task it must have been for you all. If all my teams were like you boys, the scheme would be judged a success, you are the only team up to now that has not been in big trouble, indeed some of the supervisors have been dismissed on the spot for various serious misdemeanours. Thanks again boys, you finish your drinks and Norm can get the details of your next assignment, I have made sure you have the best task."

"Blow me down Norm I was not expecting that!" said Punk rocker.

Our next job was even further away from Barrow, over the Kirkstone Pass every day, in hail, sleet or snow to travel to a place similar to an outward bound school. This white painted detached building was I think, owned by the church and young people came from the Manchester area every weekend and holidays. This was great for us because we could work undisturbed all week, and not have to pack up all our gear every night. So the first day we set off to find the place, the boys in a great state of excitement looking forward to visiting their first outward bound school. The journey was tedious for the boys, no side windows to look at the spectacular scenery, so they did what they did best, sleep. Coming down the steep hill we could see our goal, a large building with various sheds, a wall surrounding it, and best of all alongside a large lake or tarn. "We have hit the jackpot boys", I said "somebody is looking after us."

I pulled into a car park and spent some time marvelling at the beautiful scenery all around us, surrounded by fields full of new born lambs. I had an envelope containing a heap of keys for all the various buildings, the boys were acting like it was their first holiday, hang on it was. Opening the door to the biggest outbuilding we gasped in amazement, along the back wall was racks of canoes, paddles, and lifejackets. In the middle of the room was a full-size table tennis table, and on the wall a dart board, complete with darts. We were all suitably impressed and ready to look into the main building. Inside on the ground floor was a large lounge, all sorts of wet weather games were provided, a cracking table soccer game which the boys started to fight over straight away. The kitchen was well fitted out, the place wanted for nothing except a good coat of white emulsion inside, skirting boards and doors glossed. Outside the complete house was required to be painted with white masonry paint, and the steel fire escape wire brushed and painted. Upstairs the bedrooms were full to bursting with bunk beds; already they had the boys lying down on each bed claiming which one was theirs. The praise they had from the manager was going to their heads; today they could enjoy the facilities, and tomorrow start work. We unloaded all the various step ladders, extension ladder off the roof rack, and the many gallons of paint I calculated we would need. This made more room in the back of our van for the boys to stretch out on their long road journey to get here from Barrow.

Over the next couple of weeks the boys got stuck into the job and progress was being made, the outside was finished except for painting the chimney white. This needed scaffold erecting to paint it safely and for the sake of one chimney I was not going to bother. While I was supervising inside the house, Punk rocker was lowering down one of his work mates on a rope, who was carrying a bucket of white paint and a paintbrush. When I next appeared and looked up at the once grey chimney, it was now pristine white. Of course I gave them a telling off about safety procedures; secretly I was proud of them. We had used all the sporting facilities over the weeks, except for the canoes and the next day was a day off from work. The day dawned perfect for our canoe expedition; we each carried a canoe down to the tarn edge. Lifejackets were fitted, paddles handed out and off we went. The boys took to canoeing like ducks to water, what a great day we all had, I tried to get them to leave at our normal going home time, and could not persuade them to leave until darkness fell. Our office told us we had permission to stay all week and sleep there in order to finish the job, my nerves would not stand being responsible for them for that length of time, so declined the kind offer. It was about this time that I noticed small bags of little mushrooms drying on the dashboard from the heater of the vehicle. Asking what the horrible looking things were for, "Punk rocker said they were for putting on salad sandwiches to flavour them, and were an acquired taste."

Never having seen mushrooms like those before, I was just used to picking the usual white button ones with the boys around the outward bounds school perimeter, and the outlying fields. I smelt a rat here, none of the kids had ever had a piece of lettuce, fruit or a sniff of anything but junk food in their lunch boxes since we met. It was jam, or cheese sandwiches, crisp and chocolate bars on a daily basis. I strode into the lounge, and picked up a large size dictionary of United Kingdom mushrooms and toadstools. Finding a good quality picture of a Psychedelic mushroom, or magic mushroom, I read they can be dried, chopped up and boiled for twenty minutes, then the contents drunk. Alternately they can be eaten raw. Throwing the bags of magic mushrooms onto the fire, I called all the lads together for a pep talk in the lounge. Whether me talking to them helped I do not know, no bags of mushrooms were ever seen by me afterwards, so maybe it worked. The six months were nearly up for the boys which meant back onto the unemployment register. Pauline told me to bring all the boys back to my house on their last day at work for a slap up roast dinner. There were candles on the table, bottles of wine and beer. Pauline knew I would be upset at losing the boys, over six months we had become a great team and good friends. They had even clubbed together and bought Pauline a present, which started her off crying. Did the scheme work? All I know is when we started working together they all seemed a little demoralised and lost; now they seemed happier, they had all learned basic skills for when they achieved homes of their own. They had testimonials from all the various agencies we had worked for, to help in their next job applications. My own team benefited in my opinion, I cannot speak for the other teams in Cumbria. On Monday morning I would start all over again with new faces. Many times over the years I have met some of the lads in town, some have children of their own and invariably come across and shake hands with me and it feels good.

CHAPTER TEN

WE BOUGHT YOU A CIGAR

It seemed every new team I started with had a genuine punk rocker complete with green or blue hair, always sitting in the front, and ending up as my assistant supervisor. We finished the last fiddly jobs at the outward bound school, managing to drag the new team away from the attractions. Next task was an amateur rugby club in a large village; we had to paint the changing rooms, the club lounge complete with bar was securely locked thank God. The spectator stand was also painted, quite a big job on the whole, and this village was one hour drive away from Barrow. Getting the boys different personalities to gel and work together was another nightmare I had to overcome. I received a phone call at the premises one lunch time to call at our office in Kendal. Asking why, the manager said I had to take some equipment from the office to another of our teams working at Arnside. I told him I had three teams spread around my large site and was reluctant to disturb them. The manager insisted that I left them working and come to Kendal immediately and no argument. Knowing this was a stupid idea I left the Punk rocker in sole command. At Kendal I received a lecture on how I should learn to trust the boys and give them responsibility, what a dick.

Arriving back at my work site, a head count revealed one lad missing. After convincing the boys that it was not funny, and they had one minute to tell me where he was, they pointed to the tiny grounds man's wooden shed at the bottom of the rugby field. I could not put my finger on quite why the boys were acting out of character, they seemed giggly and devil may care. When we all reached the shed, I opened it to reveal the most timid boy of our team; he was tied to a chair. The lenses of his heavy black spectacles were painted over with white paint, both his work boots were also painted white. I untied him asking him the names of who did this to him, he told me it was just a bit of fun and that he was not bothered in the least. The boys could plainly see that I was very angry, and they had gone a step too far this time. I made the lads clean all the paint off the boy and apologise. I knew it was a stupid decision to leave my team unsupervised for that length of time, and they were acting almost like they were drunk. They all were smoking a cigarette each which was very odd; usually they had to share one. I got them all into the vehicle and went to investigate the lounge where the bar was situated. Looking carefully around the bar shutters, I could see that the locks had not been tampered with. I breathed a great sigh of relief to know the boys had not broken into the bar and got drunk that way, I concluded that with time on their hands in my absence, they had clubbed together and bought some tins of beer and enjoyed a party, it got out of hand,hence picking on the timid boy. Another lesson learned by me, if I was ordered to leave on an errand by higher authority, all the team comes with me. The next morning the atmosphere in the van was a little subdued, the place stank of bad breath and loud farts punctuated the silence, even more than usual,we had to have all the windows open wide. When we arrived on site, Punk rocker wanted to apologise for all the upset the day before, and thanked me for being lenient with them. In fact they had all clubbed together to buy me a box of Castella cigars to thank me. To say I was touched would be an understatement, I nearly had a tear in my eye when I thanked them, knowing how expensive these cigars are, and how poor these boys were. Over the next week work progressed, the boys again had periods of giddiness, but I kept inspecting the bar to check for tampering.

The last week of work on this project the boys were showing odd signs again, and I could smell beer on some of their breaths. I phoned the bar steward, and asked him to inspect the bar again with me to see if we could see any signs of forced entry. The committee man examined the locks minutely, and said that there was no chance of my lads gaining entry to his bar, he told me to stop being suspicious. The trustees of the rugby club were very pleased with the painting and high standard of workmanship and another letter of appreciation came to me and our office. The manager said we were his flagship team and wished his other teams could emulate us. Driving home I was offered another cigar from Punk rocker already lit, puffing away I remarked how much I appreciated the team clubbing together again, but their kindness was not necessary and they must save their hard earned money.

"Bloody hell Norm you are naive, this cigar you are smoking and all the other ones are from the bar. It was a piece of piss getting into the bar for us over the past couple of weeks. One of us pretended to be stuck on a job on the far side of the field, and whilst you were diverted, we nipped behind the bar and filled up our coffee flask with beer, or whatever we fancied. We were not greedy Norm we only took enough for ourselves each day; we could have cleaned them out, but did not want to get you into trouble. We all agreed how well you have been to us, and we enjoyed seeing you smoking our gift of cigars! We looked on this as getting a little pay for all our hard work, and we know that we have saved them a small fortune in labour. We are only letting you know because we all agree you would not grass us up, what do you say?"

Automatically chucking my half smoked cigar out of the open window I said, "Holy cow you little sods, you could have had us all in deep shit, and me receiving stolen goods off you. How could I have missed all the signs, the team have gone from Hero's to Zero's in no time? Just tell me how you did it, I can't say anything because I want you all to have a chance of a decent job one day, and you have all got one last opportunity to redeem yourselves."

Punk rocker explained that the window in the bar needed only the flat blade of a paint scraper to slide the locking bolt across, to gain quick easy access. After listening to all their experiences over the last month, these boys have had a bloody hard life and deserved decent jobs, not just temporary ones. One thing was for sure, I would watch them like hawks on the next job.

Our young team were getting a good name for doing a decent job, no complaints from the clients, always a letter of appreciation and sometimes a gift each from a grateful committee. A vicar bought us all an expensive slate gift with built in clocks each after we had completed painting a church hall, this was an extremely kind gesture and the team was very proud. I have often wondered if any of the boys ever kept their souvenirs, and still have them at home. For a treat one day we had a day off and I drove us all to Blackpool visiting the funfair, to show my appreciation for the way they had shown respect to me, they could have given me a hard time. I had a whip round my mates and we collected enough money for a day on the funfair with fish and chips afterwards. I would have been sacked if found out but what the hell, it was worth it! Thinking it was the right thing to do at the time.

CHAPTER ELEVEN

THE FISHING TRIP

One of the boys was a little grafter, always ready on time and always wanting to assist me. He had a hard time at home, yet always had a smile for everyone. He seemed mad keen on hearing about my trawler man days and all the adventures I had, when I fished out of the port of Fleetwood. When he heard that I still owned a small trawler he kept asking when I was sailing again. One Friday on the way home from work I relented, and told him that I would pick him up at seven the next morning. Pauline and me picked him up and drove down to where my boat was moored in Walney channel. He insisted on rowing us all aboard and turned out to be a good oarsman. It was a beautiful sunny day and perfect for heading across Morecambe bay on the ebb tide. Junior, it was the name he wanted to be called, took the wheel and steered a course I gave him. Junior was bright as a button, picking up any new skill remarkably quickly. Pauline handed us both bacon butty's and mugs of coffee, whilst I started to prepare the trawl and repair a few small holes. It was a day to blow all your cares away. We steered across Morecambe bay and up Ulverston channel as far as we could go until we were in danger of running aground. I explained to Junior that we were going to shoot away our trawl net and tow slowly out with the tide, trying to catch the plaice draining off the top of the banks as the high tide drained out. Pauline steered the boat in the wheel house as Junior and I threw the trawl over, then the otter boards which were designed to keep the mouth of the net open when the water pressure was on them, finally paying out the required amount of trawl warp each.

The depth of water was so shallow that you could see the sand trail the trawl net kicked up, as we looked behind the boat the orange net floats were showing on the surface. Junior was getting very excited and could not stop talking and asking questions, he reminded me of my younger days when I was just like him. The net had been fishing for about an hour, Pauline passed us both another mug of coffee and an egg butty. I said we would be hauling the trawl in after we had finished our brew. Pauline was just as excited as Junior and they could hardly contain their impatience. I thought it was time we hauled and crossed my fingers for luck, there was nearly two hundred square miles of sand and sea in Morecambe bay and only local knowledge could put you on the fish. Just then the orange buoys on the trawls headline disappeared under the water, the two trawl warps went from being horizontal to a steep angle. This showed we were towing the net through deeper water; this was where there was a good chance of catching a nice amount of skate. Hold on for another twenty minutes I said we have found 'Bog Hole' a famous skate mark.

"Bloody hell Norm I am getting excited now, this is the best day of my life, and I do not want it to end!" said Junior.

The seagulls were gathering around the boat now, it is always amazing when they seem to know that it is time to haul in the net. I put the engine out of gear and as the revs dropped to a quiet murmur, I told Junior to start hauling on his warp in the stern and I hauled from the bow, swinging the boat broadside on to the weakening tide. I told Junior to slow down I could not keep pace with him, we each pulled an otter board in, and the trawl lay spread out alongside the boat. We could see fish of various types flapping about in the mouth of the net which was a good sign, in the final length of net where the fish collect, called the cod end, we looked set for a decent catch. I said we all looked the part, kitted out in bright yellow fishermen's bib and braces and smocks. The din from the gulls was deafening, wheeling and diving to catch any small fish that were shaken out of the meshes as we three all hauled at once. Flaking the net on the boats side deck neatly, the weight of the accumulated fish in the last section of net became apparent. The boat had a good list to starboard with all the weight on that side, I passed a rope lifting strop around the net, placing in the hook from the lifting derrick and started to heave. We had no winch on the boat so all the hard pulling was done by hand, hence having to fish in shallow water and that was graft enough. Pauline and Junior could now help me pulling on the block and tackle to lift aboard the full cod end of fish, hopefully.

The full bag of swinging fish had to be held whilst I reached underneath to pull the two ends of the special fisherman's knot that never jammed, no matter what heavy weight was in the cod end. My two crew members were whooping with joy when I released the knot, and a huge cascade of fish spread into the deck pound, maybe one foot deep in various species of sea life. Now normally somebody would tie up the cod end straight away, a man on the wheel and the other would get ready to shoot away the trawl immediately, the net was not earning money lying on the deck idle. My crew had other ideas; they were so excited they threw themselves into the fish pounds, shouting about cod, plaice, Dover sole, skate, and a huge angler fish fought its way to the top of the heap. Pauline shouted and picked up a huge blue lobster, placing it alone into a basket. I had lost total control of my crew and I must admit it was a fine sight to see such a colourful and varied variety of fish species on our deck. I placed some baskets around the deck with instructions to use the measuring board to check any fish size they thought were under the legal length. I made us all a brew and watched their reaction to seeing so much fish for the first time, juniors face was a picture. It was indeed a colourful sight to see bright sea- anemones, sea-cucumbers, whelks, crabs, various types of jelly fish, starfish, sea-urchins, lengths of kelp, mermaids purses (the egg cases of the spotted dogfish) Now all this catch had to be sorted into what was saleable and what needed to be thrown over quickly to aid their survival, the small fish returned to the water swiftly would be the next seasons catch. The gulls were even walking around on the deck, pinching any fish they could when your back was turned.

Deciding that another tow was not necessary we had all the fish we needed, and enough for me to get rid of for one day, I asked who wanted to take the wheel and head the boat toward Walney Lighthouse in the far distance. The two amigos refused to leave the fish pound and Pauline was showing Junior how to gut the fish cleanly and efficiently to remove any liver and guts which would spoil the fish. So I was voted to have the boring job steering the boat back to my mooring at Barrow channel. The plus side was Junior wanted to crew for me, and I wanted to see the look on his face when I gave him his share of the money from today's catch, which would be quite considerable, it was all prime fish. He could also take the lobster for his grandma whom he lived with. I remembered to explain that some fishing trips did not earn a penny because of the possibility of ripping a big hole in the net, lack of fish, and many other imponderables. Over the coming months Junior learned how to splice rope, tie knots, steer a compass course and best of all make a bloody good mug of tea. When it was time for Junior to leave the scheme I was particularly concerned about his future, and even asked the senior manager if we could get some kind of special dispensation to keep him on longer. He had shown his willingness to work hard and learn new skills, was a great time keeper and never missed a day's work and was a great influence on all the other trainees. He and his girlfriend crewed for me for a while on my trawler and eventually they got married and raised a family; on the rare occasion when we meet up in town he shakes my hand and gives Pauline a big hug.

I badly needed a holiday so arranged for my team to all take the same week off to make it easier for me. We went to stay in a cottage at Port Patrick in Scotland a lovely fishing village. Pauline wanted a walk along the cliff path and packed a flask and sandwiches, the sun was shining, and the blue calm sea was shimmering in the sunlight, all in all a perfect day for walking. Far below us was a remote cove accessed by a very steep path, it looked ideal for a secluded picnic, we had not seen another human being all morning only a vast variety of seabirds wheeling and diving off the cliff face. The cove was truly magical, when we reached the bottom we were surrounded by grassy ledges, some bushes and small trees. Ahead of us looking out to sea was a very small grassy topped island, and all around us was flotsam and jetsam washed up on a high shingle bank after the winter storms.

Pauline unpacked a travel rug and the food whilst I explored the tide line; beach combing was a childhood passion of mine. Amongst the kelp and wood an unfamiliar object stood out, it was to my surprise a funeral urn, unscrewing the top I could see the poor souls mortal ash remains still inside. Some small holes had been drilled in the top to enable the urn to sink but obviously not enough. There was still an undertakers label on the side which stated who the person was, but the emersion in the seawater had made the ink run and was now illegible. The family must have been giving them a sea burial thinking that the urn would sink, but unfortunately it had not sunk but drifted away on the tide.

Pauline and I discussed what to do with the remains and we concluded that the remote beautiful cove was the ideal place to bury the urn, just above the high water mark. If we had been able to get in touch with the relatives it might be upsetting for them so decided in our humble opinion it was the right thing to do. We dug a deep hole in the shingle and placed the urn inside. We both stood with bowed heads and said the Lord's Prayer; Pauline said "This seems a little inadequate Norm I think we should sing a hymn 'All Things Bright and Beautiful,' seems appropriate."

I agreed thinking that nobody is around to be offended by my total lack of a singing voice and Pauline has a lovely tone to her singing having spent years in the local amateur dramatic society when younger. Actually I was a little overcome with the emotion of it all; as we sang this lovely hymn tears flowed down my lovely wife's face. The skylarks were singing, overhead seagulls swooped and dived with a backdrop of perfect blue sky, and the gentle swell rolled over the shingle, a perfect fitting resting place for anyone.

We were startled to hear someone cough nearby, not twelve feet above us on a flat grassy ledge four people were staring at us in amazement. Two children and two adults sitting on a blanket, did they realize what we were doing or did they think we were two people that had completely lost their marbles performing some kind of weird secret ritual. To say we were embarrassed would be an understatement, we were mortified. Quickly throwing all the picnic things together we hurriedly raced back up the cliff path, never looking behind once. At the top of the cliff pausing for breath Pauline gasped "Would you not think one of the family would have said something when we first appeared into the cove, how bloody embarrassing!"

CHAPTER TWELVE

A SAD TIME

All the trainee boys were working hard, and seemed to be enjoying the variety of work coming our way, nobody pulling any sickness days so I must have been doing something right. Our latest job was a community hall in the Ambleside village next to Lake Windermere. Glossing and emulsion required, so nothing the boys would find too difficult. The only problem I found was me having to accompany the boys to the village shops at lunchtime to keep them from getting tempted to shop lift, and having to leave the odd boys behind in the village hall each day on trust. Only the day I decided to return early to check on the two boys, presumably having their lunch in the hall, I found one outside on watch, and pushing passed him caught the other boy about to have sex with a local girl. We had seen this rather pretty girl hanging around all week at the hall. I could feel my hair turning greyer by the minute, I did not know what surprise was coming my way next, this must be the hardest way to make a living ever.

It was Friday evening, time for me to wind down in my extensive garden, three lawns to cut, hens to feed, crops to pick to feed our large family. Dad loved living here, planting everything imaginable, and our two large greenhouses being put to good use. I picked up a lot of gardening skills from dad that would come in handy in later life. Anyway this particular warm evening Pauline wanted a brisk walk to watch the sun setting over the Irish sea, and we left dad watching his favourite cowboy film. Our two youngest girls were having a chat and my mother was fetching them cake and coffee, all was peaceful, just as it should be. Twenty minutes into the walk I had a premonition that something was wrong, it was a dreadful feeling of foreboding and a voice in my head was telling me to return home. I told Pauline that we needed to go back. She was enjoying the walk and we had an argument about me spoiling the evening for her, she told me not to be so silly and carry on, the sunset would be spectacular tonight. I turned back for home, and all the way Pauline was complaining that I had spoilt her walk. We entered our lounge and everything was normal, the two girls still chatting away, dad enjoying his cowboy film. Pauline gave me that smug luck that proved I was being silly and said if we hurry we could still see a beautiful sunset. I looked at dad knowing that something dreadful was going to happen. Mum passed dad a cup of tea, he suddenly stood up and carried the cup and saucer into the kitchen and laid it gently on the work top without spilling a drop. I followed him into the kitchen, he turned and put his arms around me and collapsed into my arms. Thick blood poured out of his mouth in a great gush, I lowered him gently onto the floor, and he had lost all his life's blood in seconds. He looked into my eyes and a small flash of light left his body, it was like a spark of electricity and he was gone. In that split second I knew it was dad's soul leaving his body, and in a strange way that was comforting, because ever after I have believed our souls go on forever in some other form. I also believe that I was meant to be there when the tragedy happened, the voice that told me to return home was a voice I could not possibly ignore. The two girls took mum upstairs out of the way, and Pauline cleaned up all the blood from the kitchen floor. The ambulance men knew straight away that nothing could be done, it was the undertakers that took over and removed poor dad from the house. This was the first death I had ever experienced, and the first funeral I had ever attended, we were all distraught. They had had their golden wedding and been together many years, both having very hard lives until their later years. One nice touch was when the funeral cortege was passing Vickers shipyard, where dad spent his last working years, all the Vickers security men standing at the entrance gates took off their hats and bowed their heads. After the funeral we did what we thought dad would have wanted and had a wake in the local pub.

In the weeks following I could not bear to live in the house any longer, all the work dad had done in the huge garden made me realise that I could not carry it on myself. We decided to move and mother said she wanted to go as well, so the three of us picked a lovely terraced house the other end of Walney Island, the house had lovely views down the channel towards Piel Island and the castle. Our new neighbours had a panic attack when I turned up with a van load of assorted punk rockers, bedecked with chains and various piercings, who insisted on giving us a Saturday's free labour helping us to move in to our new home.

CHAPTER THIRTEEN

PROMOTION AND DEMOTION

I was called into our Kendal office and promoted to senior supervisor, overseeing four supervisors, each one expert in Construction, Painting and Decorating, and Horticulture. Our workforce consisted of thirty young trainees under the Youth Training Scheme and responsibility of putting together training modules and actual training on the job. This entailed me travelling around Barrow and South Cumbria setting up various village halls, sailing clubs, churches, and a long term assignment at Ruskin's, Brantwood home on the shores of Coniston Lake. We supplied a greenhouse for the horticultural team in the grounds; they spent months cutting down and burning the rampant growth of rhododendrons and restoring original pathways in the extensive gardens.

I had my own office in Barrow and hated not being with my team anymore, the fun had gone out of my job, I was spending all my time doing paperwork. The time had come for me to get back to sea. Like I pointed out in my first autobiography book, just when you need it most fate deals you another hand. My eldest brother who had been telling me for years to join him at Barrow docks, informed me of a vacancy as a marine port operator. I thought it was easier than buying a large trawler again, and sensible to at least give it a try, so I applied. I was asked to go for an interview at the Port office and given an interview by Captain Jackson the harbour master, one of life's gentlemen; he did not need a panel of experts to help him assess a candidate. Straight to the point he said "Are you by any chance John Pascoe's brother?"

"Yes Captain I am, his younger brother actually."

"If you are half as good as him, you will do me, when can you start?" he said.

After giving one weeks' notice to my employers, I left with glowing references and embarked on a career that would give me ten years of quite an adventurous life. Working for the docks was like going back in time; I took a long time to adapt to this slow pace of life and at first could not believe my good luck. Big brother advised me well, I thought I had died and gone to heaven. Promotion at the docks was dead man's shoes; you started in the harbour yard working under a foreman responsible mainly for the maintenance and replacing of the many channel buoys that marked the long dredged channel leading into the port of Barrow. I was part of a pool of men that every Monday morning could be assigned to any marine department on the docks, mainly to stand in for a week for anyone on holiday or sick. This could mean being assigned to the Rhymney, the old port dredger (which had two grab cranes on board) as a crew deckhand, or cook. Another possibility was deckhand on the survey launch Dova Haw, or aboard the backup launch called the Silurian. A job on shift work assisting opening the lock gates or pier head duties was another task. Last but not least, helping in the engineering workshops, mainly doing various task involving manual work. So life down the docks was never boring, on a Monday morning you could be travelling to Fleetwood, Ayr in Scotland or just dredging in Barrow channel for a week. Associated British Ports owned several docks up and down the country, and had not long issued shares to all their employees, which would prove to be very profitable in future years.

When not assigned to other dock duties, it was good old fashioned graft working on the small inner channel buoys and the huge steel outer buoys which weighed several tons. The first stage in renovating the buoys was out at sea changing the old buoy for a new one. This was done in various ways; we adapted our own system over the years. When the huge outer Bar buoy was towed in and locked through the dock system, and moored alongside the harbour yard quayside. Our team waited for the vintage dock mobile crane to arrive. Now this old crane's four stabilising feet had to be wound out manually by hand using a ratchet, heavy blocks of wood were placed under the feet to cushion the weight. No hydraulics only a long lattice framed jib, we placed the wire sling on the buoy and the crane took the weight and slowly lifted the heavy buoy. The crane then held the buoy at head height just at the very edge of the quayside, the three or five harbour yard men donned their waterproofs and did a very stupid and dangerous practice. We stood underneath a very old crane, and using wide steel scrapers on wooden poles to reach up under the buoys bottom, dug into the mass of weed, mussels, eels and assorted sea life that had made their home there for up to three years. After scraping this mass off and letting most of it fall into the dock, the rest still on the quay was pushed into the dock using wide yard brushes, sometimes we picked a feed of mussels to take home. The next dangerous stage was to somehow lift the buoy from one side so that it tilted, and using a long rope with all of us pulling like idiots try and pull the buoy over onto its side, before slipping a disc. This usually resulted in strained backs, and lots of bad language directed at the harbour yard foreman for these age old practices. Six times out of ten doing this job resulted in mayhem trying to control manually, tons of unstable buoys. When the buoy was at last chocked up on its side with wood baulks, the crane dismissed, and us all knackered; we all had an extended brew in the buoy shed foreman's office wondering how somebody had not been killed. When the boss was fed up with our moaning he kicked us all out to start cleaning off the bottom and top of the buoy with a powerful hosepipe. Next a noisy diesel high pressure compressor was started, and sets of vintage needle guns were coupled up to chip off the thick black tar on the base and the red or green coloured gloss paint off the buoy's superstructure. It was our foreman's policy to chip down to the bare metal each time, very labour intensive and unnecessary in our view, but maybe the boss wanted to keep us busy until a few of us were required on other jobs. It was a few years before the new regime started to make sweeping changes to our working lives. We wore ear defenders when chipping the buoys; the noise was terrible when four of us were using needle guns at the same time. First the bottom had several coats of black tar, then the topsides primer, undercoat and finish gloss, red or green depending on port or starboard hand channel buoys. Years later when the Trident submarine project started, and getting money out of the Ministry of Defence was no object, they paid for all new lighter plastic buoys, so the end of another dangerous traditional working practice was over.

One particular task I found quaint, it had to be done at low tide on the edge of Walney channel, and I was carrying a huge five feet long metal screw device with a ring on the top. My two pals were carrying a six foot long steel round bar, hacksaws and large shackle. After we reached a small channel buoy after a long walk across the mud flats, our foreman explained the object of our mission. He pointed to the heavy mooring chain and said "It is knackered that screw eye that is in the ground, cut the end links off, screw the new mooring into the ground and shackle the good chain to the new eye, piece of piss for me, get working, the tide will be flooding soon!"

Now I knew what everything was for, I held the five feet long screw upright, the long bar was put through the hole, and two men walked around like old time sailors working a ship's capstan. The ground was a mixture of clay and mud, so the effort needed to get this steel screw down to sea level was considerable; sweat was pissing off my mates so we had to take turns, excepting the Harbour yard foreman of course, he always wore a uniform, complete with brass buttons, peaked cap, pristine white shirt and black tie. When the screw was in the ground far enough, we had to take turns with the hacksaws to cut through the rusty chain, God help anyone who snapped an hacksaw blade and this was not easy. When our task was finally done, a long walk carrying our tools back up the marshes to Biggar Village, where we had parked our lorry. We had a lighter load coming back, no heavy shackle and no heavy mooring screw. Only a few of these channel buoys were accessible at low tide, the ones in deeper water the tide never fully left had to be kept in position by using heavy cast iron and later cheaper concrete sinkers. After a couple of weeks chipping and painting bloody channel buoys, you would be getting very peed off, and prayed on Monday morning for a week as deckhand or such like, any job was more interesting than the buoy shed. One consolation was the huge size of blackberries that grew in the compound, when Pauline wanted to make pies or crumble I could pick the blackberries in the firm's time when the foreman was not around.

CHAPTER FOURTEEN

THE TORPEDO

One morning I was told to report to the twin grab dredger to train as a crane driver on the Rhymney, a one week at least post, the grab driver had phoned in sick. I reported to the ship moored at the deep water berth, the skipper said I was to train on the aft end crane, my eldest brother had the forward crane this week. The ship pulled over to the deep hole, dredged for the newly launched submarine to lay in if an emergency arose that prevented the tugs getting her into the dock entrance. The Ministry of Defence paid the docks a lot of money to keep the hole dredged to a certain depth, because Walney channel's swift tide bought in large amounts of silt. The skipper put the boat in position and disappeared to his cabin situated under the bridge wing, my brother explained what the various clutches and levers were for. The first problem was me being short arsed, my right leg could not reach the pedal that was used to brake the jib slewing to right or left. The cab was very greasy and my boots were sliding on the chequer plate floor, my brother had to get the ship's engineer to bolt a block of wood onto the pedal so I could reach it. "Your bloody hard work Norm," said my brother.

"It is a pleasure to work with you too John," I said. He stood behind me for about thirty minutes and turned to climb out of the cab. "Last words of advice Norm do not let too much cable run out after the grab hits the sea floor, if the wire runs slack and runs off the sheave it may jam, the grab is out of action, and the ship's engineer will probably kill you."

With those kind words big brother buggered off back to his beloved forward grab. I got cocky after a short period of time and had visions of earning big money driving the grab full time, assuming of course the permanent driver stopped off work. When the skipper of the boat thought you were qualified enough to competently drive the grab, he phoned up the port engineer, who stood on the quayside watching you working the grab for ten minutes and if it was a cold day soon walked back up to the office. In a few days you received a letter saying you had passed, simple. I never received a passing out letter; because unfortunately my foot slipped on the greasy wooden pedal and the full grab of channel mud flattened some of the ships rails. I received a rollicking form the extra work the ship's engineer had to do. The next hour went well I thought it was just like operating one of those fairground grabs that fall down and hook a cuddly toy. Never been successful with them either, but at least the bloody controls were not greased up to hell! Well my party had to come to an end, just when I was beginning to enjoy it. I slewed the jib around to my left rather too quickly; my boot slipped off the greasy pedal I lost control and the huge jib hit the ships bridge house. What a bang and a crash, a huge bloody great dent was put into the ship's bridge. I realised that my accident had been noticed when all the crew appeared from every nook and cranny where they had been idling, whilst me and my brother had been doing the only work. The skipper came out of his cabin onto the bridge wing, leaned over and angrily said, "You bloody imbecile are you trying to dismantle my ship bit by bit, the impact of the jib crashing into the bridge shot me out of my bunk. Hell will freeze over before I let you drive one of my grabs again!"

"But skipper the cabs full of bloody grease my foot keeps slipping!"

"No more feeble excuses get out of that cab now you are deckhand for the rest of the week!" skipper said.

It could have been worse he could have sent me back to the harbour yard to paint and chip buoys. I got to work with my brother that was nice, the only fly in the ointment was the second engineer had to drive the crane which pissed him off, and I discreetly kept out of his way. In those far off days the work force was so easy going, everyone seemed to get on well, no hassles or stress. I had been used to grafting and this job seemed unreal. Loads of variety and interesting jobs to do each day, and I could not believe how lucky I was to do a job like this. One lovely summers day I had been painting buoys and the skipper of the dredger was walking passed, "It is too nice a day to be stuck here Norm go ask

Frank the foreman if you can come on board the Rhymney, we are full up and going out to sea to the spoil ground to dump. We are not back until early evening and you can steer the boat there and back if you like!"

Well Frank said no bother but he could not pay overtime after my official finishing time, it was only two o'clock in the afternoon and I finished at five. That's how flexible the docks were in those days, Frank knew how bored I was with the painting and how much I would enjoy going for a trip out to sea on the dredger, I did not dream of getting paid after teatime. It was great being on pier head duty, we worked the tide times, two hours before high water until two hours after, then the dock entrance gate was closed and shipping had to wait for the next high water time. The variety of ships using the port varied and sometimes we locked them through to the inner dock system, nuclear submarines, new built warships, cargo ships in fact anything that floated. The docks are manned twenty four hours a day every day of the year, and I worked several Xmas days over the next ten years.

The Rhymney was dredging near the new nuclear fleet submarine HMS Torbay in Barrow docks, when in the grab emerging from the muddy water was firmly grasped a long torpedo. The grab driver gently lowered the torpedo onto the deck of the Rhymney; to say he was surprised would be an understatement, rumour was he had to quickly get a change of underpants, for all he or the crew knew it could have been ready to explode at any moment. This would be 1986 in December, the skipper was told to move the ship to the least populated area of the various dock systems. Vickers was informed and the Royal Navy explosive team from Plymouth were on their way, blue lights flashing and police escort up the motorway. Meanwhile the torpedo was covered in old carpet and my brother John was delighted to work overtime keeping the torpedo company and playing the deck wash hose onto it to keep it cool. I phoned my sister in law to tell her our John will not be home until further notice. When she asked why I said "He has dredged up a possible live torpedo and he is playing a hose pipe on it as we speak." She did not believe me and put down the phone thinking I was playing a joke on her, only being convinced when it came on the local radio station.

The bomb disposal team arrived after a long motorway drive to declare it harmless. It turned out to be a long lost Mark 44 torpedo dummy which sank in 1975 during deck launcher trials from the Type 42 destroyer Hercules, then being built for Argentina. The torpedo had sunk after the sixth and final firing during harbour acceptance trials. It had developed a leak and a nylon rope used to retrieve it parted as the torpedo left the vessel. The dummy disappeared into the mud of the dock bottom, remaining there for ten years despite the efforts of divers to locate. The torpedo was removed to Vickers tip on the North end of Walney Island and blown up by the Navy. Some excitement for the crew of the Rhymney and a few hours overtime, and still all here to tell the tale...

The dock office phoned our buoy shed asking for a deckhand for the Rhymney, it so happened that all the pool of men were out on different assignments except for me. Our foreman was happy to send his last man; it meant nobody in his department left to bother him for a week at least. He could put his feet up on the desk and snooze in peace, dreaming about his next holiday in Madeira. Well I struck lucky the Rhymney was working in the dock dredging the newly built ship fitting out berth by the High Level Bridge, under the giant dockside crane. This berth had not been dredged ever to my knowledge, and when the grabs came up they were both full of various scrap pieces, namely very valuable copper and brass. Now the deckhands had a full time job pulling out the valuable metal before depositing the oily silt that was left into the hold, where when full would be dumped out to sea and lost forever. The managers at Vickers who were paying the docks for the dredging contract were not happy when each grab bucket was carefully held over the side deck for us to delve into each grab and triumphantly pull out a huge lump of copper or brass.

Where all this valuable metal came from was well known to local people for years. This being the fitting out berth for grand ocean liners, and warships from the time of the docks opening, craftsmen and apprentices threw over the ships side into the dock any jobs they had made that did not fit correctly for various reasons, then go back to their workshops and make another. When the buckets came up with steel, iron or steel wire it was dumped straight into the hold. What came up was fascinating, vintage oil lamps, ornately worked brass fittings from Victorian times; unfortunately all damaged and crushed by the grabs. It all became a free for all; the stack of valuable metal was growing very substantial. Our dock office was receiving complaints that we were scavenging in the grabs like scrap metal merchants and holding up the contract. On the next trip out to the dump grounds the bottom doors that were opened at sea to allow the spoil to drop out of the ships hold got jammed with some of the enormous amount of steel wire dredged up. This necessitated hiring a team of divers to clear the doors of the wire jamming underwater. This gave the skipper an idea to use a Vickers barge tied alongside the dredger so that any wire could be pulled out of the grabs onto the barge, the wire disposed onto Vickers tip by them. A perfect excuse for us to pull out our valuable metal onto the deck of the barge at the same time, which made us very happy, if we had more time I am sure we would have found something better than scrap value. The oily, slimy mud clung to us like a coat and the smell was awful, but we knew we all had a substantial bonus coming our way. This was a once in a lifetime opportunity, I had been fortunate to get my foreman to let me have an extra week. The mate on the Rhymney said the crew were having a meeting in the mess room to vote on my share of the loot. I told him whatever cash received would be appreciated by me, it beat the hell out of working in the harbour yard chipping and painting channel buoys. When we were moored up Friday evening after the scrap dealers lorry had driven off with the golden cargo, the mate handed me an envelope stuffed full of cash, telling me this was my share. I must say it was a very welcome and generous addition to my wages, like I have said before they were a grand bunch of men.

The next week a plum job on the Rhymney came up again, a trip to Fleetwood dock dredging the Roll On, Roll Off berth in Wyre Channel. This was another chance to earn a lot of money for a two week trip, Frank said I could stay on board if I liked, not being greedy I passed the deck hand job to a mate in the harbour yard that I knew was struggling financially. That was the least I could do after my profitable time aboard collecting scrap. I was gradually going up the pecking order as people died, got sacked or just left for pastures new, the first in the harbour yard were being promoted to the next permanent positions, like I said dead man's shoes, the next man on the list was offered the job and rarely was it refused. If you declined the job your name went to the list bottom and you had to work your way up again. Getting back to the top could take years of chipping buoys, waiting for your ideal dock job to appear just when you had reached the top of the list again.

CHAPTER FIFTEEN

SKIPPER AGAIN

There came a new regime, out with the old and in with the new, Captain Jackson a greatly respected Harbour Master retired, things were never the same again. The company policy was multi tasking and a job was given on merit, not dead man's shoes anymore. In many ways it was better but bloody hard to get used to the new ways. Wages were calculated on how each individual worker multitasked, and each individual could be paid a higher or lower salary. This did not bother me unduly because working in the harbour yard you had always been on call to learn most of the dock jobs over time. The skipper of the port survey vessel had just retired; the harbour yard foreman and the entire crew of the port's dredger took redundancy. The dredger had developed a leak and instead of repairing her, she was sold. Possibly the first time a dredger had not been permanently based in Barrow.

I applied for the skippers job on the Dova Haw which was an all white painted catamaran used for surveying, small buoy changing, and a vast variety of jobs. In Captain Jackson's time at Barrow if the skipper of the Dova Haw was caught towing a channel buoy or using it as a platform to work off, he would have been severely reprimanded. When I got the job it was used for a workboat, towing work etc. in fact anything, I would never be bored. The area I had to survey with a dedicated small team of hydrographers was vast. From Scarth Hole at the north end of Walney Island to Lightning Knoll buoy a few miles off the south end of Walney Island, also the huge area of Barrow dock system. My new contract also included towing work, buoy changing, servicing all the Leading Lights and transportation of personnel. Routine maintenance of my vessel and be expert in using a boarding dinghy in the rip tides of Walney channel when the Dova Haw is left on a mooring. We also had a standby spare survey boat called the Silurian; we did not use this old boat if we could help it. My survey team had to do an awful amount of overtime when the trailing suction dredger was doing the annual full channel dredge; this dredger sucked up the silt like a Hoover, filled the holds and headed out to sea to dump. Our survey boat was called out at all times in order to make sure the right amount of silt was being removed. The docks seemed a lot quieter with all the staff that was made redundant gone, the heart had gone out of the place and it never seemed as easy going anymore. The docks decided to buy their own pilot boat and employ a permanent dock pilot. I also became the skipper of our new pilot cutter boat called the Gertrude, she was sent from our sister port of Hull, forty feet in length and very fast. She was capable of sailing through really bad conditions and with her powerful twin diesels gave you confidence in stormy weather. I had to organise another mooring in Walney channel for when we needed to get down channel to meet a ship early off Lightening Knoll buoy.

This also meant having a small boarding dinghy light enough for the pilot boat skipper and deckhand to drag up and down the beach; this was sometimes done in pitch dark conditions and at all hours of the night. Sometimes it was very dangerous to row aboard the Dova Haw or Gertrude on the moorings, when experiencing wind against tide on the flood it required very skilful handling of small tenders. Obviously we preferred to have both boats inside the dock where we could just step aboard in complete safety, this was not possible on occasions as the main gate being tidal could only open two hours before high water until two hours after, which made access restricted. Later on a tragedy happened, two men were rowing at night to board the pilot boat using the small boarding dinghy, and when they got near to the Gertrude the dinghy overturned throwing both men into the freezing water. One man died and the other rescued by the bravery of a shipyard worker who heard his cries for help, a little more on this story later.

The method of surveying the Barrow channel approaches using line of sight visual positioning was about to change dramatically. For many years the side of Walney channel had posts and perches set up, this enabled the coxswain of the survey boat to steer from point to point across the channel using an expensive paper recording echo sounder to show the seabed contours. This entailed a man standing at the tide gauge at the dock entrance entering the time and the tidal height every few minutes. This manual method of surveying was very skilful and sufficed for many years until it was decided to build a new generation of monster sized Trident submarines. These leviathans were too big to be launched on slipways into Walney channel; a huge covered ship building hall was constructed and a giant ship lift was commissioned to lift the enormous submarines in and out of the dock. Also the length of Walney channel needed to be dredged a lot deeper for the passage out to sea of these new Trident submarines. Massive new facilities were needed at their new base at Faslane in Scotland. So the survey work became crucial and the old methods too inaccurate, the whole project would eat up millions upon millions of pounds, our small survey team needed to be trained into the computer age. A complete new dock entrance needed to be built and millions of tons of silt removed from the channel. I had to learn how to use a micro fix system to steer a course along a channel divided every ten metres for several miles out to Lightning Knoll buoy. Going across the channel from the dock entrance out to sea doing all this was called a full channel survey, and the Ministry of Defence paid Associated Ports the owners of Barrow docks for a full survey every month for several years. Depending on weather it could take two weeks or a full month to achieve this, and our small team never failed to have a full up to date chart produced by the month end ever. This was a great undertaking considering boat break downs, illness and constant malfunctions of the Micro fix stations which were set up at various points around Barrow and Morecambe bay; we even had a Micro fix on top of Barrow town hall.

This repetitive survey work was mind numbing and I was glad to have the other variety of seagoing work I loved more. It was a nice change to take the electricians out to the buoys and leading lights to change bulbs and batteries. The Dova Haw was also used for the inside channel buoys replacing them with a new one and towing the old one back to the harbour yard. We fitted a steel lifting derrick in the stern and using rope pulleys heaved in the old chain by hand, no health and safety just using brute force, no power winches. Sometimes I and Michelle my young female hydrographer would have to be at sea manning the boat on our own, sometimes due to lack of crew or nobody was willing to do a sixteen hour day crewing for us in order to finish off a particular urgent survey, my surveyor friend Alan had left by this time. Having a lifetime's local knowledge enabled me to survey in a gale of wind because I could find a lee somewhere in Walney channel to complete a section in relatively calm conditions. One particular day in a howling gale after finishing a survey at low tide, I ran the Dova Haw aground under the lee of Walney lighthouse for our lunch. We switched off the two noisy engines knowing the tide would not be around us for a while, the steep sand bank above us had the wind howling above us and we were lying snug. The pier head whose call sign was Ramsden dock radio called us up worrying about the strong gale blowing and if we were all right. The sky was blue, the sea was blue, huge white combers were rolling in at the entrance to the channel, and Michelle was commenting on how the two seals alongside our boat were very partial to her sandwiches. One could not help but think we were getting well paid to be here and many workers were slaving in factory environments, not seeing what we were experiencing. I thought that this job would never equal trawling for a living but it was the next best thing. To one side of us the open sea, huge waves pounding onto the groyne, in front of us Walney lighthouse its white tower appearing above the sand dunes, where my good friend Peggy, England's only female light house keeper used to live. On my right hand side the magnificent ruins on Piel Island with its majestic medieval sandstone and cobble built castle standing proud, this beautiful view bringing back my childhood memories of long summer camping trips. Playing truant from school and rowing our small dinghy all the way from Ferry Beach loaded to the gunnels with camping equipment and fishing gear. When the flood tide started and our survey boat began to drift off the sandbank it was time to start both noisy diesels, disturbing the tranquillity and wakening the dozing gulls sleeping on our wheelhouse roof. I said to my friend Michelle "We will look back on these days in the future with nostalgia."

A swift journey back up the channel, Michelle handling the helm like a professional enjoying the rough sea being kicked up, this because of the wind going against the tide, heavy spray shooting high over our wheelhouse. I was down below checking that everything in the two engine rooms was working right, listening to Michelle whooping with joy every time an exceptional wave hit the bows. We put the boat back on her channel mooring ready for an early start the next day, and I rowed us ashore in the dinghy before the channel became too rough for our frail dinghy, what you would say was a good day at the office!

CHAPTER SIXTEEN

THE PILOT BOAT

This chapter explains the feeling of being a coxswain in charge of a modern twin screw fast pilot cutter having to leave harbour when other boats are running for shelter and in all weather conditions, in order to put a pilot on or off various types of ship. The boat must be strong enough to resist turbulent seas and tolerate being crashed into the side of larger vessels. Pilot boat operators face many formidable challenges, from their control position they must gauge exactly the right moment to move alongside the vessel so that the pilot can safely grab the rungs of a rope ladder or hand holes. The pilot boat deckhand usually assists the pilot onto the ladder. The coxswain must be constantly alert because the situation can become dangerous very quickly, especially in heavy seas and at night. Sometimes I would have to abort the approach and try again, letting the vessel know what my intentions were. When the cargo vessel or whatever was high out of the water the pilot would have quite a height to climb, they needed to be very fit, in the old days before new safety laws were bought in, the vessels boarding ladder could have rungs missing or frayed rope that needed replacing. The laws about unsafe boarding ladders are strict and very large fines and prosecution is now inevitable for unscrupulous ships captains or owners. After only being used to heavy slow single engine fishing trawlers and tugs, it was a revelation for me to skipper a very fast, twin engine pilot boat, the speed and enormous power amazed me. They are designed to cut through waves cleanly and not have to reduce speed; from the dock entrance out to Lightning Knoll where the ships were waiting took no time at all.

The pilots were a special breed of men; I do not recall a woman pilot ever at Barrow. The harbour pilot is an expert in his local waters and advises the ship's captain entering port about his speed and direction. Ship's pilots know their area and can visualise the underwater area, the sandbars, and tidal effects and how local rainfall affects the water level.

The ship's captain always has command of his ship and thus ultimate responsibility for the ship and crew. The pilot has the conduct of the ship in the pilotage district and upon boarding the vessel provides a safe passage plan for the transit, directing the course and speed. He handles the vessel on and off the port wharfs and facilities, ensuring the safe transit of shipping in and out of the port. This is recognised as the high risk element of a ship's passage. The responsibilities involved in handling high risk cargoes, gas condensate, fuel tankers, nuclear flasks or ships with poor manoeuvrability can induce high stress levels. The ability to keep a clear head and stay calm is a desirable quality in a good ship's pilot! There needs to be a manned boat and pilot available twenty four hours a day, every day on call. The maximum draught of vessel able to enter Barrow dock entrance is ten metres.

The worst trip out in my experience as been following a nuclear container ship out to Lightning Knoll buoy off the coast of Walney Island. The pilot had boarded in Barrow docks and we were heading out in a fierce gale, the wind against a ten metre tide ripping out of Morecambe bay. The waves were steep and vicious, we ploughed into a particularly big one, there was a loud bang and a solid wall of water dropped on us. The mast and all the wire rigging was swept overboard, this was serious because it ended up around our stern end and threatened to get wrapped around our twin propellers. Immediately knocking the engines to neutral I rushed to help my best mate hanging over the side with a pair of wire cutters in his hand. Luckily for me Gary was on board this trip learning the pilot boat coxswains job and being an ex fisherman knew what to do without panicking, having any other deckhand I would really have been in trouble. Soaked through, his head under water for much of the time, he managed to cut free the aluminium mast and rigging from around our stern. The pilot could not see us in the wave troughs, and called us up on the radio to ask what the problem was and if we wanted them to turn back and give us a lee. The pilot boat was broadside to the waves and drifting near to shoal water, it was looking a bit dodgy for us, if we got any nearer to the bar we could be rolled completely over. Finally both soaked through we had the mast aboard and lashed to the deck, we heaved a sigh of relief when both propellers engaged and we headed into the waves again in the direction of our nuclear ship. It was hard enough picking the pilot off in severe weather without him getting hurt, never mind our boat nearly being disabled, it was one of those days and I was extremely lucky to have had Gary on board. On another hairy occasion we were steaming outwards to pick the pilot off an outward bound tanker. Instead of waiting to disembark at the Lightning Knoll buoy the pilot tried to save time by getting off early. This was the worst possible spot in the narrows for us at Bar buoy, wind against tide, bad visibility and snow showers. This was two am in the morning and I had decided to give up the pilot boat job, after concentrating on my survey work all day, I needed to be out here like I needed a hole in my head! The tanker could not alter course to give us a lee because of the constraints of the narrows. The breaking waves were on our bow and the first run in I ended up under the tanker's rudder, just as the transom of the ship was coming down. This was white knuckle time, managing to avoid the pilot boat being crushed I came in again; Gary put our search light onto the tankers quarter where a rope ladder was being blown nearly horizontal with the wind and sea. The visibility was still poor and the hunched up figure of our pilot could be vaguely seen trying to access the first few rungs of the rope ladder. The pilot boat's windows were misting up making it difficult to time when to pull into the ladder, I was having problems you might say. Gary from his position looking from our wheelhouse door was waiting to go forward to grab the pilot when he had climbed far enough down the tankers hull. A massive comber game screaming down the side of the tanker, the pilot boat took a lurch to starboard, and just when the snow became thicker Gary shouted that he had lost sight of the pilot! To say I nearly had kittens would not be exaggerating; we both thought the pilot had gone into the tide in the dark. In those conditions with the heavy seas and the tide ripping out of Morecambe bay I would not give much for anybodies chances. A scrambling noise on our wheelhouse roof and a relieved Gary helped the pilot onto our boat's side deck. Our pilot explained that when our boat rolled to starboard he jumped and grabbed the first thing he could, which happened to be the handrails on our wheelhouse roof. Steaming for home on full power ready for our nice warm beds we all agreed it was a shitty job sometimes. On a lovely calm summer's day the pilot department seemed the best ever career choice, but wintertime in the early morning darkness heading out in the teeth of a westerly gale you begin to wonder! Gary went on to be a good safe pilot boat skipper until he too decided to pack the job in, becoming a full time owner/skipper of his own trawler.

CHAPTER SEVENTEEN

CHOCOLATE BOX COTTAGE

Relieved that my mate Gary was now skipper of the pilot boat, meant that I could concentrate on achieving our full monthly channel survey as well my other launch master duties, rarely crewing on the pilot boat. On a rare weekend off Pauline suggested a walk in the very beautiful Duddon estuary, a narrow estuary with a panoramic view of the Lakeland Mountains. Jutting out into the channel is a huge lump of limestone rock looking like a flat topped aircraft carrier from a distance. It is a twenty minute walk from Askam village car park to reach and it is called Dunnerholme rock, the view from the top is breathtaking. On the leeward side of the rock nestled snugly against the cliff are three chocolate box ancient cottages. The end cottage had a for sale notice stuck on a pole in the front garden. I knew instantly that this cottage was going to be ours and we just stood and stared. A voice startled us, "Are you interested in buying this cottage?" A tall man from the garden of the middle cottage asked, in an accent we learned later was Canadian.

I thought about his question for about thirty seconds then said "Yes."

"Hold on I will give the owner a knock they are having their lunch but I am sure they will see you, it is their holiday home and I know they are leaving for home shortly," the tall man said.

Pauline was speechless, she is the type of lady that likes to make viewing appointments with the estate agent, and give a lot of thought to how we are going to finance our house purchase, in short she is very sensible, the exact opposite to me. After quick introductions we were shown into the cottage and us apologising profusely for interrupting the couple's lunch.

The cottage was everything I had ever dreamed of, horse brasses adorned the original dark oak beams across the ceiling, and a blazing log fire filled the room with a rosy glow. We were shown up the mahogany staircase and saw two cosy bedrooms, complete with oak beams and lovely views out of the windows. The man said he was a builder so all the house from top to bottom had been totally renovated. The tour took all of ten minutes tops. The owner said if we were interested to let his estate agency know. I said "Have you had a firm offer yet?" The owner said that he had an offer of one thousand pounds under his asking price. I do not know what came over me, a voice in my head told me to give him his thousand pounds extra and shake hands on it. So I did, telling that my word was my bond and as far as I was concerned it was now my cottage and my solicitor would contact him the next day.

"In that case I will pack my personal possessions in my car now and leave everything in the house that you see now; we will not be back ever!"

While this was going on Pauline had stood watching, her face white as a sheet and speechless. We both shook hands with the couple, I popped in next door to thank the tall man who had insisted that we enquire about the cottage, I told him we were the new owners and looked forward to being his neighbour. It felt like being in a trance the whole time and that I had no control over my actions.

Pauline after walking back along the beach for five minutes said "Jesus Christ Norm what have you done, you have totally lost all your marbles, that was not normal behaviour even by your standards! You will have to go back and apologise to that poor man, he might at this minute be packing his personal belongings into his car, what you just told him was cruel and no way can we afford to keep two houses. This cottage is a mile from the main road and you will have to open the unmanned level crossing gates, you need to live near your work at the docks."

I said "For now we will use the cottage for a holiday home and a bolthole away from my mother, she is getting harder work by the day and we need a break away from her." We did not realise mums increasingly strange behaviour was due to the early stages of dementia. My time needed on survey work was becoming even more demanding for the new generation of Trident nuclear submarines and my pay increasing accordingly, I needed something like the dream of my cottage to keep me going the long hours I needed to work. We did not have a mortgage on the house on Walney Island so financing the cottage was not a problem. We did not realise how much Dunnerholme was going to affect our lives over the next years, and the adventures we were to have with the nine grandchildren at that time.

We found out later that the three cottages used to be one ancient farmhouse, the first cottage under the lee of the rock was the farmhouse and the two cottages adjoining used to be a barn for livestock. Some say it used to be the ancient guide's house that showed travellers and packhorses safely across the treacherous sands of the Duddon estuary. This was a shortcut from Askam to Millom instead of going the long way around the estuary; it also explains all the small pony shoes I have found nearby over the years. A stone's throw from our cottage is three ancient lime kilns, one reputed to have been used by the monks of Furness Abbey who lived in an ancient monastery a few miles away in a secluded valley near Dalton. The ancient hedge lined lane leading from the main road to our remote cottages is one mile long, two farms were situated along the first length of tarmac track, and the rest after the last farm was unmade road owned by the farm. The farmer filled in the potholes when they became too deep for our vehicles to negotiate safely.

The first farm on the right is called Guards farm and the second is Marsh Grange a grade two listed building. The farm was built on an ancient site developed as a monastic grange by Furness Abbey; the 17th century house was the birth place of Margaret Askew the wife of George Fox founder of the Quaker movement. The final stage on our route to Dunnerholme is to cross an unmanned railway level crossing after first phoning the manned railway level crossing in the village of Askam to receive his permission that a train is not imminent. This may sound a right palaver and I suppose a rather unusual way of reaching or leaving your house, you surprisingly get used to the routine. Anyway back to my description of the route to our new holiday cottage, after receiving permission to cross the rail tracks, remembering to shut both gates firmly behind you to prevent the farmer's flock of sheep getting onto the tracks. It has happened in the past where somebody inadvertently left a gate open and sheep have been killed on the railway tracks. The old railway cottage used to be manned by the level crossing keeper but is privately owned now.

After shutting both gates behind you and looking towards the huge lump of Dunnerholme rock you can see a row of three white cottages nestling under the rock. The ancient buildings were cleverly built in the lee of the rock face to be sheltered from the prevailing westerly gales that buffet this coast. All the area this side of the rail tracks is a Site of Special Interest containing a rare colony of protected Natterjack toads. The sheep are useful in keeping the grass cropped down which benefits the toads. Also from the level crossing the land belongs to Dunnerholme golf club which has a ten hole course, they also own the rock on top of which is their number six hole thirty feet up the cliff. The unmade track leading to our cottage is bumpy but the views are stunningly spectacular of the estuary and the Lakeland Mountains. Clumps of yellow flowering gorse bushes abound around the golf course fairways, rabbits and sheep grazing alongside each other in perfect harmony. We had a glimpse of a huge barn owl diving into the rough grass and soaring away with a mouse or vole clutched in its claws heading towards a faraway old stone barn to feed its young no doubt. Pulling up at the chocolate box cottages in front of the old peat houses and the three added on outside toilets, I remembered reading on our deeds that we now held ancient peat cutting rights and the right to take sand and gravel from the beach for our own use.

All the cottages seemed to have nobody at home and we enjoyed having a nosy around our new house and the other cottages. We had a nice area of garden surrounded by a dry stone limestone wall in front of the cottage, and separating the gardens from the cottages is an ancient sea cobble laid floor which in the past served to keep mud and such like from being walked into the houses. At the back of the cottages there was a small ladies tee and surprisingly a recent tide line of seaweed and suchlike that proved the high tide came to within twelve feet of our cottage back door. Now this was a little disconcerting for me being an expert on tides and realised that even though we were told the cottages had never been flooded in recent times, I had my doubt about this. The view from our kitchen door was unbelievable to a man like me, who had been bought up in an overcrowded Victorian row of terraced houses near the docks. To own this house as a holiday home was totally alien to me and I had to pinch myself to make sure I was not dreaming. My wife was feeling emotional and wiped a tear from her eyes. "I love this house Norm and cannot believe I hold the keys in my hand, let's go in and see what has been left in the house."

I noticed Pauline's hand was shaking has she opened the storm porch door and then the inner door, we walked in to our lovely cosy lounge and were surprised to see all the furniture still in place, even a small television, carpets, curtains. The former owner had done us proud, even all the different horse brasses along the dark oak beams were still in place. The kitchen had all the electrical appliances including washing machine, fridge, cupboards full of crockery and cutlery; in short the owner had just walked out and left everything. Going up the beautiful varnished mahogany staircase to the two upstairs bedrooms we were pleased to see the rooms furnished with beds and furniture. "Wow" was all Pauline could say. We returned the favour to the lovely couple who bought our cottage years later as a holiday home.

On the right of our cottage was a huge area of marsh which sheep grazed on stretching all the way north to the village of Soutergate and then Kirkby. In front looking out of the back door was the end of the rock and the start of the sandy estuary leading across to Millom, only the deep channel separating the estuary at low tide. On a high spring tide the sea rushed into the Duddon estuary faster than a horse can gallop a very dangerous place to be if caught out without local knowledge. Sheep grazed everywhere on the golf course, marshes, among the gorse bushes and even roamed onto the beaches. Depending on the wind direction, sometimes you could open the kitchen door at night step out to fetch some coal and fall over a ewe sheltering from the storm outside our backdoor, this give us quite a shock I can tell you. In short the area around our cottage was one great adventure playground and we could not wait to have all the grand children stay with us. All of our children and grand kids lived in Askam village or nearby, and the walk along the beach to Askam took about twenty minutes, longer when you decided to beach comb and over the years we found many interesting things washed up after a storm. I decided to buy three canoes and a rowing dinghy for the grand children because when the tide was out, a shallow fresh water beck ran out to sea through the marsh at the back of our cottage. This was safe to teach them how to paddle a canoe and learn how to row a boat. Also it was at the back of my mind that I might need a boat to rescue somebody cut off by the tide some day. The place had calmness about it and I knew that one day we would live here permanently.

CHAPTER EIGHTEEN

A BUSY TIME WORKING

For the moment I had to concentrate on earning enough money to pay off the mortgage as soon as possible, which meant practically living in the Irish Sea working all hours surveying Barrow approaches for the Trident submarine program. Between repetitively crossing to and fro across Walney channel hundreds of times every month I had other duties to perform, including taking divers out to lay wave and current indicators on the bed of the dredged fairway. I enjoyed taking out the divers to change the batteries in the recorders, we could have a good laugh with them. Electricians still had to be taken to the leading lighthouses to change batteries and the days just flew by. We had requests from different firms for other types of surveys and I had to rig up my boat to handle special sonar equipment for the laying of gas pipes from the new gas rigs to come ashore from the Irish Sea through Walney Island and under Walney channel to the Barrow gas terminal. Never a dull moment and rarely at home much, the docks were booming and doing very well. Operating a slow survey boat I likened it to driving a transit van, operating a pilot boat was like driving a Ferrari. To keep myself awake during the long hours surveying I found playing Freddie Mercury albums at full blast was the best way to handle the boring work. It was like painting the Forth Bridge, when I finally finished a monthly survey and my survey team were proud to have beaten adverse weather and boat breakdowns, we had to start the whole process all over again. The good side to this job was you were left to get on with it as long as you achieved your goals.

Heading for home after a long day three miles out and beyond Lightening Buoy, we spotted near the end of Walney Island, two strange heads above the water. This certainly looked strange and out of place, it was getting dusk and hard to see what exactly it was we had spotted. I slowed the boat down and going past us caught in the outgoing tide was a deer and her baby. They were obviously at the end of their tether and stressed out. We took the quick decision to go alongside them and with great difficulty lift them both onto our side deck. This was one time I was glad that our boat was low in the water. I laid a blanket under them and headed for shore straight away to minimise the mother deer's stress. Luckily the tide was still high enough so I could ram the boat ashore under the lee of Walney lighthouse, quickly lowering mother and baby onto the sand. To our utter delight they headed up towards the sand dunes and some grass I knew was nearby. It was days like this that always cheered us up knowing that if we had not been coming in at that exact moment the deer would have been swept well out to sea and no doubt perished. Actually the same thing happened a couple of years after this, we received a call from Ramsden dock radio to tell us two young deer were being swept towards us in Walney channel and could we rescue them!

That reminds me of the time everyone in the marine workshops had left for lunch and I was just about to jump into my car and follow them. I saw and heard a hell of a commotion and squawking coming from the middle of the dock basin. A flock of gulls were forcing a pigeon into the water by dive bombing it and generally scaring the life out of it. They must have been protecting their territory I suppose. Anyway they succeeded in making it crash into the water and then left it to flounder, the poor bird flapping its wings and not possibly being able to take off again. I thought what a shame and got into my car, my lunch would be on the table waiting for me at home and my granddaughter Francesca would be waiting to see me. Halfway up the docks road I knew what I had to do, turning around I headed back to the docks, and I could not leave the bird to die. The pigeon was feebly flapping and I knew I would have to hurry before the gulls decided to eat it. I climbed down the quayside ladder and boarded the pilot boat which was the nearest vessel. Starting up the two engines I ran onto the deck and cast off the forward rope and then aft to throw the stern line ashore. Steering the forty feet long pilot boat alongside the pigeon was not easy but luckily eventually the bird drifted within reach. Unfortunately for me being on my own I had to hang upside down with nobody to hold on to my legs. Nearly losing my grip I came very close to dropping into the dock myself, and just when I was about to give up the pigeon flapped its way towards my hand. I grabbed it with one hand and somehow managed to pull myself back onto the boat without harming the bird. Thank God there was nobody around to see how daft I had been, the only man on duty was the pier head man, and after the main dock gate was closed he usually put his feet up for a break. Getting the wet bird into the wheelhouse I let the boat drift while I dried off the contented cooing bird with paper towels, to my delight I saw a numbered tag on its leg, it was a racing pigeon. Our son in law Gary raced pigeons so he would know what to do. Putting the bird in a small cardboard box I put the pilot boat back where I had stole it from. Congratulating myself for a successful rescue mission I climbed up the access ladder onto the quay, seeing a pair of highly polished boots and looking up seeing my boss, he was not looking best pleased.

"What the hell do you think you are doing Norman?" he said.

"Rescuing a drowning racing pigeon" I replied.

"You have spent an hour in the middle of the dock just to rescue a bloody pigeon!" he said.

"Now let me think, oh yes you have broken every safety rule in the book, no lifejacket, no deckhand on board, taking the pilot boat and using fuel unnecessarily without asking permission, I could go on. What have you got to say for yourself Norman?"

"Whoever or whatever was drowning in the dock I would do exactly the same because that is the way I am!" I replied, and went into the mess room for a brew even though my lunch hour had finished.

The lucky bird turned out to belong to an avid pigeon racer in Wales and was duly returned to him in good health. The next bird I rescued was a poorly seagull from the dock one lunchtime, I put it in my car and drove to a rescue centre, due to being in a hurry I had no cardboard box to put it in so sat the gull on my back seat, the bird lost bowel control and shit all over the inside of my car. Two hours it took me to clean the car that evening after work, Pauline stood shaking her head lost for words!

We had some bloody good laughs down at the docks; I was on duty in the old pier head when it was just a basic shed before the brand new up to date money no object pier head was constructed. My feet were up on the table and I was answering the VHF radio, sun streaming through the window, me warm as toast. Next moment a jet of water soaked me and half the pier head floor, looking up in angry surprise I saw my friend Gary the skipper of the pilot boat had pushed a powerful water hose through the partly opened window. He and a few other workmates were pissing themselves laughing at the drowned state of me. "You bastard Gary I will get you back for this!" I shouted.

The next day I pretended that I had got over the joke played on me and watched for an opportunity to have my revenge on Gary. I was reading my newspaper at break time in a crowded mess room when I saw my chance. Gary stood up and said to no one in particular that he was going for a number two (poo) if anyone needed him. I gave him a minute and followed him to the toilet, there was a row of several cubicles each one had the door shut, and I knelt down and saw a pair of boots and trousers down, he was sitting on the toilet. Got him I thought, this is perfect. Tying the door handle tight with a length of strong rope I put the hosepipe over the top of the door and turned it on full blast. You should have heard the angry shouting and swearing. I shouted back through my tears of laughter, "I told you I would get my revenge Gary you sneaky bastard! How do you like a taste of your own medicine?" It must have felt like being in a car wash for him. Just then a figure emerged from the far end toilet cubicle, "Oh my God it was Gary!" I rushed to turn off the tap.

"What is all the noise about Norm?" said Gary.

Then suddenly it dawned on Gary that there was an innocent victim involved and that meant I was in deep trouble, he started laughing and rushed to see who my victim was.

Now the loud screaming abuse had stopped I recognised who it was, the voice shouted out "Pascoe you are a dead man walking."

I ran outside and headed for my car, the man in question was a real hard nut and hired on an occasional basis by our firm. This was not the time to try and explain the circumstances of why he was suddenly doused with ice cold water by an idiot who had never checked all the toilet cubicles properly, visions of me lying in intensive care flashed in front of me. Discretion is the best part of valour they say and later that night I called at my innocent victim's house baring a bottle of expensive malt whiskey. His wife opened the front door and immediately said "You must be Norm, please come in I know all about what happened today and I have never laughed so much in years, I wish I could have seen my husband's face it must have been priceless!"

"Take a seat I will put the kettle on, we will have a nice cup of tea then you can tell me exactly what happened from the beginning."

There was never a dull moment down the docks, heading out to survey the channel off the Walney coast a youth on 'Work Experience' stumbled on the survey boat's after deck as the boat slammed into a wave. He grabbed the nearest object which happened to be a 'Man Overboard' orange marker flare off its bracket on the back of the wheelhouse. Billowing dense clouds of bright orange smoke swept around the boat, in no time at all the wheelhouse filled with smoke and fumes. The young man ran around in panic shouting "Is it poisonous?" covered head to toe in orange stain. I managed to throw it overboard and call Liverpool Coastguard on the radio to report a false alarm before a lifeboat was launched to rescue us.

What a sight we all looked coated in orange, I cancelled the survey, and the white painted boat took the rest of the day to clean off and ourselves. A similar problem happened later but was a fire extinguisher that caused chaos when we headed out to sea. The survey boat hit a big wave; the fire extinguisher flew off its bracket and set off a wall of foam which proceeded to fill the wheelhouse. Another big mess to clean up that I could have done without!

CHAPTER NINETEEN

ESCAPE TO THE COTTAGE

When I realised how high the tide reached towards our new cottage it seemed a good opportunity to bring my three canoes and rowing boat to keep there permanently. My thinking was the grand children could use the canoes in the beck that ran past near the cottage and out towards the estuary, the rowing boat would be ideal to use in an emergency for anybody who was unfortunately trapped on a sandbank near our cottage, God forbid that I would need to use it.

The first weekend that I was free from work we explored the area around our cottage, walking on the marsh towards Kirkby we came to a long fence that ran onto the sands for several hundred yards. I realised that its purpose was to keep the two different flocks of sheep grazing on the marsh separate. On the far end of the seaward end of the wire fence was what looked like a bundle of white rags hanging off it. Just out of curiosity me and Pauline walked out alongside the fence onto the sand thinking we should hurry up the tide was coming in fast. When we walked nearer we could see that the object was a sheep hanging off the wire fence, her wool was firmly entangled and her skin was bleeding from the wire cutting into her. We knew that this end of the fence was covered at high tide, all the seaweed and flotsam trapped in the fence was evidence of this. We had to work fast to save the ewe from drowning, and not for the first time I was grateful for the very sharp penknife I had carried in my pocket since being about eight years old. Pauline held the ewe firmly to stop her struggling and making the wire dig into her deeper. I swiftly hacked at the wool until the tide was swilling around both our knees; Pauline was getting a little panicky by this time shouting to me to hurry. At last the wool around the wire was cut off the sheep's back and Pauline helped the ewe onto her legs and guided her in the direction of the higher ground and to safety. We were wet up to our knees but elated knowing if we had not been passing at that exact moment the ewe would have certainly drowned. We phoned the local farmer and he came out on his tractor to check the ewe and give it some treatment, she was easy to find still limping and looking sorry for herself. It was a good way of introducing ourselves to George who would learn us all about the ways of sheep and become a very good friend and neighbour over the years, that was to be the first of many sheep incidents over the years.

George was one of life's characters who had a dry sense of humour, would help anyone in trouble and was a very strong man. He certainly did not suffer fools gladly; we gave him many a laugh over my townie ways. We had a lot in common his job being outdoors and mine coming from a hard seagoing life we always had plenty to talk about. Over the years George taught us how to spot the symptoms of ailing ewes, and over time we had many adventures involving his beloved flock, he knew every individual ewe and their different personalities. He used to call me his unpaid shepherd when we eventually lived at Dunnerholme full time and once after phoning him to inform him of yet another sheep in trouble he said, "Norm one day it would be nice if you phoned with some good news!" George had a son who also worked the farm with him but we saw George almost on a daily basis roaming the marshes or the golf links with his sheep dogs checking his flock.

Being a town dweller all my life I did not realise how difficult it could be for a sheep farmer to keep his flock safe. The tidal marshes were an obviously dangerous environment for sheep and lambs, one minute they would be contentedly grazing the short marsh grass, then be cut off by an exceptionally high tide caused by a sudden south westerly gale of wind making a much higher sea level. Another danger for the flock was deep gullies haphazardly crossing the marsh running in all directions. Even on the golf course there was danger from golf ball injuries and the steep sided drainage ditches that ran through the links. Over the years I witnessed sheep suddenly and unexpectedly coming out of the gorse bushes and struck dead by a golfer teeing off and not being able to stop himself. The ball on rare occasions hitting the sheep between the eyes and killing it stone dead. The golf club members had insurance to compensate for any mishaps, the farmer had grazing rights and accidents happened. So we were learning that sheep were in danger from not just walkers letting off their dogs allowing them to scare and chase sheep, but sheep found many other ways of self termination.

A rare week off from work saw us and my elderly mother looking forward to having a relaxing time at our cottage. It was peaceful until there was a loud hammering on the cottage door, followed by shouts of hurry up. I answered the door with my mouth full of food, we were having lunch and I was just about to pour the wine, thinking this is the life. Four irate and excited golfers were all shouting at once and pointing out to sea. There were two men and two women, the two women were crying.

"Calm down I can't understand what you are saying, what the hell is going on?" I said.

One of the golfers managed to calm the others down a little.

"Look out there on that sand bank, a ewe and her two lambs have been cut off by the high tide, already the two lambs have drowned and the waves are washing over the mother's head, soon she will drown!"

I knew what was coming, "Have you contacted the farmer," I asked, this was before mobiles became affordable. "No" was the answer, so I asked Pauline to phone the farm, there was no reply.

"Stop buggering about and launch your rowing boat they all shouted at once, before the poor sheep drowns."

The two men then started to drag my rowing boat down to the tide line, the oars and rowlocks were in place in case of an emergency, meaning human's in danger not daft sheep. I looked out into the estuary, it was quite rough and a fair distance to row against the strong wind. There was no way I was going to let these golfers take my rowing boat out. I called to Pauline and she jumped into the stern of my dinghy. I pushed the boat out before the golfers realised that I was taking over the rescue. I knew that I was not being very sensible, and was reluctant to see another sheep drown, knowing that not many people could handle a dinghy better than me, especially in these adverse weather conditions. On the long row out to the sheep I explained to Pauline that I would back the boat's stern up to the ewe and she could grab the two curved horns and hook them over the stern of the dinghy. When she had done this I would tow it back to shore slowly. Pauline got very upset when she saw the two white corpses of the poor lambs that had already drowned beginning to float out to sea. We could tell when we reached the mother sheep that she was nearly giving up paddling getting tired, sinking lower into the sea as her wool became waterlogged. Pauline did a great job of grabbing Flossie, she had given her a name already, and even though Pauline was soaked with the cold spray coming over the dinghy she managed to hook Flossie's horns over the transom stern of my rowing boat.

"Alright love head for shore I have her secure," she shouted.

I got the distinct impression that my lovely wife was enjoying our little adventure. We reached terra firma eventually to a thunderous applause of clapping from several golfers who had all stopped to enjoy the spectacle of our sheep rescue. As for Flossie she gave herself a severe shaking to get rid of some of her accumulated seawater, coughed quite a bit, looked a little confused, and the poor thing trotted off to find her two lambs seemingly already forgotten about their fate for now.

This was the first but not the last dinghy rescue we did over the coming year, and only the start of our sheep adventures.

Never have I seen such beautiful sunsets or dawns as we frequently saw holidaying at our newly bought cottage. Sometimes I had to pinch myself to realise that we actually owned a chocolate box ancient cottage including our very own peat house. Also the original outside toilet was still functional, a key was always left in the lock and all the golf club members informed that they may use it at anytime; it was particularly useful to the lady members. Over the years we have had many request from golfers, from use of our phone, have we a sticking plaster for a cut, a drink of water, even on occasion first aid or a run to hospital after a ricochet from a rebounding golf ball hitting a dry stone wall boundary, had bounced back into their face. The blood spurting out of the cut was not a pretty sight and on at least two other occasions this happened in the years spent at the cottage.

Of course living within the boundaries of a golf club where a tee was at the front of the cottages, and a tee only four metres from the back caused us residents some dangerous moments over the years. This was a down side to owning a house on a golf course. When often strangers passing would remark that we were so lucky to live in such a dream like place, with stunning scenery to die for, I would say it was ninety five percent paradise. A few golfers were very safe when teeing off, some were downright dangerous and near misses occurred, sliced shots hit the windows, slates were hit and one's patience would be sorely tried on many occasions over the years.

On one memorable occasion on a lovely sunny day we were sitting enjoying the sun streaming in through the front door in our lounge; our youngest daughter Susan was bringing us all a tray of coffee in. A white blur of a golf ball flew through the storm porch at great speed just missing our daughters head. It proceeded to ricochet around the lounge for quite a long time, bouncing off our lovely mahogany staircase many times. How it missed us all and did not break any ornaments or do major damage I will never know. We sat and our daughter stood in amazement holding onto her tray of coffees not spilling a drop.

A cheery voice shouted "Can I have my ball back I saw it going into your house?"

I looked at the golfer thinking the cheeky sod the least he could have done is make his self scarce after his bum shot! I was just about to give him a rollicking when our daughter started to laugh and greet him like an old friend. It turned out that they were in the same form at school so all was forgiven, it seemed. Our daughter even offered him a brew and a slice of Pauline's fruit cake! He certainly had a good story to tell in the bar at the clubhouse later!

I was pottering in the front garden one Sunday morning near our dry stone wall boundary, when a golf ball flew past my nose and buried deep in my lawn. Standing up to give the golfer a piece of my mind I saw my elder stepson Tammy walking towards me laughing, he was a member of the club and must have been in the competition.

"Sorry about that Norm my ball did not hit you did it?" he said.

"I am playing rubbish this morning after last night's beer session; I will give you a knock on the way down for a cold drink and fruitcake for me and my three mates!"

At that I gave him the ball that was embedded two inches deep in my lawn and watched them all trying to get the balls up the rock and onto the green with varying success. I smiled to myself and thought of a good way to get my revenge on our Tammy.

The very next Sunday morning competition when our Tammy was playing up the rock again, I was waiting patiently to get my own back on him. Lying down on top of the rock out of sight of the four golfers teeing off below me, I saw my stepson teeing off first. He hit the ball perfectly high in the air dropping about ten feet from the flag, the golfers down below could not see the green because of the lip of the rock face. Crawling commando style I grabbed the golf ball and placed it in the hole, then retreated out of sight and made my way back to the cottage. Listening at my front gate I heard them shouting "Tammy has a hole in one lads; the drinks are on him back at the clubhouse. It is his bad luck that the course is busy today, hope he's plenty of money in his wallet!" I enjoyed listening to our Tammy ranting on about the cost of getting a hole in one, and how it always seemed to happen when the golf club bar is packed!

We seemed to have an extraordinary knack of finding sheep in various difficulties around the golf course gorse bushes, or on the marshes where they loved to graze on the short tidal washed grass. The marsh was cut through with deep gullies and the sheep could get cut off by a fast incoming tide. Mostly they managed to wade or swim across the gulleys but occasionally they got into difficulties and we were able to help rescue them. Over the years we managed to learn from George a little of sheep's ways and when to phone him and not be wasting his time. He taught us to lift sheep back onto their legs when we found them lying on their backs with all four legs in the air unable to right themselves, or when they needed a calcium injection after finding them lying on their sides among the gorse bushes. The crows were always keeping watch on the sheep flock and if they spotted a sickly sheep or lamb we learned that the sheep's eyes would be pecked out before the beast had even died.

When I phoned George up to tell him any bad sheep news, he would always say "I wish for once when you phoned it could be good news Norm!"

Shortly after we started using the cottage as a holiday home, we stopped this particular weekend enjoying the peace and tranquillity, me wishing I did not have to get up for work this Monday morning. The bedroom seemed much lighter and it seemed to be so quiet, the alarm went off at five and I glanced out of the window. A magical scene met my eyes, the large snowflakes were drifting silently down, covering everywhere with a deep mantel of snow. Pauline put on her dressing gown and joined me, saying what a wonderful sight to see our first sight of snow for several years. Where our and the neighbours cars were parked was a huge snowdrift much higher than the top of the three cars. The wind was blowing south easterly which meant that the snow drift was building up at the front of all three cottages, making the access to our front doors impossible without hours of shovelling.

Pauline pointed towards the gorse bushes which looked like giant snow mounds; a fox was gamely trying to hunt any rabbits hiding under the bushes. Clustered in the lee of the gorse were dejected looking sheep getting what shelter they could, each one looking rather strange covered in ice and snow. We knew the farmer would be out after breakfast to bring them some much needed fodder and sheep nuts. Looking down our long access road we could see a three hundred yards length was covered in a snowdrift at least to a depth of six feet, most of the rest was about a foot deep. This would have to be the month for a new channel survey to begin and the survey department would not be best pleased if I was off work for any length of time.

We were excited as school children and dashed downstairs to look outside the back of the cottages. There in the lee of the cottages lay about fifty ewes sheltering under the high walls, patiently waiting for the snow to stop falling. The tide was out so as far as I could see was white all the way to the sea edge; visibility was only to the end of Dunnerholme rock in the gloom. Pauline started to cook some bacon and eggs and I was looking forward to a couple of days off work, it was a good job my mother had come with us for the weekend, so we knew she was all right. We both could not stop smiling as we gazed out at our winter wonderland of snow.

We heard the tractor before we saw it ploughing its way along the road with a trailer of fodder for the sheep. When the sheep heard the tractor they came from all directions jumping through the drifts of snow hungry for their treats. George dropped off small bales of hay and spread armfuls around, Will his son spread out the sheep nuts evenly distributing them, so all the sheep had a fair share. All the ewes were pregnant so needed the nourishment even more. I put on my wellingtons and warm gear and went out to follow all the sheep tracks that had left the back of our cottage towards where George and Will were still feeding and counting the sheep.

George saw me and said "Have you seen anymore sheep this morning Norm we have around thirty still missing."

"No I have not but if you like I will circle around the rock and look for them there George," I said.

"That's all right Norm, me and our William will head over to the boundary fence and search there, I think they may be together under a snow drift, see you later."

Going around Dunnerholme rock was difficult, sometimes the snowdrifts were higher than my head and a slight detour was required. After sweating profusely and filling my boots full of snow which melted, and my feet felt like blocks of ice, I reached the summit of the rock. From the top I had a panoramic view of the estuary; I looked for signs of the sheep and George. Then I saw them over by the dry stone wall digging frantically into a huge snowdrift, 'Bess' his sheepdog must have found them and was running around, tail wagging and barking.

I collected a spade on my way passed the cottage and headed towards George who was hauling out the ewes from the drift. When George had accounted for all his precious ewes, we all walked back to the tractor closely followed by the thirty hungry ewes more than ready for their fodder. George gave me a lift back to my cottage and Pauline handed out hot tea and freshly baked hot scones at the back door. George said he would be back later to clear a path for our vehicles so we could make it for work the next day, there was I thinking we were snowed in for a week at least. This was our first example of kindness shown to us by the splendid neighbours that lived in and around Dunnerholme cottages. George said our next door neighbour had been spotted passing his farm early this morning heading for Barrow using a pair of skis, well he is Canadian. Over the next years we saw a lot of our rural neighbours and became firm friends and were enriched by knowing them all. We had two working farms, a small holding and a few cottages as neighbours so were never lonely.

Over the different seasons we saw the way of life of country folk and in time photographed and recorded my experiences. Sometimes when we took our evening walk down our lane towards the farm George would be in a field training his sheep dog. If we were lucky George would lean on the gate and tell stories from the old days and these could be very funny. A relation of his loved taxidermy as a hobby and needed a badger to complete his collection. He said to George if you see a road killed badger that was not too badly damaged on your travels could you put it in your freezer until he could collect it. As luck would have it George was travelling home alone across the high fell one night and came across a badger lying at the side of the secluded road. Getting out of his car he found the badger was still warm and looked in remarkable condition considering it had been just hit by a vehicle. George felt really pleased about being able to phone his relation with the good news so quickly and placed the unfortunate creature in the foot well of the front passenger seat.

Continuing down the steep narrow road off the fell, George heard a sniffling and a snorting sound coming from the badger. George thought bloody hell the badger must have been only stunned it was coming back to life and sounding a little pissed off, not only that but was attempting to regain its balance to stand up. Now George was really getting worried, trapped in the car with an angry badger was not to be recommended, it was baring its teeth and starting to look around, looking a trifle dazed. He stopped the car and placed both of his legs onto the dash board to keep them out of the badger's way, knowing the damage its teeth could do. He tried to reach over to open the passenger door to give it an escape route but was unable to reach the door handle. He then opened his driver side door wide hoping the angry animal would see daylight and run under his legs and escape to freedom. George was really worried the badger was staring at him and being so near to those yellowing teeth and smelling its bad breath, its front claws looked enormous close up, would it jump up at him? He had seen how quickly they could move. George heaved a great sigh of relief, the disorientated badger choose to run under George's legs and out of the door to freedom. George quickly slammed the door shut and saw his hands were shaking, after composing himself he drove home thinking in future he would just drive pass road kills ignoring them altogether.

I finished work early one Friday lunch time and drove to our house on Walney Island to pick up Pauline for a quick and unexpected trip to the cottage. My mum was at my sisters so we had just to pick our yappy tiny Yorkshire terrier up for our trip out. We had Penny from when she was a pup; she was so tiny she fit into my pocket. Everybody adored her and every holiday she was never left behind, it was a full time job keeping her alive. People who have yorkies will understand what I mean, for a female who was too small to have even one litter of puppies she was as brave as a lion or daft. If a Doberman or Alsatian came towards us, her ears would pin back she would run straight towards them to defend us, barking and growling like a dog possessed. Of course this was tantamount to committing doggy suicide, I would have to run after her and pick her up before the larger dog could bite her. I always said that our Penny was put on earth to make me stressful, and I seemed to spend an enormous amount of time rescuing her from dangerous situations.

Back to the day in question we drove along the top fell road looking down on the Duddon estuary, the row of three cottages nestling snugly under the cliffs of Dunnerholme rock. The afternoon sun lighting up the whitewashed cottages, everywhere seemed to be bathed in glorious technicolour, it was always so calming to look at that scene. Driving through the farm we pulled over to let the milk tanker pass and had a quick natter with George in the small field where he was training his new sheepdog. When we finally tore ourselves away we looked forward to lighting the fire and putting on a brew.

Penny was barking with excitement and was obviously anticipating chasing rabbits around the cottages. Nobody else was at home the other two single cottage owners were still at work, Bridget who owned a bonnie black Scotty dog and Graham who owned a particularly clever black tom cat. The sheep asleep outside of our kitchen door did not even deign to move when Penny raced towards them, maybe they thought that she was a rabbit like creature or a rat. Either way they were not in the least bit bothered by this tiny ball of fur racing around, indeed when the ewes bought their new lambs to shelter at the back of our cottage in sunshine or storm, they totally ignored our Penny also. In fact later on Penny laid in the shade side by side with her best friends the lambs.

After lighting the fire and settling in we noticed Penny was not around anymore, one minute she was sniffing the sheep the next gone. Now when I whistled her she always came running and on this occasion she did not.

Pauline said she might have chased a rabbit into the sand dunes or gorse bushes. We split up both calling to her. Two hours later and we were both frantic with worry and still no sign of her. We had to face the possibility that a fox or hungry feral cat may have got her, just when I was about to call off the search and go and get some volunteers from around the golf club I heard a faint bark. The sound came from the sand dunes I thought. We heard it louder when Penny must have heard our voices. Suddenly we realised that the muffled barking was coming from down a rabbit hole! Penny must have followed a rabbit down the hole and got stuck, unable to go forward or backwards. From elation at realising a fox had not eaten her to thinking how the hell were we going to rescue her, these thoughts raged through my head. Penny was part of the family and needed to be rescued quickly, we could sense her becoming stressful.

I asked Pauline to kneel down in the sand at the entrance to the rabbit hole and to try and sooth Penny, meanwhile I ran back to the cottage to fetch two shovels. Back at the rabbit burrow we frantically dug the sand away for maybe two hours before seeing any progress. Then suddenly looking up the burrow I spotted black fur and two tiny stick like back legs, reaching in at arm's length I managed to slide my hand in and gently ease our beloved dog backwards out of the hole. It was licks all round from Penny and tears of joy from me and Pauline realising how near we had been to losing her. If I had not heard her faint barks and the sand being so soft and easy to shovel we could have easily lost her. A damp cloth to remove the sand from her eyes and Penny was good as new, a little subdued for a day or two maybe but we noticed she never stuck her head into a rabbit hole ever again. Penny had plenty more adventures over the years where she needed to be rescued on many other occasions.

A ewe became particularly friendly with our Penny and this partnership went on until Penny passed away. The grand children named her 'Flossie' after finding her collapsed outside the cottage door one rare blistering hot day with, we assumed, heat exhaustion. We got her to her feet and gave her a bucket of cool water which she greedily drank; it always amazed me seeing the capacity of water sheep can drink. Penny made a concerned fuss about Flossie sensing she was not well. The grand children were so happy that the ewe recovered so quickly and George the farmer said they had done the right thing.

The next morning, Laura our eldest granddaughter, opened the Kitchen door after insistent knocking was heard. She opened the door and started to laugh, we heard a loud baa-baa, and your right it was Flossie, cheeky ewe was butting the door to get some attention.

"Laura fetch a bucket of water for her, who said sheep are daft it looks like this may become a regular habit on a hot day!"I said.

Well this made the children excited with something to tell their class mates in school. Then when Flossie's two lambs were born she began to bring them to our back door for a refreshing drink of clean water and to see Penny. One day I took a photograph of our Victoria and Francesca giving Flossie and her lambs a drink at the kitchen door, I wrote a short article and sent it to a magazine, the children received a cheque for some pocket money, and took the magazine to school to show their teachers.

Our Francesca found a length of fishermen's drift netting washed up on the tide line near to the cottage door after a particularly stormy night, and enmeshed in the fine netting were several large eating crabs, to her surprise they were all still alive! Pauline said "That is our next meal Francesca we can boil them and have crab sandwiches for dinner, my favourite food!"

"No nana I found them and after I get them out of the net I am going to set them free in the estuary, granddad Norm can come with me, you are not going to boil them that is cruel!"

Two hours later after cutting the crabs free from the fine netting without being nipped by the strong claws, we walked out to the middle of the estuary finding a deep pool to release them. Francesca wrote a short article about her find and posted off a photograph of her and the rescued crabs to a magazine. In due course receiving payment for her feature proving that kindness does pay!

CHAPTER TWENTY

THE GRAND CHILDREN

Our nine grand children at this time thought that the cottage and the beautiful surrounding area was their own special adventure playground. We could not say no to them, they wanted to stop with us every weekend and have adventures; it was like a second childhood for us. Cliffs to climb, sand dunes to play hide and seek, and cockling out on the sands at low tide, canoes and rowing boat, miles of marshes to explore, abundant wildlife to amaze, the list goes on. It was like being in our very own 'Enid Blyton' story, but this was for real.

The grand children became a common sight at Dunnerholme, two adults with nine children of various sizes following behind like a gaggle of ducks. We had two bedrooms, the spare one was full of bodies and a mattress on the floor slept the others. The proverbial sardines in a tin came to mind, but the cottage was always filled with laughter and I had the best time of my life with those wonderful children. Weekends and holidays went by in a blur, always adventures to be doing. New Years Eve we had all nine staying, my step children thought Pauline and myself were mad, but nobody could have had a better time than our gang.

Our fun started when we had got rid of the grownups, and sleeping bags and spare clothes were stowed away. Pauline made a huge buffet and laid it all out on the kitchen table. Whilst she was doing this I took all nine of the grand children down to the shore at the base of the rock. They were sent to comb the high water tide line to collect driftwood to make our bonfire when darkness fell. Old newspapers were put in the centre of the huge woodpile ready to light up when we were ready, not until after our delicious buffet was enjoyed by nine hungry, excited children. The nicest sound ever to me was listening to the excited squeals and laughter as the children ran along the beach trying to find the biggest logs that had been washed up in recent storms. When the bonfire was judged by the children to be big enough and dusk was falling, I said it was time to go for our buffet. I had to persuade the children to leave the bonfire and convince them that nobody would come in the dark to set fire to it whilst they were in the cottage. Our cottage was the only one with residents in that night, so nobody could hear the vast amount of noise coming from our small cottage, only the usual sheep resting in the lee of the cottage walls to disturb. Then it was time to put warm clothing on and wellington boots for everyone. Each of the children had a torch and I carried a huge box of fireworks that unknown to the children we had saved from bonfire night.

Outside was pitch black, Pauline led from the front up the steep path leading up to the top of the rock and then downwards onto the beach, I followed behind making sure they stopped in the centre of the track. You can imagine how excited they all were, a proper adventure just like the 'Famous Five' they had all read about. A match was quickly put to the pile of newspapers and the sea breeze soon had the fire fanned and blazing, sparks flying up into the sky. We switched off all the torches and could get our night vision better; the children understood the reason we had to build the bonfire in the daylight now. We had set up huge logs around the perimeter of the fire so we could all sit down together and enjoy the moment, the six girls all holding hands and the three boys throwing more wood on the fire.

The tide was out and nobody around but us eleven people and about one hundred randomly scattered sheep, our own private party and I would not have swopped that evening for all the money in the world, and I am sure Pauline felt the same way. Over the other side of the estuary the lights of Millom town twinkled in the frosty air, the glow from Askam village where the grand children lived could also be seen. Suddenly snowflakes began to fall and the scene became even more magical, everyone started singing carols and holding hands. Thin twigs were put to good use toasting huge marsh mallows and we opened our flasks for a hot drink.

When is it midnight granddad? They all kept asking and eventually it was time to set off our rockets. We could even hear the ships foghorns in the far distance coming from Barrow docks clearly on the still night. To a chorus of loud cheers all the rockets were set off and erupted in the skies amid all the other colours and patterns illuminating the night around our estuary. Eventually the children became quieter and began to yawn, time to make our way home, the tide was beginning to put out the fire and wash away the glowing embers. A cup of hot milk and Pauline got them ready for bed while I washed and tidied away all the dishes from the buffet party. After a kiss and a hug from the children they all climbed up the stairs to bed, their parting words were "We all love this cottage Granddad and Nana, but especially you two!"

We both fell into bed exhausted and slept until about three am when two little blond heads appeared by our bed. "Nana Rebecca has been sick all over my head!" said Sinead.

We could see sick in Sinead's hair and down her night dress, also Rebecca was smeared in sick. The smell of vomit was overpowering, Pauline told me to stay where I was and she would see to them. I was too tired to argue and promptly fell asleep again.

Next morning after breakfast Pauline asked me to take them all hunting for golf balls around the perimeter of the course, something they all loved doing. Pauline wanted to get everything ready for the parents calling for her traditional home made meat and potato pies or cheese and onion if preferred, mushy peas and gravy. Also to take the entire gang of grand children home with them to give us a rest, it had been rather hectic to say the least. When we saw the state of all the parents we were not sorry we had stayed at home with all the children. Boy oh boy they looked rough after the parties they had attended, never again they all said, and we are giving up alcohol was mentioned often that afternoon. Headache remedies were freely handed out and glasses of water passed around.

Of course all the children sensing that their parents were grumpy with headaches, wanted to stay at the cottage another night and have more adventures. Looking at the bags under our eyes Pauline and me bundled everybody out and threw the children's belongings into the cars, closely followed by nine children, it was time to relax for us. When the last car drove off the silence in the cottage was deafening. Something seemed to happen at Dunnerholme all the time to keep all the children excited, mostly we tried to limit three or four staying at the cottage each weekend or school holidays and taking fair turns. My mother wanted to stay occasionally but mostly preferred to stay in the house at Walney Island to be near my two sisters.

My eldest sister who also lived on Walney Island loved the taste of cockles and when we accidently found a bed of giant cockles lying near the middle of our estuary she could not believe her luck. Our Mark, Kristian and their sister Katrina were exploring the sandbanks and gulleys with me at low tide. Mark spotted some huge cockles that were so big they had difficulty digging themselves into the sand deep enough. These cockles were the size of golf balls and were by far the biggest I had ever seen, these cockles were near dying of old age. I had a couple of plastic carrier bags in my coat pocket so we had a pleasant thirty minutes of walking around just picking the cockles up without having to dig for them. When both bags were soon filled up we had a wander around to see how extensive the cockle ground was. The children loved every moment of being out on the sands in the fresh sea air, only the distant sound of the waves breaking on the bar and the cry of the gulls. Being in the middle of the dangerous Duddon estuary with a granddad they trusted gave them a taste of adventure.

We taught them to respect the sea and the tides, to tell how to read the sands to avoid dangerous patches of sand and gulley's. We knew eventually they would be fishing bank lines with the other village boys, on the sands digging bait in the early hours of the morning. They needed to be shown the safe way to use this dangerous estuary so that we could trust them. Their fathers were good seasoned fishermen so between us all they had good tutors. The tide was beginning to flood back in it was time to make for shore, heading straight for the limestone mass of grey rock of Dunnerholme in the distance. We took turns carrying the bags of cockles home and were looking forward to showing their nana Pauline our bounty.

This small cockle bed we found kept us and our extended families going for a long time in prime cockles. Until one day a sharp eyed bait digger who lived on Walney Island spotted us carrying our cockles off, when he saw the sheer size of them, he and his friend came every day for a year collecting them. We found out that he was boiling them at home and putting them into glass jars in vinegar, selling them around the

Barrow pubs. Of course the cockle grounds could not sustain this level of removal and before long there were none left on this particular spot and not been any since. Never mind we all enjoyed them whilst they were on our doorstep.

The grandchildren were gradually learning about the variety of nature that lived around the cottage. One day we found a dead adult hedgehog just outside the back door; three babies were waiting patiently for mother to wake up. Our elder granddaughter Laura and sister Victoria were staying with us this particular day and were upset to see the dead hedgehog. They fetched a cardboard box and filled it with hay, then opened a tin of cat food we always keep for stray cats. The baby hedgehogs started to eat the cat food and sip water from a dish eventually. The girls looked after them until they were big enough to fend for themselves and set them free one warm sunny evening.

Sometimes when looking out of the cottage window the children would spot a stoat or weasel stalking a rabbit, or occasionally a deer that had crossed the estuary at low tide. Foxes came down from the Kirkby fells hunting on the rabbit warren alongside the golf course, and at night the farmer sometimes would shoot the foxes to keep down the numbers. We kept dog and cat food in our cottage for the odd stray or lost pet that ended up at our door. It was unfortunately a fact of life that there are some very cruel people in this world. Late at night we would occasionally see the headlights of a car on the track, a car door opened and then quickly slammed shut, and then they usually drive off very fast. In the morning a frightened cat or dog might be cowering at our door, even on at least two occasions a pure black or white rabbit hopping about. Why they dump their unwanted pets in the countryside I will never know. Once the pet rabbit gets into the gorse bushes they do not last long, foxes, stoats, weasels or dogs get them. Sometimes they manage to mate and have their young, but these offspring do not last long either. Why these people think they are doing their unwanted pet bunnies a favour is beyond me.

I kept a small pet basket in my shed just in case I could catch any of these poor frightened creatures, and take them into the animal care centres in Barrow. Three nights I spent trying to catch one very scared ginger female cat, she would come into my shed for a feed and I tried all I knew to entice her into staying in the basket whilst I shut the door. Finally I managed to grab her and bundled her into the basket, she sank her teeth into my thumb, scratched my arm to ribbons, I was in a terrible state, blood flowed everywhere. It was not the cats fault, fancy being dumped in the countryside after relying on a human for so long to feed you, no wonder she fought me. I took her the next day to an animal centre and they assured me that they would try their utmost to find a home for her after she had settled down. I left some money for her food and board, I lost my thumbnail and it took a long time for my cuts to heal. It was not the first or last animal I delivered to that wonderful rescue centre and it was a good place to donate all the stray golf balls to them to sell in their shop.

Time has moved on and my farmer friends tell me that they have to cull even more foxes because they suspect that vans are turning up in the night with foxes from other towns and cities. They think when councils start to treat the foxes as a nuisance problem, animal right's people are capturing them and releasing them in the countryside, transferring one problem to another. One morning our Rebecca and Francesca after breakfast wanted to see the crow and the seagull, I had been telling them about a funny scene I had been watching each morning for the past two days. From a grassy hollow below the rock we watched a black backed gull flying out to our cockle bed and scratch around until he found a large cockle. Flying towards Dunnerholme rock he flew high in the sky until he was above a level rock ledge. He released the cockle from his beak when he judged the right height was reached to ensure the shell broke on impact with the rock.

"That bird is very clever granddad" said Rebecca, admiration in her voice.

"Just watch what happens next" I replied.

The large cockle shell hit the rock and the shell broke releasing the contents. Before the gull flew down to eat the hard earned reward lying waiting for him, a big black crow hopped from his hiding place under a rocky ledge and ate the cockle before the surprised gull had even landed.

"Now that is clever granddad" said Francesca.

"Wait and see what happens next" I said.

The seagull set off again for the cockle bed and the same thing happened three times before the gull finally decided enough is enough, she decided to go and eat shrimps or suchlike out on the sands where the annoying crow would not bother her.

The children loved to see barn owls and sparrow hawks catching the mice and voles that inhabited the rough ground at the edge of the gorse bushes. They always had something different to tell their teachers when back at school. We all soon realised just how special and magical Dunnerholme was and that unusual adventures were always going to happen. The three boys and six girls shared any adventures except when one day Mark's dad, who was a member of the golf club, suggested that on a dark night I took the three boys on an expedition to find and retrieve the Shangri la of golf balls. This special magical place was the beck that ran nearly the full length of the golf course. His dad said to take plenty of buckets with us for they would be full in no time. I wished he had not said that because I knew the boys would not give me any peace until this expedition was organised. The girls also gave me grief because they wanted to join the boys; in short it was a nightmare.

Two weekends later all the children were staying at the cottage, we had a compromise agreed. The girls would help Pauline bake some lovely cakes whilst the boys could have their golf ball retrieval expedition. The girls became less vocal about going when it became very dark outside, and the wind was howling through the trees. The boys wanted to black their faces with soot from the chimney, just like commandos. We had eight plastic buckets waiting at the back door; the boys looked nervous but would not change their minds about going.

"Nine o'clock granddad time to go" said Mark waving his torch in the air.

The six girls were pleased that they had changed their minds about going out into the dark night, telling the boys to do exactly what granddad said.

Pauline said "Be careful you lot and watch what you are doing!"

Mark said "It is a bit like that nana, if grand dad got caught by the golf committee raiding the course he would get done!"

Picking up the buckets and torches we left the cottages heading along a secluded path towards the start of where Mark's dad instructed us to go.

Lee said "It is very scary granddad and those gorse bushes are waving about in the wind making creepy noises, I might go home and help the girls bake some cakes."

"Oh you are not leaving Lee you are not spoiling this adventure for me and Kristian!" said Mark.

Just then we all nearly jumped out of our skins, a large black object jumped out of the gorse bushes in front of us, we all dropped our torches and screamed. I grabbed my torch off the floor to see what the black object was; it was bloody 'Amos' my neighbour's rather large black tom cat.

"It is all right lads I shouted to the still whimpering kids, it is only Amos calm down, must admit lads I nearly wet my pants then, he frightened the life out of us didn't he?"

A quiet voice said "I have wet myself granddad!"

"Do you all want to go back now?" I said.

"No!" was the emphatic answer.

Amos must have been out hunting when he decided to join us and followed us all night for a bit of entertainment I thought.

We had got off to a bad start so as the song says, things could only get better, we hoped. The stone bridge across the beck loomed up in the dark; this was the spot we planned to get into the water. There was a loud splash, a startled yell and Mark had fallen head first into the beck. Luckily the pitch black was soon dispersed by bright moonlight; the full moon came from behind the clouds and it became more like daylight. Everybody cheered up then; and became braver I asked if they wanted to go home yet and a resounding no came from the lads, they said they were enjoying the adventure too much.

"We are just like the famous five granddad, now for the golf balls let's get started, we have put our gloves on."

At that everybody jumped into the beck and sank into about two feet of black ooze with a foot of water on top. Of course the wellingtons filled with cold water and sludge. You could feel many hundreds of golf balls under our feet so it was easy to just reach underwater to pick up the golf balls. The boys really were excited now, in no time at all the eight buckets were full to the top and laid on the parapet. We were all soaked with black muddy water and getting cold but enjoyed every minute of our adventure. The only dry one was Amos who walked proud as punch at the head of our column his tail in the air showing us the way home, obviously enjoying our company very much.

The reception when we finally arrived back at the cottage was not like the departure by no means. To a chorus of "You all stink! You are all covered in black slime and are not coming into the house in that condition."

Pauline was not best pleased when she saw the state of us all.

She said "Take off all your clothes and put them in a heap, they will have to be burned, next stand in a line and I will bring out buckets of hot water to get the worst black slime off you all. Then the three boys can get into a nice warm bath and into their pyjamas and have their supper. I am annoyed with you Norm the children show more sense than you!"

A chorus of "Please do not shout at granddad nana we have just had the best adventure ever, even Amos came with us. Look at all those golf balls we bought home we can clean them tomorrow and sell them, the money will pay for our new clothes, what a fabulous time, we love staying at your cottage nana!"

A busy day at Dunnerholme it was Francesca's birthday, a huge bouncy castle had been delivered complete with petrol generator to power the air compressor to inflate it. All the grand children wheeled it down to the flat grassy area under the lee of the rock, and we inflated it ready for all the other children to arrive. The sandwiches and cakes were all carried down to the picnic site; I had been up earlier in the morning carrying a big bag of toys to bury in the sand on the beach. I buried them in the sand each one about twelve inches deep, so we would know where to dig I put a large circle in the sand around them. The bouncy castle on the beach was a great success but the buried treasure was a huge disaster, I was not popular one little bit! The children dug and gave up crying, the adults dug, to no avail, not one present was ever found. I was not amused, the beach resembled a battlefield. I could only conclude that somebody was watching me bury the prizes, and rubbed out my circle and put another one ten yards away, playing a sick joke on me. Granddad had gone from' Hero' to 'Zero' in no time at all. By the end of the day the children had recovered their sense of humour and we finished off the party with a game of rounder's. An added bonus for the great gang of children visiting was that the sheep did not fail to be the centre of attention. One of the pregnant ewes had got herself trapped along a thin ledge, halfway up the cliff face in their constant quest to commit suicide. Of course that set half the children off screaming and crying, as for the others they were very excited to see if the sheep was going to fall off and die. Pauline said "For God's sake Norm tell George to hurry up with ropes and a long ladder, the children refuse to leave until they see the sheep rescued!" Good old George was here in a flash, and amazed to see an enthusiastic audience watching his every move. The ladder was put up to the ledge, one of the children's dad was a keen mountaineer, he climbed onto the ledge with a thick rope and in no time at all proceeded to lower the dozy sheep down from the ledge, to be caught by eager hands and a big cheer from all the children. That I believe was the highlight of the day and made up for the buried treasure debacle.

There was a lovely steep grassy slope running down from one part of the rock, this we found ideal for launching the children off with their sledge. The novelty was we did not need any snow, the children loved it. The only problem was that when somebody went down the slope, they soon got fed up with dragging it all the way back up again. My solution was to fetch a long length of thin rope from the peat house, tie it to the back of the sledge and hold the loose end at the top of the hill ready to pull the sledge back. A simple and fool proof way of retrieving the sledge each time, the former rider of the sledge could climb back up in their own time. Of course as the day progressed the neatly coiled rope became haphazardly dumped in a careless heap. Our Victoria headed down the slope screaming with excitement, to be extremely surprised to see poor nana overtaking her hopping on one leg, being towed behind the sledge with the rope wrapped tightly around an ankle. We had to close our eyes, the crash and tumble of nana turning cartwheels was a sorry sight to witness. The howls of rage and pain not nice to hear, we all dashed down to the bottom of the slope quickly as possible, hoping to find a pulse. Pauline was very lucky, a few painful sprains and grazes, thankfully no broken bones.

New Years Eve in cottage

Glum faces going home

Rebecca and Hayley Cockling, Dunnerholme in background

Francesca saving the crabs

Rescued lamb from the marsh

Our youngest grandson Kristian used to bring us fresh milk and bread
along the beach from Askam village on his quad bike (wearing his helmet
of course) Happy days !

Dunnerholme cottages

Shepherd George and his beloved sheep

The Hospice Christmas card we sold

On Safari in Kenya

Sheep about to be cut off by the tide

Trident Nuclear Submarine covered in secret acoustic tiles

Our cottage and beautiful view of the Duddon estuary and
Lakeland mountains

Sheepdog pups at George's farm,
this photo was featured in several different calendars

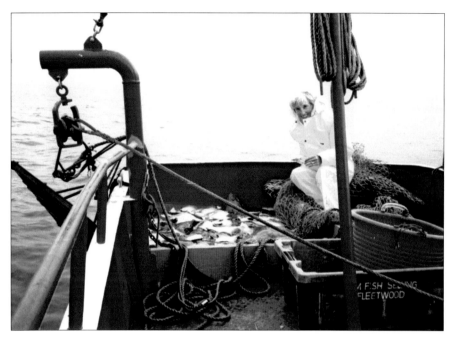

Pauline sorting the fish on our trawler

Our last trawler called 'Saltaire' which was crewed
by my lovely wife Pauline

MY FAVOURITE PLACE

BY KATRINA TYSON

AGE 11 YEARS

My favourite place is my nana's house. My nana's house is warm and cosy with the big soft chair swallowing me up and heat coming from the roaring flames of the fire. It is quiet and peaceful and the only thing you can hear is the soft humming of the warm oven in the kitchen, I am surrounded by sweet smells of baking. The delicious mouth watering taste of my granddads nutty flapjack soaked in a hot cup of steaming tea sends a warm sensation to my stomach. My granddad deals a crisp new pack of cards on the table and asks for a game of Find the Lady.

My nana dusts the fine mahogany table and places a bowl of juicy fruit onto the white lace tablecloth. The garden is like an African jungle, the rain pitter patting on the porcelain dog which looks through the window with sad droopy eyes like small pools of a midnight lagoon. It smells of flowers and wet soil. The dark soil where the lettuce patch was before the giant slug infestation. My granddad doesn't believe in slug pellets, he thinks they are the wildlife's answer to a slow death. I love their cottage so much.

CHAPTER TWENTY ONE

THE SURVEYS

Often when surveying we found odd marks on our echo sounder recordings, sometimes caused by the air bladders of dense shoals of fish, occasionally swarms of jellyfish and quite often some dick that had pinched a motor car or motor bike and drove or pushed them into the dock or Walney channel. On one memorable occasion a huge old fashioned ornate safe was found with its door still secure. When we reported strange marks on our recording paper our local diving company were called out to investigate, and usually fixed strops around the objects ready for a dock mobile crane to lift out onto the quayside. This lift of the heavy safe was a special case; it could have been stolen years earlier by burglars who could not manage to open it, and then dumped it into the dock if the police suspected them. Anyway we were speculating about Victorian jewels, gold or cash, our imaginations were running wild and the day our diver friends got the door off after a lot of hard work will never be forgotten, it was bloody empty! Everybody involved were arguing about what share each person deserved so that had been a waste of time. When we finally finished the dock surveys to loud cheers, we had instructions to report to the dock office for another assignment.

To our surprise an old chart of Cavendish dock was laid out for us to look at. Now Cavendish dock was a reservoir to top up all the other docks and make sure a certain depth of water was always maintained for submarines and other shipping. This dock was a huge expanse of water and except for padlocked sluice gates was landlocked. The Dova Haw could not access this water and the average depth maybe only twenty feet or less. The water was also pumped out and back as cooling water for the

Roose power station, this increased the overall water temperature so weed grew alarmingly fast, fish thrived and wildlife of all kinds.

We were told to do a new survey and produce a completed chart as soon as. Interestingly the old chart about 1946 showed a position in the middle of Cavendish dock where a German bomb had landed and not exploded when attacking the shipyard in 1941 if I remember correctly, and a possibility of another in the dock that was not marked on the chart. A large heavy steel open boat was to be used on which we fitted a small outboard motor. This did not work because every five yards run the engine became clogged with weed, I tried rowing but the heavy boat and the long distance to row made us return this outfit in disgust. We bought a small light rowing tender and a set of oars, tied a transducer to a pole on the side of our dinghy rigged to a paper depth sounder, powered by a car battery, this would have to suffice.

Alan had the privilege of being the first hydrographer to survey and produce this new chart since 1946. Alan said he would be proud of being the first man in all these years that could put his name on the bottom of a new chart.

I said "What about my name on the bottom as well."

Alan said "Get stuffed I am doing all the brainwork Norm, a monkey can spend all day rowing a little rowing boat up and down a calm dock."

"You cheeky sod" I said "It is probably the equivalent of rowing to the Isle of Man and back and you show me a bloody monkey daft enough who would do that!"

When faced with a mutiny Alan agreed to my request but lied, when I last looked at the chart only his name was credited on the bottom.

Even though most of my working day was spent doing a full Walney channel monthly survey I did have to squeeze in several other tasks. Sometimes working evenings or weekends and quite often sixteen hour days, very annoying for my wife, even having to cancel a planned holiday to Tenerife on one occasion due to a nuclear submarine leaving earlier than planned. I loved the constant variety of tasks that came my way as the launch master, taking out a diving team to change the batteries in the underwater wave recorders off Walney, taking electricians to the many channel buoys, all the ports leading lights needed regular servicing, all had to be accessed using the dock launches. Sometimes after a long day surveying, and finally relaxing at home, a phone call to ask me to turn out on the pilot boat in the early hours of the morning might come, the regular coxswain being off with illness. All in all I considered myself very lucky to have such a responsible, varied job and so well paid.

The downside was under the guise of flexibility you were expected to do anybodies job and the management took full advantage of this. One particular day our new pilot boat arrived from Hull on a large low loader lorry at the Nuclear Terminal. I supervised the unloading onto the quayside and our foreman turned up with gallon tins of red anti-fouling paint and two brushes for the deckhand and me. It was blowing a gale of wind and around the boat was like being in a wind tunnel. I said "You are bloody joking?"

He replied that we had signed this new flexibility labour clause so get painting boys! My pal Gary said that if we hurried we could get the hull painted and finished for lunch time. Of course the paint blew off the brushes and coated us with millions of bright red paint spots, my spectacles were coated, it was in our eyes and our boiler suits looked as if they had been dipped in it. The manager of the Terminal played hell and we like all the prison guards said, "We are only following our orders!"

The manager replied "Have you no common sense you are the Launch Master for heaven's sake, can't you use your bloody initiative skipper, painting in a gale of wind is stupid? Our office windows are being speckled with windblown paint.

The hydrographer then turned up saying "What the hell are you doing lying under the hull of that pilot boat covered from top to toe with bright red paint?"

"It is a long story but something to do with my new contract about being flexible at work, what do you want Alan?"

"I want you and Gary to throw down those bloody paint brushes and get the survey boat ready in twenty minutes, the dock gates are opening and the dredger skipper is screaming for a quick survey of the dock entrance. The Ministry of Defence is paying a lot of money for your service; by the way you will both have to work over the lunch hour, so get a move on!"

"Too many Chiefs and not enough Indians that is the bloody problem, we should not have signed those contracts, our working life has changed for the worse Norm!" said a very annoyed Gary.

It was the week after this that Gary was called out to take the pilot boat out in a heavy blow in the early hours of the morning, after a severe collision with a large ship in a heavy sea, he limped back to port with a severely disabled pilot boat. I could not believe the damage that was done she would be out of commission for some considerable time. This was a major boatyard repair, the starboard engine was moved off its mountings and needed to be sent away for repairs, the forward bulkhead was cracked and displaced, the huge heavy bow fitting had ripped off and the stainless bolts bent in half. The cracks in the starboard side revealed that the hull was suffering from osmoses a form of fibreglass rot. With one of the engines out she had a huge list to one side and could not be delivered to the boatyard over Morecambe bay at the port of Glasson dock. To get her on an even keel temporarily for the trip over on one engine I got the crane to lower a concrete mooring sinker into the engine room to compensate for the missing engine. The weight was just right if the weather forecast said no wind, it would be an acceptable risk. Of course nowadays with the new health and safety culture it would not happen. Gary buggered up the pilot boat so he had to sail her across the bay to the boatyard, where eventually she was treated for osmosis, painted up, and the reconditioned engine put back in. Meanwhile the docks hired another pilot boat at great expense.

The job we took for granted was dangerous at times but dealing with the sea sometimes took you unaware. To board the Dova Haw or the pilot boat in the middle of the dangerous rip tide of Walney channel needed a boatman of special skills. Two men in a small dinghy, rowing out or from, a big boat moored in midstream, dealing with a ripping tide and high waves takes an exceptional skill not many people possess, especially in darkness.

The reason I am labouring this point about rowing skills is because we lost a great friend and work colleague one dark night attempting to board the pilot boat. Our friend used to be Captain of the ports bucket and grab dredger, he had worked at the docks for many years and was now assistant dock master. On duty this night he and another man who was on pier head assignment, decided to go to the harbour yard boat club and launch the small rowing boat to board the pilot boat moored midstream, the object was to bring the pilot boat into the dock to have some work done the following day. The dinghy overturned in the swift flowing tide, the dock master and the other man were washed down tide being kept afloat by their inflatable lifejackets. The two men were spotted by a young Vickers shipyard worker named Douglas Moore who with no thought for himself waded into the freezing tide, pulling one man ashore safely; he quickly removed the man's lifejacket and putting it on jumped back in the water bravely swimming out to the dock master, and with great difficulty pulled him ashore. Unfortunately the dock master did not survive the accident. This tragedy of course cast gloom over all the dock work force and things never seemed to be the same again. We all mourned a good and loyal man who was sadly missed, and never had the chance to do all the things he had talked to us about when he retired, and which was not too far off. The young man who behaved so bravely that night rightly received an award for his outstanding efforts.

CHAPTER TWENTY TWO

SKIPPER PAULINE

One of the rare days I had off Pauline said she would like to catch some fish to fill up our freezers, and supply our family and friends with a stock of prime fish fillets for winter. This particular morning was perfect, the sun was shining and the tides were just right for sailing out on the ebb tide. It was so calm that all the boats on their moorings were perfectly mirrored in the still water of Walney channel. Pauline rowed me across to our boat lying quietly to the large orange mooring buoy; two seagulls resting on the wheelhouse roof reluctantly took flight at our approach. Pauline expertly pulled our small boarding dinghy alongside the trawler called 'Saltaire.'

I had bought her recently from Amble on the east coast; she was what we call a mini trawler being only twenty six feet in length. She was steel built and fitted with a powerful diesel engine, on her deck was a trawl winch, next to the wheel house was fitted a net hauler. She had two small bunks fitted, and a gas cooker to make a brew and cook using two rings. She was fitted for fishing just like a larger trawler and only needed two crewmen to handle her. Pauline loved fishing this boat with me and was the best crew I ever had. The routine was that while I checked the engine for oil and water, Pauline tied the dinghy to the buoy and prepared to cast off the mooring when instructed. When the engine was running and everything stowed secure we headed down channel, another fishing trip was underway and on a perfect day we normally only dream about.

Pauline took the wheel and steered her under the great span of Jubilee Bridge that connects Barrow to Walney Island, expertly avoiding yachts and a myriad of assorted mooring buoys that tended to obstruct the fairway. Mean while I had to decide whether to trawl or set a trammel fixed net, it was a gamble and the choice would dictate the type of fishing ground Pauline steered towards. We had reached the channel mouth and could take several directions. "Which course skipper" asked Pauline?

"Head north up the coast towards West shore we will put the trammel net down instead of trawling today love."

Pauline knew exactly where we were heading; we had been shown this particular fishing mark by our Tony my stepson the year before. We had sailed out of the Duddon estuary from our village of Askam with our Tony using his small open boat with two hundred yards of net onboard. He had put his net on to a reef he had found to be prolific with fish. We hauled his net and saw bass, mullet and plaice were in abundance, a couple of lobsters and some crab, all in all a profitable days fishing. That was not to say we would be successful today but this mark of Tony's boded well for us. On the way to the reef I prepared the net for fishing, when it was ready I fried some bacon and made butties and coffee. By this time we had reached our fishing mark not far offshore, knocking the engine out of gear we idled over the reef whilst having our lunch in peace. The scene was idyllic, pristine white gulls floated on a flat calm blue sea under a perfect blue cloudless sky. The happy shrieks of children could be heard playing on the nearby beach; it just seemed to be too nice a day to be sweating pulling nets in and out, but old habits die hard they say.

Our new paper recording fish finder was fascinating Pauline, she could see the individual marks of each fish recording onto the paper and the rough outline of large rocks on the seabed. I did not know what type of fish was there except that they were big and plenty of them. Pauline took the wheel again to steer the course I gave her, at very slow speed we passed along the reef as I paid out the trammel net in a straight line, all one thousand yards. We would be fishing on sand as well as a rocky reef, with about ten feet of water under us. After all the net was shot overboard and marked at each end with a marker flag, I knocked the engine off and let the boat just drift slowly to have some peace and quiet on this beautiful day. I set two folding chairs onto the deck and started to doze off in the heat. We both had shorts on and I would put my fisherman's oilskins on when we started hauling the net in. The day was so still you could pick out what people were saying on the nearby beach. Pauline kept looking at the fish finder and getting extremely excited seeing all the fish marks coming and going around the underwater reef.

Two hours later I woke Pauline up, truth be told her snoring was doing my head in. I started up the engine and ruined the silence, we motored up to the first flag and I picked it up with the boathook. Pauline stayed on the wheel and I operated the net hauler and commenced with the usual trepidation about what was likely to be trapped in my nets. Looking downwards into the sea watching the first net come into view in the clear water, large fish enmeshed in the fine mesh were coming into my sight. When these huge fish came bouncing over the net hauler nearly braining me, most about six feet long and weighing God knows what. Pauline spotted them and was screaming with happy delight, "We have done it Norm what a haul we are going to have, look at the size of those fish they are enormous!"

A huge mound of net and fish was building up by the net hauler, the heap was so heavy the boat was tilting over to one side. I could not believe our bad luck; Pauline was doing some kind of celebratory war dance around the deck wondering why I was not joining in. Thinking that she must be told of why I was not as enthusiastic as her I said, "Sorry Pauline I do not want to rain on your parade but we have a haul of shark "Tope" to be precise, not giant cod or bass but bloody useless bloody tope, no good to sell or eat, a great big tonnage of rubbish. To top the day my nets are ruined, by the time I disentangle all these huge fish my net will be in ribbons."

Pauline was really disappointed she thought we had caught a boat full of high value fish, I explained that the tope were probably chasing mackerel or herring and our net got in their way. The day was roasting hot and that meant that the tope would need to be released quickly or would all die. There was no time to waste I had ruined my thousand yard of net but was not prepared to let these fine fish die on my deck.

"Why are these fish special Norm" she said. "Well there are a lot of fish around six feet in length and weighing up to one hundred pounds, they are slow growing and anglers would dream of catching fish like these and release them back into the sea unharmed, then go home thinking it was one of the best days in their lives," I explained. These tope, a member of the shark family are a remarkable fish. They are slender in shape with a sharply pointed snout, and sharp triangular teeth within their under slung mouth. The colour is grey brown on their backs and sides with a white creamy underbelly. They attack shoals of cod, mackerel and herring but will also feed on the bottom eating flatfish, crustaceans and molluscs. They come into shallow waters to give birth in summer, so some of the large females could be carrying up to forty young. Tope is not eaten in the United Kingdom but is used for certain dishes in Spain and is on the 'Vulnerable' status. So you can see how keen I was to save these lovely creatures. I suggested that Pauline steered the boat home and the extra breeze of the boat moving will help them cool down a little, meanwhile I played the hosepipe onto the great heap of tangled bodies. The sizes of those fish were unbelievable and I only had one shot of film left in my camera so I could show my colleagues at work. The afternoon was spent cutting the mesh away from the tope and putting them back over the side quickly as I could. The sweat was pouring out of me and my back was killing me, my mood was steadily getting worse. I looked up and saw Walney lighthouse passing by, hell the time is going quick but only the last few fish were now left on deck. This had turned out to be a waste of a perfect day; we would have been better off going down channel to Piel Island, anchoring the boat and rowing ashore for an afternoon sitting on the grass outside the Ship Inn drinking a cool pint of lager. Well I can honestly say all the fish were returned to the sea alive despite the hot day; my net was completely knackered, cut to shreds. I was in a foul temper and had a really severe back problem. Back safely tied up to the mooring, Pauline rummaged around the locker bringing out a string of mackerel feathers. Standing on the stern of our boat she started to pull in five mackerel every cast.

"Turn that frown upside down Norm! Every cloud as a silver lining put the kettle on fresh mackerel for our supper coming up!"

I began to think taking up yachting might be a bit less like hard work, maybe it was time to relax after work instead of hunting fish when I did not need to anymore. The advert was duly put into the old faithful fisherman's publication 'The Fishing News' and I awaited the usual outcome, from the time wasters to the deluded who expected the boat for peanuts. Knowing a genuine fisherman would eventually turn up I sat back and waited patiently. I had owned and sold many boats of differing types and sizes over the years, this was the newest boat and in the best condition I ever sold. I was to do a survey job in Walney channel and a dramatic rescue with this boat before she was sold. I was in the pier head on duty one day when a man knocked on the door asking if I was the skipper of the port survey vessel. When I said yes he offered me silly money to charter my own boat for the weekend to survey part of the channel near the lifeboat station. I asked my buddy to crew for me and it was done to this man's satisfaction. He gave me the money and disappeared, strange but at this time many contractors were involved with various activities relating to building new lock gates and the complete channel being dredged for the new generation of Trident submarines.

The week after I was relieving somebody in the pier head again, a radio call came in from a jack-up rig that was sited around Halfway shoal off the coast of Walney Island. It was taking core samples of the seabed; the three men on board were in a right panic threatening to call out the lifeboat to rescue them. It was an hour before low water and wind against tide kicking up a big sea. The men on the rig thought the waves were undermining the rig making it unstable and it was going to topple over. They had a small tug tied below the rig reached by a rope ladder; they abandoned the rig and boarded the small tug. Finding the engine and boat swamped with heavy spray and an engine that would not start, they climbed back onto the platform and began to scream for help over the radio to us. I explained all this to my boss who suggested instead of launching the lifeboat, would I be prepared to fetch them off using my boat. It was suggested that I put a bill in for my fuel etc. to the firm who owned the rig, and to check that the rig was in no danger and the men were panicking for nothing.

Collecting my pal Gary again as deck hand, we boarded my boat and headed at full speed on our rescue mission. It was a dismal afternoon, grey skies, rain showers and a fresh wind blowing. The seas looked high sweeping under the jack-up rig but the men would be safer staying onboard than climbing down the flimsy rope ladder. Certainly calling out the lifeboat was not necessary and as we thought the men had had enough, and wanted to go home. They insisted on climbing quickly down the ladder, and it was difficult to get them onto our deck safely when large breaking waves were sweeping passed underneath the four jack-up legs.

When they were safely aboard we then concentrated on getting a towrope onto their workboat, before the tug was battered to pieces against the legs, already she was damaged and would not have lasted much longer. With the men holding a steaming hot mug of coffee to warm them up, we towed their workboat to Roa Island and put her onto a safe mooring. My pal said that it was a bit hairy that rescue, and we were lucky not to have done serious damage to our boat, but it all ended happily.

The next week I showed my boat to a retired fisherman in Wales, gave him a run out and he wrote me out a cheque for my full asking price. He wanted to use her for shrimping and was delighted with her, taking her away a couple of days later.

We looked at my first sailing yacht the next week, she was called 'Ann Doreen' was twenty three feet in length, four berths with a petrol engine. It was very strange stood looking up at this quite sizable twin bilge keel fibreglass yacht, sitting snugly on a four wheel trailer. My only experience of sailing was with an old friend in an Enterprise sailing dinghy, and crewing occasionally on the first fibreglass yacht to arrive in our area. This was a brand new 'Hurley 'fin keel twenty two footer, with an auxiliary outboard motor. This man was called Stan and he had the boatshed next to ours, he was a gentleman, never swore and thought a lot of me and my friend Brian. Over the long winter nights Stan patiently taught us the art of navigation over numerous cups of coffee. At weekends if we were not out fishing because it was too rough in our boat, Stan insisted we crewed for him sailing his yacht 'Dinah' out to Morecambe Bay light vessel in the most appalling weather. We were absolutely petrified and frequently wondered if Stan had some kind of death wish. We had reefs in the mainsail and a storm jib up, our little yacht climbing up the high waves and down into the troughs. It was when we saw Stan at his happiest in those sea conditions that we realised that he was a great sailor, and completely in his element.

The boat healed over on her beam ends, me holding onto the tiller for dear life, Stan saying "Hold that course, hold her steady Norm, well done!"

Brian looking at me with genuine terror in his eyes, and Stan singing to himself down below making yet another cup of coffee, me in relief shouting "I see the lightship Stan are we turning back now?"

Stan's reply "Well done Norm we are going to sail around it!"

Stan had won many races with the large wooden yacht he owned and sold the boat to buy this small yacht he could use single handed if needs be. He won many races with his new Dinah, he was a great yachtsman, a gentleman and respected by everyone who knew him.

I never really took to sailing my heart was into tugs and trawlers, trawl nets and fishing. Big winches and noisy big diesel engines and it would take some getting use to a relaxing hobby of yachting. Thinking it would be a good idea to purchase a land rover to tow my new yacht the ten miles home to Askam, I did what I always do fall for the salesman's patter and blarney. The land rover had been used in a back street garage as a tow truck, only had fifty thousand miles on the clock; a hundred thousand had been wound back using an electric drill. This I found out later when asking around, but what the hell it was cheap, and it was diesel. I rounded up six mates to help me very early on a cold frosty Saturday morning; everything went well except that my land rover was reluctant to start, and when she did condescend to fire up the resultant black cloud had nearly choked us and several passersby. To be fair to the engine when warm, the black smoke turned a nice blue colour.

When coupling the land rover to the yacht trailer my friends seemed a little apprehensive, and voiced some concern about whether my old crock of a vehicle could pull the heavy yacht up the very steep hill that we needed to negotiate on the way to my village. "That is why I asked all six of you to help me in case of any unseen problems; you don't think your all getting your bacon butties that easily." Driving along Abbey Road caused a bit of a stir, a land rover pickup truck with six cold men sitting miserably in the back towing a rather large yacht at a top speed on the flat level road of twenty miles an hour, my foot was hard down to the floor! Vast clouds of blue smoke was emitting from our exhaust pipe. I began to feel very apprehensive about the outcome of our mission; a bad sign was the lack of piss taking that would normally be coming from my mates in the back. Our convoy stretched for miles behind us, buses, lorries, vans, taxis, well you get the picture. Horns were being used like we were in Rome and not our rural little sleepy town, nobody dared overtake us because they could not see to overtake for the dense cloud of exhaust emitting from us.

"For God's sake pull over and let this traffic overtake us Norm, this is bloody ridiculous!" shouted somebody from the back. Up ahead I spotted a place to pull in at last and we all heaved a sigh of relief. The long row of traffic passed us and it was a good job none of us were blessed with a sensitive disposition. My pal Brian sitting in front of the cab with me said, "That is all the swear words known to man that are being shouted at you Norm, they are very inventive with their insults don't you think?"

"Not really Brian I have not heard anything new that I have not heard before."

The long stream of traffic gradually thinned out and it was safe to move on, ahead was the first steep hill and then would come just one more with a bigger gradient, and then all the way to our village downhill. At least this hill ahead had two lanes so traffic could pass us safely when they could see through the exhaust cloud. Our speed reduced to a barely susceptible crawl and slowly but surely after what seemed to be forever we reached the summit. No police in sight as yet, that is the lucky part of the day so far. Down the hill and a sharp left turn that took both sides of the road up, forcing passing cars to use the pavement, passing the Red Lion pub the incline started to get ever steeper. Cars were parked on either side of the road leaving no room to manoeuvre, I had to go forward foot flooring the accelerator, shit or bust and it was looking awfully like bust!

Thankfully cars stopped at the top of the hill when they saw this battered land rover towing a large yacht up the hill, trailing a jet of blue exhaust. It had to happen, just when I thought we might have been getting towards the peak of the hill the land rover stopped and refused to move forward. The engine was still working but was not powerful enough to move us further up the hill. To compound the problem the weight of the yacht began to pull us backwards. "Put the brakes on quick Norm and the bloody handbrake we are sliding backwards!" said somebody in the back, stating the bloody obvious. A few yards behind us was a convoy of cars following closely up the hill, and no place for them to get out of the way? I was having a panic attack; the lads in the back were all shouting at once, all I could think was the carnage that would be caused when we destroyed all the cars below us, the news headlines, BBC news, and the shame.

My foot was on the brake, the handbrake fully on and still we were sliding inexorably slowly backwards towards the first car only six feet behind the trailer. The first car was blasting on his horn, followed by other panicking drivers doing the same, as though the noise of the horns was going to stop our descent down the hill. Of course all this racket fetched hoards of inquisitive people to stand and gawp, delighted to see a free disaster happen on their very own doorstep. Three feet away from the nearest car and I angrily shouted to the six lads sitting in the back to stop sitting on their fat arses and jump out and put their weight behind the trailer, it might give me time to think of something. They held us for a few minutes with help from some sympathetic bystanders, until Brian said "Try the four wheel drive Norm it just might be enough to get us going again and reach the summit!"

"Good thinking Brian if that does not work I am well and truly goosed! And bankrupt, I have not had time to get the boat insured."

With my heart in my mouth I put it into four wheel drive and foot hard down on the accelerator released the handbrake taking my foot off the brake. A great cheer went up from the crowd. We started to go upwards once more, at a snail's pace but definitely moving in the right direction. Somebody up there was looking after me as usual. A disaster was averted for me and we had not even seen a policeman all this time. We reached the summit then it was all downhill to our village after that, a terrible smell of burnt clutch and overheated brake pads and a relieved group of men reached our destination.

"Bloody sailing boats you can keep them Norm, they are nothing but trouble, you should stick to good old fishing boats!" said Brian.

We had some lovely sailing trips all over the Irish Sea with this yacht, visiting many different harbours and spending weekends anchored off Piel Island overlooked by the ancient castle.

Possibly the most embarrassing day of my seagoing life was with Pauline on our second yacht. This rather bigger four berth yacht I named 'Pauline,' after all our village shop was called 'Paulines Fruit & Veg' shop and it bought us luck! One sunny summer's day we motored down channel at low water due to not having a wisp of wind to fill the sails. Our intention was to have a few drinks with our friend Ronnie the landlord of the pub called the Ship Inn on Piel Island, and afterwards find a secluded place near the castle to sunbathe, away from the hoards of tourist bought over by the ferry boat. Picking up a mooring in Piel anchorage to save lying at anchor I pulled in a few yards and saw it was good mooring rope and thought how lucky I was not to have a hundred foot of anchor chain to pull in later in the day. The spring tide that day was ten metres and starting to flood in now, if I set off back one hour before high tide the three knot current would take me home quickly, I would need to have Jubilee Bridge lifted and that was no problem.

So we rowed ashore looking forward to having a good crack with our mate Ronnie, he had accompanied us on a few adventures over the years when he was a diver and used our boats. After a few pints sitting outside on the grass watching the ferry disgorging twelve tourists at a time, the pub was filling up so Ronnie had to get back behind the bar. We said we would go onto the other side of the Island to sunbathe in peace. The first thing I heard when I awoke in the hot afternoon sun was Pauline snoring alongside of me, the second was a loud man's voice shouting "Where the bloody hell are you Pascoe?"

Thinking I know that voice I stood up and saw Ronnie, sweating like a pig, face bright red and looking pissed off!

"I have been all over the island looking for you Norm, your boat is drifting up Walney Channel, it is still attached to the mooring complete with concrete sucker, you have put your boat on Tom's winter mooring, it is only on a short rope to mark its position he took the riding rope off yesterday!"

Oh bugger I should have checked it properly, only last week at high tide a forty foot long yacht was moored on it, a complete amateur mistake I would not be able to live this down in any of the local boating clubs for a long time to come. Ronnie shouted "You better get your arse into gear Norm and start rowing after it, if she reaches Jubilee Bridge her mast will be ripped out!" It was a good job my boat was big enough to lift the concrete mooring sinker a smaller boat would have been pulled under as the tide flooded in. Running as fast as we could to the jetty where our rowing boat had been left, we launched it and Pauline sat in the stern. Our yacht was a dot in the distance making about two knots heading in the direction of Barrow and Walney Bridge. Looking around I saw typically no boats around when you needed a lift only the ferry which was busy commuting passengers to Piel Island. So I rowed like the devil was after me and realised that Pauline was excess baggage, I should have left her ashore and picked her up later. Another elementary mistake I had made this day, the sweat was running off me but I could see progress was being made the tide was helping me. After what seemed ages I caught up with the yacht Pauline, she was bow down with the weight of the heavy sinker tied short to the front of the boat and her stern high out of the water. Finally just before the dangerous bridge structure I boarded my boat, and leaving my embarrassed wife to secure our rowing dinghy started up the Volvo diesel and put the engine onto full power. Against the tide I had no chance to return the mooring back to Piel Island, so headed inshore to the shallow mussel beds where I cut the mooring loose to drop onto the seabed. Watching from the bridge many pedestrians were wondering about the funny antics we were doing, the mooring would have to be returned another day in the near future and hope my grovelling would be enough to placate the owner of the mooring. All in all a pretty shitty day but it could have turned out a hell of a lot worse, like my yacht being dismasted or sunk at Jubilee bridge.

CHAPTER TWENTY THREE

THE BUMBLING SPY

We spent the morning surveying the dock basin where lay the enormous bulk of a Trident submarine. The sheer size of this black 'Leviathan' never failed to amaze me, knowing that like an iceberg most of her vast bulk was under the surface. This 'Vanguard' class was built here at Barrow by the highly skilled workforce in our small town. In this dock I was surveying, the submarine was called Vanguard and the three others are Victorious, Vigilant and Vengeance. These boats are the sole platforms for the United Kingdom's nuclear weapons. Each one costing £1,500 million each and the total programme cost £15 billion, and have been in continuous service since 1993. These nuclear-powered ballistic submarines displace 15,900 tonnes submerged, are 491ft 10inch in length- beam 42ft.0 – draught 39ft 4in. The Vanguard's submerged speed is an incredible excess of 25Knots and her range only limited by food and maintenance requirements. With her complement of 135 men she can roam the world's oceans with stealth anywhere she chooses, each submarine is armed with up to 16 Trident missiles, plus torpedos.

When we finished at lunch time a friend phoned to say that our friend had been arrested for being a spy! To say I was shocked would be an understatement, our pal and his friend would be the last people you imagined would be involved with breaking Official Secret Acts. Our pal used to drink with our gang for years, with his beat up old car we would roam around the local pubs and drive up to the Lake District, always ending up drunk. Of course this was in the days when many people did drink and drive and the law was more lenient, this was something I never personally would do. He worked at the local paper as a type setter, using lead type in those days, a highly skilled job. All his holidays he spent crewing on our trawler, he absolutely loved gutting fish and meeting the Fleetwood lads when we landed in Fleetwood fish dock. A visit to a Chinese restaurant and then a drunken tour around the many thriving fishermen's pubs, and getting fixed up that suited him fine. He was very popular and everyone thought he was a Walter Mitty character, a bit like this time next year I will be a millionaire, sort of person.

He came down to our trawler one day saying he had packed his job in and was going down to London to become a private Investigator. Seemingly his brother, who already did this job, had arranged it for him. He came back to Barrow often to visit us and everybody started to call him Joe Cool, on account of him always wearing large sunglasses. He was bloody good fun and never a dull moment when he visited; with his lurid tales of London life he told a good story. I remember saying to him that we needed some new heavy duty batteries for our boat but we were stony broke.

"No problem Norm I will get you some tonight when it is dark, I know the perfect place the plant hire firm must be replacing them with new ones they might do your needs," he said. In those far off days you usually went out in your best suit to chat up the girls, especially in the posh hotels. We toured around the Lake villages, and managed to both get a date for next week in Coniston. On the way home in the pouring rain my pal drove me to a plant hire site that was not even fenced in yet, where lay all types of welding machines. Pulling up he proceeded to pick up four batteries from a big heap of them, "Saying don't just stand there like a spare part Norm, give me a hand to put them in the boot, it is not like stealing they are scrap value only."

It was piddling down, freezing cold and we were very drunk, he drove to our boat club and we stashed them into my shed.

"I don't want to seem ungrateful pal but these batteries seemed a bit rough and covered in grease and goo," I said.

"You ungrateful brat after me going to all this trouble to get your trawler sorted out with batteries, it is the last time I help you out," he said.

"I can't help thinking we could just call tomorrow and ask to buy the best ones in daylight?"

Well it turned out an expensive night out for both of us, when I got home; as usual I hung my best suit on a hanger behind my door before jumping into bed in a drunken stupor. Mum woke me up shouting about my suit, drunken nights and I needed my arse kicking. Opening my blood shot eyes I saw an angry mother holding up a string of rags on a coat hanger. A strange sight, I thought where did those shredded rags come from, and who is inside my head causing so much pain.

"What has happened to your suit Norm? It is bloody ruined!"

I felt sick and could not even imagine what might have caused my expensive suit to begin to shred itself to death after a normal piss up with the lads?

Oh hell it began to dawn on me, it was the bloody batteries they must be all leaking acid, my suit and trousers were eaten away, I checked my shoes they were goosed, both my bare legs were red raw with acid burns. Well it served us both right, a lesson to be learned here, of course my friend's gear was buggered too. The batteries were no good, I persuaded him to take them back the next night and leave them where they came from. One of the many stupid daft things we used to get up to before he went back to London.

Anyway back to the 'Two Bumbling Spies' they had concocted this hare brained scheme to try and get a shed load of money through the sale of a secret acoustic submarine tile to the Russians. My friend had come back from London a few years later and become a local taxi driver for amazingly named 'Trident' taxi firm. His partner in crime who had worked for the shipyard for fifteen years and was a security guard had access to these secret tiles. They drank together in the local Conservative Club where they were both members and over a few pints put this mad idea together. Their aim was to get enough money to retire to Spain and live a good happy life on their share of the vast proceeds they hoped to receive from a grateful Russian government, assuming the Russians would be daft enough to give them a load of loot!

When I heard what my friend had been accused of, this surprised me because we had lost touch since I had got married and gone back to my seagoing career. Indeed not seeing him for years I assumed he was still in London working as a private investigator. The headlines all over the world when the infamous two were convicted said 'British Foil Plot by Two Bumblers to Sell Secrets.'

From the start it went so wrong, at Preston Crown Court in the north of England it was told that "someone" had informed the police that an unidentified man had phoned the Soviet Embassy. The caller had offered to sell the embassy a secret acoustic tile used to cover the hulls of Britain's giant American designed Trident nuclear submarines, being built at Vickers shipbuilders at the huge docks at Barrow-in-Furness, this top secret tile made the submarines practically undetectable to the Soviet sonar systems.

My friend's partner in crime said "Do you want to buy a rubber tile that goes on the outside of a sub?" was the jocular approach made. He was a security guard at Barrow shipyard. The remark was made to a Russian man who informed the pair that he was an official of the Soviet trade delegation in London. The pair said they also called an assistant naval attaché at the embassy trying to interest him. Using the name John Stuart they asked for a sum of ($4.8 million), the court was told, and the Russian laughed so hard that the would be Barrow spy had to hold the telephone away from his ear.

This of course was no laughing matter to the British Security Service who wondered who the hell this man could be, also what other secrets he had or what else did he have on offer to the Russians. The police and MI5 knew the phone calls had been made from around the Barrow dock area and that the Russian had laughed at the men's first approach, something a decent spy should never do.

The police and MI5 took out advertisements in the personal columns of local newspapers that made it look like Mister Madrichyk had had a change of heart about their proposal. One said 'Please write' "John Stuart, last heard of in the Cumbria area," one advertisement said. "Don't take what I said at face value. Please contact Alexander M. Calling the telephone number you have may cause problems. Please write to me at Box 110, Mail, Barrow, so we can get in touch again."

"John Stuart from Alexander M." Began another "I repeat that you should not telephone us on our London numbers. Please understand that they cannot be used to discuss such matters. Also I am not an expert in this business. Instead please telephone my colleague Nick who wants to help you on 0836 632363 any weekday between 1600 hours and 1700 hours starting Wednesday 29th August."

Our two bumbling would be spies had almost forgotten about the plot by then, perhaps because as they explained to the court, they had dreamed it up over pints of beer in the Conservative Club of Barrow-in- Furness, where both were members.

My friends pal and partner in crime who had worked at the shipyard for fifteen years, told the court that the acoustic tiles were stacked out in the open all over the place, he spotted the advertisement and contacted 'Nick' on the 0836 number, a mobile line, from a telephone booth in Barrow. It was the first of nine telephone calls that would have done credit to a 'Brian Rix' farce according to what was said in court. Nick (the British agent) tried to imitate a Russian accent in his negotiations over the acoustic tile but kept forgetting that the Russian word for 'yes' was 'da,' not 'ja.' He also could not pronounce the word 'Moscow' properly. Both would be spies pleaded guilty in court.

The two Barrow men kept using the same telephone booth so the police and Security Service soon caught up with them, even taking photographs of the pair of bunglers. The Security men even forgot to take the lens cap off the camera first on one occasion! They were even spotted by my friend in his taxi when they were driving away, he saw them dusting for fingerprints at the booth. You could not make it up!

Incidentally Pauline and I were driving passed that very same telephone box and saw men dusting the booth as though for fingerprints, it sticks in your memory, especially in broad daylight with no temporary screens put around it. This sort of thing does not normally happen in a small town like ours; hundreds of people must have spotted them doing it and talked about it all over Barrow.

After the ninth telephone call the hapless Barrow duo was now demanding $3.2 million in used $:50 notes and then the police finally arrested them. Both pleaded guilty to making damaging disclosures in breach of Section2 of the 1989 Official Secrets Act. My friend the taxi driver, then forty one years old admitted handling stolen goods, the ex Vickers security guard then forty seven years old admitted stealing a sonic tile. The judge sentenced them both to fifteen months in prison; they had hoped to be spending the rest of their lives living the good life in Spain.

A few years after they were released I had a surprise visit from my taxi driving friend and a woman. He came knocking on our cottage door at remote Dunnerholme, introducing the lady has his girlfriend. Over coffee and cake we talked all afternoon, the version of his espionage arrest inevitably came up. His version of the story that made headline news all over the world was very different to the newspaper accounts and the official story. In prison he said they were known to their fellow inmates as 'Glasnost' and 'Perestroika.'

My friend said he had a patent out on a new way of scoring 'Bridge' and was hoping to make his fortune getting somebody to mass produce it, and would I like to invest, of course I declined his kind offer. His girl friend seemed a lovely person and as we were chatting at the cottage door he saw my four canoes lying in the grass.

"I am renting a cottage at the side of Lake Windermere Norm, would you mind letting me borrow all your canoes for the week, I have visitors arriving next week and could take them all on the lake. I will bring the canoes back next weekend, I promise" he said.

"I can let you borrow two canoes plus paddles but need to keep the other two for the two grand children visiting this weekend," I replied.

He tried again to get me to give him all four canoes but I was adamant. Off they drove into the sunset with my rope lashing the two canoes on his car roof, two sets of paddles, and a box of Pauline's cakes in his boot. That was fifteen years ago and I have not seen the robbing little sod since! I have seen my canoes, it was a picture in our local paper the Evening Mail of a canoeist paddling on Lake Windermere, yes your right it was him. So much for giving somebody a second chance, a lovable rogue!

CHAPTER TWENTY FOUR

FLOTSAM AND JETSAM

All my life I have lived on the coast, my holidays are always spent on the sea shore; I always love to beach comb and over the years found many interesting things. You never know what you may find after the last tide ebbs away. When I was a child camping for the full summer school holidays in an old leaky tent on the shoreline of Walney Island, the receding tide left us enough wood for our campfire. When we inevitably ran low on food the shoreline had cockles, mussels, winkles, crabs and the odd lobster. The fields bordering the coast were a source of mushrooms, blackberry bushes abounded, nearby farmer's field's containing potatoes and turnips. Of course you would expect a clip around the ears if you were caught!

We always took a bank line with us with thirty hooks attached; dug worms for bait and set the line out at low tide, we buried the hooks under the sand otherwise the gulls would pinch our bait before the tide came in. Getting to the line before the tide had not quite receded was essential before the gulls did, otherwise all the fish eyes would be pecked out and the bellies eaten by the ravenous birds. We have had a fish on every hook at times, codling, bass and flounders, if this happened we could sell some to the locals who lived nearby. For twelve year olds we were very independent not seeing our parents for weeks on end. Once we were all pinching a certain Walney farmer's potatoes and he spotted us, normally he would shout and wave his fist at us, we knew we could outrun him so were not overly bothered. On this occasion he fooled us, around the hedges came the young farmer's sons on a tractor, they drove after us and we ran like the very devil was after us. Running in the direction away from where we were camping, of course the tractor soon caught each one of us up as one by one we collapsed on the grass panting and gasping with fear and exhaustion. We all knew perfectly well what coming next, we all received a good leathering, the farm lads putting the boot in. The farmer strolled up and said "You won't be pinching any more of my potatoes for a long time boys will you?" Not in broad daylight anyway we thought.

Back to beach combing, I have always found interesting objects washed up by the tides over the years. Valuable wood which was carried as deck cargo, and washed overboard in storms, messages in bottles one from the last ever full time lighthouse keeper at Skomer, and when a young boy corresponded with a Irish radio merchant navy officer name of Patrick Edward Regan for a long time. He sent postcards and letters from all over the world to my little terrace house in Glasgow Street. Actually our Francesca found one last year washed up at Askam beach, and we keep in touch with a lovely man Peter a retired school teacher from Hull who threw the message overboard from the Isle of Man ferry!

After buying our cottage at Dunnerholme we found unusual items here that came in useful washed up along the estuary shoreline. One morning finding hundreds of plastic tubes of sun tan oil, they kept all our family and friends supplied for years. We heard that a coaster had sunk down south in the English Channel somewhere, and this was part of the cargo sweeping up the Irish Sea on the prevailing wind and ending up on the West coast of the UK. Cans of Guinness to my surprise one morning were deposited around our beach, I tasted one and it tasted fine, I distributed them to my drinker friends and became very popular until I ran out of them. Many small boats and rowing boats, trawl nets, and large valuable and useful orange coloured mooring buoys, you name it we have found it at some time beach combing. I helped to keep the fire in our cottage burning using the pieces of coal washed in after a storm. I assumed the coal was used in the old steam ship days, when coal fired dredgers, tugs and hoppers used to operate out of Millom. They dumped the ashes and clinker overboard into the Duddon estuary and good coal ended up falling off the decks when loading up their bunkers.

One stormy night a cargo ship was sailing from Scotland with a cargo of logs all about ten feet long, to be used for wood pulp. The sea's were on the beam of the ship, the constant rolling broke all the fastenings holding the ship's deck cargo of logs, the high stack of wood tumbled into the Irish sea off the coast of our Walney Island. What a bonanza for the locals thousands of logs washing up along our coast and estuary. Tractors and four by fours were on the beach for days collecting the bounty. The ones washing up around Dunnerholme were quickly collected for firewood, and Askam village all had their logs for winter.

Recently my eldest stepson Tammy found or rather Pippa the family whippet found, washed up in the Duddon estuary near Askam village, a turtle. It turned out to be one of the worlds's most endangered 'Kemp's ridley' sea turtle, usually spotted around the warm waters of the Gulf of Mexico. It was assumed the turtle was cold stunned because of sea temperatures dropping on the east coast of America, leaving the turtles becoming lethargic and unable to swim against the strong currents or even feed. Kemp's ridleys are so rare that it is thought there are only one thousand breeding females in the world. They reach about 65cm in length and 45kg in weight; have a triangular head and a greenish-grey colour.

Our Tammy took the turtle over to Walney Island where he passed it onto the warden of North Walney National Nature Reserve, and they in turn passed it to Maryport Aquarium where facilities were better. If the turtle recovered back to full health it was planned to fly it to the United States and released back into the Gulf of Mexico. Unfortunately efforts to nurse it back to health failed and the poor turtle died.

Another example of keeping eyes open around our shores, was the day a large shoal of mackerel at high tide chased a smaller shoal of tiny sprats into the gulley's, that run up to nearly our cottage back door. In the mackerel's feeding frenzy they became stranded in the shallow gulleys on a quickly ebbing tide. Thousands of fish were quickly stranded and cut off from deeper water, seagulls came from afar attracted by the noise made by the gulls screeching and squalling over the fish bonanza. I had heard of this happening occasionally over the years but never seen it myself, apparently old records show a massive shoal of herring did the same thing at Millom across the other side of the estuary many years ago, and many people took away baskets of fish from the beach.

Hundreds of gulls swooped down picking up fish and dropping them all over the place, on the top golf hole on the summit of Dunnerholme rock the green was covered in dead mackerel, also some of the fairways.

Some golfers picked up plastic bags or borrowed a bucket to take a feed home. Some volunteers helped to save thousands of fish using buckets borrowed from the cottages to put the heaps of fish into the odd deep gulley still ebbing into the estuary, so some did get their freedom. It was a sight we will probably not see again in our lifetime and one rare day indeed. A hell of a lot of people had fresh fish for their tea that night in the local villages.

A very old fox started to hang around the cottages and feed on the many rabbits that lived amongst the gorse bushes; we named him 'Bushy Tail'. You could tell that he had arrived to see out his last days at Dunnerholme, he was very slow and hunted in broad daylight seemingly not afraid of the proximity of the walkers or golfers. You could get up really close to him and he became a regular sight around the sand dunes. Then one morning walking along the sand dunes we came across old 'Bushy Tail' seemingly fast asleep curled up in a cosy little nest in a hollow amongst the dune grass. The old fox had passed away peacefully in his sleep; we buried him in a sandy grave where we found him.

Never a dull moment, we arrived home at the cottage nearly at midnight after seeing a show at Barrow, it was a dreadful night, heavy rain and a strong gale blowing. The heavy wooden level crossing gates were a swine to open in the strong wind, and I was looking forward to a hot drink before bed. Our two neighbours were both away so the cottages were in total darkness until I put our lights on. Sitting nursing a hot cup in our hands getting the last warmth off our fire, we were startled out of our wits hearing a loud banging on our back door. We heard the Kitchen door burst open, a cold blast of air blew into our lounge, and a weak voice shouted "Help us please!"

To our utmost surprise two bedraggled young teenage girls staggered into our lounge and fell in front of our fire both shaking like leaves. They were both soaked to the skin, seaweed hung from their coats and their jeans were black with mud. Pauline took charge right away peeling off their wet clothes and putting warm blankets around them. I switched on the electric fan heater and rushed to get them a hot drink, explanations could come later. After they became drier and warmer they explained how they had attempted to cross our estuary from Askam to their home in Millom and become disorientated in the dark. They misjudged the tide times and the fast incoming tide cut them off, they had no clue of where they were until they saw our light go on, they swam across several deep gulley's following the light to get to us. Two very lucky girls, the incoming tide was sweeping in faster due to the south westerly storm, if we had not got back when we did and put the lights on, they would probably be another drowning statistic to be recorded. The girls explained that they had been visiting relatives in Barrow and spent their train fare, thus being forced to walk home and take a short cut across the estuary. This was in the days before mobile phones; their parents assumed they were staying with their relatives in Barrow for the night, so the alarm was not raised. After drying their clothes and feeding them we put them in our car and drove them around the estuary to Millom, we had to knock up their surprised parents who proceeded to run a hot bath for them and leave all the recriminations until later. The main thing was the girl's guardian angel was looking after them that night; they got away with it and hopefully learned a hard lesson. We drove home from Millom mentally and physically exhausted and dived gratefully straight into our bed; it had been a long day! Waking up the next morning it seemed to have been all a dream, until walking into our lounge to see two sets of muddy footprints and bits of seaweed on the carpet!

CHAPTER TWENTY FIVE

THE ROWING BOAT

Some days in summer we stayed in the cottage and I left for the docks early in the morning leaving Pauline, my mother and Penny our tiny Yorkshire terrier, to enjoy a sunny day relaxing at the cottage. Having to set off early I had a stretch of unmade track to crawl along because of the potholes and the railway level crossing gates to open, but first having to phone to check no trains were imminent. I was never ever late for work or missed a tide, even though I was held up occasionally by a flock of sheep blocking the lane, or some sheep walking on the railway lines when a train was due, these needed to be coaxed off the lines before at last I could proceed towards the main road.

I remember one summer morning about five am we were awoken by the sound of somebody chopping wood. Looking at my watch I said to Pauline that it was a bloody strange time for our neighbour to be doing a chore like that. This went on for about thirty minutes and curiosity got the better of me, looking out of the bedroom window I was amazed to see the culprit making the noise was not my neighbour as such, it was one of George's ewes. I dragged Pauline out of bed to see what this mad sheep was doing. The bloody sheep was looking at her own reflection in the side of the car and thinking it was a strange sheep kept butting the car, and these sheep have big horns. That is one dozy sheep, it has been circling around the car for over half an hour and still not sussed out it is the same reflection she is butting!

Pauline said "It's your fault Norm you cleaned the car yesterday, normally it is covered with a thick layer of dust!"

I rushed out in my pyjamas and chased the mad sheep away, and she only reluctantly moved. My lovely car looked like a colander everywhere was a mass of dents and deep gouges. After counting two hundred dents I gave up counting. After breakfast I phoned work and explained why I wanted a day off, saying the reason was a mad ewe has trashed my car caused merriment in our office. The next call was to my car insurance broker and I had to hold the phone away from my ear he was laughing so loudly. Just a moment he said "I have got to tell the others in the office about this it will cheer them all up!"

"Sorry about that Mister Pascoe we have heard some reasons for claiming for car repairs, but never one about a mad sheep with a personnel vendetta against you!" he chuckled. Driving my mum to Askam village later that morning passing through the farmyard, George the farmer stopped me and asked who the vandal was who had trashed my car. When I told him it was a ewe of his, he said "Let me deal with the insurance Norm and you will not lose your 'no claims' bonus." This was really decent of him and showed what a great friend he had become to us. The golf club were great they let me build a fenced coral to keep my car in to stop it happening again. I suppose it would have been easier to keep my car dirty and cheaper!

The sheep were a bane in my life, we or the grand children found them all over the place trying to commit suicide in one form or another over the years. We had the grand children walking on the marsh and our Laura spotted a lambs head sticking up out of the grass. It looked a strange sight, and looking closer could see the poor lamb had walked down a narrow 'V' shaped gulley to the end, and now could not back out again, she was jammed in tight. She was in a bad way and been there for some time, all the grass she could reach had been eaten. We sent the eldest girl Laura to fetch the farmer, the three others to go to the cottage to fetch a pick and shovel to dig the lamb out. We dug all around the lamb removing the peat, and saw its little hoofs had sunk deep in the mud of the gulley bottom. George arrived with his quad bike and trailer, our Laura feeling very important standing in the trailer. George finally extracted the lamb and said the girls had done a good job of spotting the lamb in danger. George also pointed out the old skeleton of a lamb in the gulley bottom, it had happened before. Now we had dug out the narrow

'V' shaped gulley it could not happen again. He put the mud caked lamb in the trailer with straw packed around her to take to the farm. He told the children that the mother had waited so long by the lamb, but then left her because she had another lamb to look after, he would match them up later when he had cleaned up this one. He told the children that they were his unpaid shepherds and his flock of sheep at Dunnerholme were safe with them around.

Having our lunch in the cottage one extremely windy day thinking to ourselves it is nice and cosy here sitting in front of a roaring fire, our peace was shattered by a very loud hammering on the back door. Three golfers were shouting all at once about two sheep that were cut off by the high tide and it looked like one of them had drowned. Can you phone the farmer one asked, and tell him about the sheep in danger? I explained that the farmer could not do anything about his sheep being cut off far out on the marshes, and that it happened all the time and mostly they got themselves ashore safely. It was much too dangerous to try and rescue them, it was a hazard that marsh grazing sheep put up with from time to time.

"You have a rowing boat outside, we can borrow it and save at least one of the sheep, I can row" said his friend, "I am always rowing on Barrow Park boating lake!"

"With due respect the Park Lake is a lot safer than the strong tide and waves that we have here" I said to them. My mother joined in then telling me to go and rescue the sheep myself, "It is not like you have not rescued some before Norm, go on the other sheep is in a bad way, hurry up!"

Talk about pressure, on one hand mother and a gathering of golfers stacking up outside the cottage, all urging me to row out in a gale of wind to rescue a bloody sheep. Pauline telling me not to be so stupid and come in to finish my lunch, I had enough.

"This is the very last time I row out for a sheep in peril, the dinghy is going to be put up for sale tomorrow, and that's the end of it!"

We dragged the dinghy the short distance to the tide, Pauline jumped into the stern and we headed out to sea. I said "Same as last time Pauline, I will back the boat up to the sheep, you hook her horns over the back of the dinghy and I will tow her slowly into shallow water."

The poor drowned sheep had drifted away on the current, and our barely still alive survivor stood up to her neck on a raised sandbar, her fleece sodden. The waves were beginning to knock her off her feet and we knew we had to be quick. It was a struggle to row against the wind and waves; it was further out than it looked from the shore. Next moment the ewe was alongside our boat and Pauline made a grab for the horns hooking them over the back. "Alright Norm I have got her now take us slowly into the shore," she said a relieved look on her face. It was quicker rowing in than out; the wind and waves were pushing us in. The lucky sheep could feel terra firma under her hoofs and started to hobble up the beach, shaking the water off her fleece.

We felt embarrassed, all the golfers and a motley collection of passing dog walkers, started to clap and give us three cheers. Well that was until we heard a loud couth and the rescued sheep keeled over stone dead. I was just relieved that there were not any of our grand children visiting us, because seeing the sheep die would be very distressing for them. The dinghy was sold it was too much of a temptation when the tides were high, and the sheep became cut off, for me to be persuaded to row out to them in rough weather. We just kept our canoes they were totally not suited for rescuing sheep.

George the shepherd asked me for copies of photographs of his sheep swimming ashore, because several of his shepherd friends who farmed on the high fells in Lakeland did not believe his stories of how far they could swim in the sea. Later after showing his shepherd friends the photos at the auction mart he said they were all amazed.

CHAPTER TWENTY SIX

THE SURVEY BOAT SINKS

During my time working at Barrow docks I think some of the tasks I took on were above the call of duty, on at least two occasions I have refused to let anything stop me from fulfilling my job. In the middle of a crucial survey one day we experienced an engine problem on the port engine. Going below into the engine room I found a lift pump not working. I took the boat back to harbour for our port engineers to repair. It was no good trying to manoeuvre in the swift run of tide where we needed to survey with just one engine. The suction dredger needed to have his up to date survey results so that he could set off for another urgent contract, and could not leave until we had finished this last survey. The workshops said a new part was needed and would be delivered in a couple of days, it was ordered by the store man and everyone left for home, it was finishing time, end of story. My pal Gary and I still had our survey team on the boat awaiting developments. Gary said "You have the same lift pump on your trawler Norm; we can row aboard your boat at Ferry Beach, take your pump off and fit it on the faulty Dova Haw engine. Survey will be completed and perhaps you will leave me in peace!"

"Gary that is a bloody good idea let's do it, so we left a survey team waiting and a huge suction dredger hanging around in mid channel until we had completed our task of getting the pump off my trawler. Once Gary had fit it on the survey boats engine, the survey was completed to everybody's satisfaction. I said to Gary afterwards "Nobody else cares but I can go home knowing that we did our job well, nobody else needs to know how we did it, especially the trade union!" On a few more occasions we borrowed engine bits off my trawler to keep our dock survey boat going, the engineering workshop would have got their union involved if they knew what we were up to.

It started out just a normal day at the docks, it was December and bitter cold with an icy wind blowing off the channel. The young dock electrician and I were working on my survey boat 'Dova Haw' disconnecting the batteries for charging up in the starboard side engine room. Busy with my spanner I suddenly heard the sound of running water coming from the other engine room. Lifting the portside engine hatch I could see water running from the base of the engine seacock, climbing down into the engine room I grabbed the valve to turn off the flow of water. The complete unit which lets raw seawater into the engine to cool it down blew off and into my face. Instinctively throwing myself backwards against the ship's hull, this caused me some considerable pain. With the complete seacock blown to one side the sea started to pour in with such force that the solid bore of seawater hit the deck head, cascading all over the engine room and spraying me with ice cold water.

My adrenalin kicked in and even though I was soaked to the skin I realised the boat was going to sink, and that we needed to move fast to attempt a salvage operation. She was my boat and I was not going to lose her without a fight. I shouted to my work colleague to start getting the expensive survey equipment off the boat, and just to cut the wires and leads to save time. Luckily for me our pilot boat was moored alongside us, this made it easier to place all the salvaged survey equipment onto her side decks. I radioed the man on duty in the pier head control to arrange for a large heavy duty mobile crane to maybe lift her out of the water before she sank, and for more men to help us.

Our boat was developing a severe list to port with the weight of water in the engine room. I rummaged in a locker and located two wooden bungs which I hammered into the fuel tank vents to prevent the fuel oil polluting the dock system. Unfortunately the tanks had been filled the day before so were full; I put drums of oil dispersant into both engine rooms and shut both hatches. Still working without thinking of the consequences of the boat sinking with us on it, we continued in the wheelhouse to remove more valuable equipment. Other help now arrived and we managed to pull the boat alongside the dock wall where it was less deep, in case she sank it would make salvage easier. I was the only person left on board, and I tried to salvage the last piece of survey equipment which was an expensive depth paper sounder, the water was up to my waist by this time. The starboard hull of the survey boat was now well in the air and it looked as if she was going to capsize; voices were shouting get out Norm she is going over. I dumped the heavy piece of equipment into the water and half swam out of the wheel house door. The fire brigade arrived but too late to use their powerful pumps to bail out the 'Dova Haw' her decks were level with the sea. We decided to cut the ropes holding her to the quay wall and let her settle level when she sank, enabling the salvage divers to work on slinging her safely ready for a huge mobile crane to lift her up again sometime later. The numbness I felt from being in the cold water for so long was wearing off, and I felt severe pain all over my body. I got a lift to the doctor for a check up complaining about my neck and back. Writing my report about the sinking of my boat on which I had spent so many days and hours was quite upsetting. I could not praise Graham the dock electrician enough, he could have just left me and stepped ashore, he was not being paid to risk his life, but he did not leave and helped me save very valuable equipment.

In time he received a thank you letter from the port office, and likewise me praising me for quick thinking, in particular for saving a pollution situation by blocking up the fuel vents. It eventually cost me my career because of ill health, I had an operation to remove bits of bone from under a knee cap, had a blood transfusion and developed cervical spondylosis in my neck. My life was about to change, I was put onto long term sick leave, and I was not very happy. From having an exciting and at times dangerous career, I would have to accept that my seagoing life was going to end for certain, and due to recurring health problems not being able to work at all. Before I accepted this I booked to see two different neurosurgeon professors privately for their opinions, and had a full body scan which one of the professors suggested I took. The long term prognosis was not good and eventually I had to accept the facts. Like other people in my position who have to give up a job that was like a vocation, it takes a long time to adapt to these new circumstances, mentally and financially. The transition from working long hours to waking up every morning wondering how to fill your day is daunting; you tend to lose your optimism and sense of humour. Your confidence goes and you wonder how you are going to cope, I was lucky in having a wonderful wife that never let me down and never gave up suggesting answers to any problems that came our way. Of course you had the usual morons saying how lucky you were to finish your working life early.

CHAPTER TWENTY SEVEN

MY MUM LEAVES US

We had to sell our main house on Walney Island when I finished work due to my reduced income. We were looking forward to living in our cosy little cottage at Dunnerholme, me Pauline, mother and our tiny Yorkshire terrier Penny. Penny was over the moon about living full time at the cottage, her best friend Flossie the sheep called every morning for a bucket of fresh water, when Penny heard Flossie head butting the back door, she barked for us to open the door. When Flossie became the proud mother of two lambs she bought them for a drink also, it was a grand sight to see Penny sleeping alongside the lambs on the grass outside in the sun. Penny was fifteen years old now and moving to Dunnerholme seemed to give her a new lease of life, she was acting like a puppy again, her arthritis seemingly better.

At first my mother enjoyed the new experience of living in the country, grabbing a bag and stout walking stick she roamed the lanes looking for blackberries or mushrooms. George from the farm could not do any wrong in mother's eyes; he showed her the hidden places behind his barn where the biggest black berries grew, giving her permission to access his fields. We had to go looking for her when dusk was falling trying to find her. She could have strayed anywhere and it got to be a worry for me, many a time knocking on the farmhouse door to ask George if he had seen her recently. We would find her happily picking blackberries practically in darkness. She said to me "I don't want to go back yet, the biggest berries are on this bush, you go back and I will follow later."

Looking in her bag, half the berries were red and unripe; I began to worry about her. Mum said she used the phone before crossing the railway lines but following her one day we saw her ignoring the phone, and not even looking up or down the tracks for signs of a train coming. Golfer's started to knock on our door complaining that mum was wandering along the fairways and ignoring any shouts of 'Four!' When asked by them what she was doing wandering about on the course she replied "I am looking for mushrooms and I have found one!" We realised we had to seek help when we saw her wandering on Duddon sands with an oncoming tide, she was looking for us to say I was wanted on the phone. We took her to the family doctor to run some tests, and he said mum had the onset of dementia and it would only get worse. We had a big problem, noticing for some time odd little things she did that was out of character. She had been living with us for sixteen years and not for one moment did we ever think that this may have to end.

The stage came when mum would not stay in the house unless one of us stayed with her, if we both had to go out for hospital appointments; mum had to come with us. Mum needed a permanent babysitter at all times, and worse was to come, she insisted that we sold the cottage and moved back to Walney Island straight away. When we were still debating the best way to sort this next problem with her, mum picked up the telephone unbeknown to us and told Social Services that her life was in danger from, railway trains, golf balls, and fast running tides, she needed to leave here quickly, she told the bewildered lady. The kind lady asked mum to pass me the phone, mum very reluctantly passed it over and did not look very happy. I explained the circumstances and the lady made an appointment for the very next day to come and see us all at the cottage.

The Social worker called the next afternoon and said "They do not normally call this quick, but mum had sounded like it was a matter of utmost urgency, and when old people say their lives are in danger we have to act quickly." We said that mum had been very well cared for sixteen years and we would like to carry on even under these difficult conditions of mum's illness.

We were told that actually because mum called them it was not our decision anymore, mum was asked if she wanted to go into a care home, and said yes she would. It was as simple as that, they even got her a place on Walney Island, exactly what she wanted. The very next week we packed her belongings and with tears in our eyes drove her to her new home. Pauline and I could not stop crying, we had put my mother before everything for all these years, and it all seemed surreal. We carried her bags into her new room and Pauline went to unpack mum's bags and put her clothes away, just like she had always done for the last sixteen years living with us. We were both gently shown the door and it was explained to Pauline that her job was over now; mum was getting twenty four hour care, she was not our responsibility anymore.

My mother had shared holidays and our life for so long it was a strange feeling walking into our cottage without her. Even Penny was acting strange wondering where mum was, we knew mum was certainly happy all her final years in the care home, the last ten years of her life not even knowing who we were. We bought her home for visits and Christmas dinner until she was too frail, she lived until she was ninety two, which was pretty good, I thought she was lucky being always well looked after until the day she died.

The first Christmas day I will never forget when mum was in the care home, we had arranged for her and Pauline's dad Ben (her mother Emily had died a few years previously) to come for dinner at the cottage. It turned out to be the Christmas day from hell! We also had our Marion and Susan plus their children coming for dinner, we had prepared all the vegetables the evening before so were relaxed. After breakfast I looked out of the back door to see the estuary strewn with strange white objects. The tide had gone out so I picked up my binoculars to try and identify what these objects were. "Oh no I shouted to Pauline it looks like nearly a full flock of George's sheep have been drowned during the night, Christmas day and having to phone him about bad news like this!"

Just after I phoned George about the sheep all our electricity went off and the turkey had just been put in to cook. George was out on the sands in his tractor looking at the sheep, and shortly after knocked on our door to say the sheep were not his but belonged to a farmer that lived across the other side of our estuary. "Have a nice day he said I am going back to my dinner and to phone the other farmer," and off he drove, apparently his electricity was still on.

We phoned everyone and said we will have our dinner at Marion's house in Askam village, so we loaded up the car with turkey, pans of assorted vegetables etc. Arriving a little flustered at Marion's house shoved the turkey into her oven just as her electricity went off also, now Pauline really did have a panic on. Phoning our Susan in Barrow she said her electricity was still on and to bring everything to her place. Arriving eventually at Susan's we unloaded everything out of my car and I had to drive to Ulverston to pick my father in law Ben up, then to Walney care home for my mother. From a dinner scheduled for just after lunch time we all sat around our dinner table late that night. The electricity was off at the cottage for over three days, and all the freezer contents, which because of Christmas were jammed full of goodies, had to be disposed of. So all in all it was a Christmas to remember!

Looking back it was all for the best the day mum made the phone call to Social Services; I still wonder how she found their telephone number. I had some terrible health for a time after, and poor Pauline had enough with me to look after for a while. It was a twenty mile round trip to see mum and we managed it mostly twice a week, we became very good friends with all the staff, they were the salt of the earth and could not do enough for her over the years. This was another chapter in our lives over and like someone said, never a dull moment!

CHAPTER TWENTY EIGHT

OUR TONY'S BOAT CAPSIZES

I explained in my previous book how dangerous the Duddon estuary can be. All the numerous boats that have been capsized and sank losing their crews, attest to the dangerous conditions on the notorious bar. The story of how when a crewman and partner in a tug we nearly came to grief rescuing the crew of a coaster in a raging storm, the waves around twenty five feet high, in this very same estuary. This was also in our estuary that a tragedy very nearly occurred that involved my stepson Tony and his friend.

This incident happened on a late September afternoon on a cold, dull grey day. Our Tony and his friend launched their small fibreglass fishing boat at low water at Ronhead using his tractor; the boat was loaded with drift nets for a night hunting for bass. They headed out on the last of the ebb heading north to try their luck at Silecroft; they found the sea there unproductive so headed back southwards to try over the Duddon bar on the flood tide, hoping the shoals of bass would be feeding there. Tony steered the boat whilst his friend paid out the long length of netting, Tony noticing that the wind was getting stronger and the run of tide sweeping in fast with the wind behind it, and the swell increasing in height all the time.

The line of netting was drifting perfectly over the top of the bar where they expected a shoal of bass to be feeding in the disturbed water. This is what driftnet fishermen call a perfect shot; if the fish are there they will catch them. Night was falling but the men could see well enough the channel they were aiming for, to enable them to cross over the bar in safety. They were nearly through the safe channel when a rogue wave hit them from nowhere, the boat heeled sharply over on her beam ends; and before the boat recovered they were hit by another steep curling comber which flipped over the boat completely.

Tony's friend was thrown out of the boat into the sea, the boat settled in the water completely awash, but had enough buoyancy to float level with the sea. Tony surfaced after being underwater and held onto the edge of the boat, he could feel his waders filling with water and starting to drag him under. He spotted his friend in the gloom and shouted loud to be heard above the howling wind and the booming noise coming from the combers hitting the bar. He shouted "kick off your wellington boots or you will be dragged under!"

The boat's fuel tank floated past and Tony's friend made a grab for it, Tony had managed to kick off his heavy waders and his trousers went also. His friend was a well built lad and did not have a lifejacket on, he was struggling but managed to kick off his boots and trousers, he had on a fishermen's smock top. I must have had a premonition of danger earlier because I had given Tony a pilot jacket with a built in lifejacket a few days before, and I made him promise that it would be worn all the time at sea. That promise saved his life and that of his best pal. Tony knew that the nine metre high tide would push them into the estuary, and it was a matter of surviving until the early hours of the next day before anyone would realize they were overdue, Tony was experienced to know the odds of surviving much longer were very slim indeed, exposure would soon set in.

The next rushing comber washed the boat away from his frozen fingers into the darkness and he soon lost sight of it, then in the gloom he caught a glimpse of his pal holding onto the petrol can. Blowing some more air into the lifejacket Tony realised that his friend would have to hold onto him, and share the lifejackets buoyancy. They were both in a bad way now, Tony's friend was not coping very well, and both were feeling the cold numbing their bodies. Tony estimated that they had been in the water for one and a half to two hours and they were getting very weak. An added problem was the combined weight of two of them being kept afloat by one lifejacket, seemed to be causing the jacket to start losing air.

Tony's friend said to him "Let me go mate the air is leaking out of the jacket and I am having trouble holding on to you, there is no point in both of us drowning."

Tony said "Hold on as long as you can, we can't give up yet, we must have drifted half way up the estuary by now, with this run of tide."

While all this was going on in the middle of the estuary, we were lying in our bed at the cottage unable to sleep because of a strange feeling of dread we were both feeling. The wind was blowing the curtains, we could hear the branches of the tree's making loud creaking noises, and I mentioned that I hoped our Tony was not at sea in this weather. Never realising that at the very time, not a half mile away, our Tony and his best friend were fighting for their lives and were close to giving up!

The lifejacket was losing air fast and Tony had to keep blowing into the mouthpiece to keep it firm enough to support them, but he realised it was a losing battle. Just when his friend said "Let me go Tony!" he thought his numbed feet touched the seabed, a moment later they touched again. They realised the strong wind and current had pushed them onto a sandbar, and that it may lead possibly to shallower water. I can imagine the relief they must have felt thinking how near they must have been to disaster. They held each other up and in the dark waded up the sandbar towards the lights of the shore, the waves getting smaller has they neared the beach. When they both realised that they had both survived and were now safe ashore, they hugged and sat down on the wet sand, hardly believing their good fortune.

Tony said " This is lucky mate, my flask is washed up here in the water a couple of yards away" and on unscrewing the top steam came out, "Would you like a hot coffee?" he said.

His pal said "You have the first drink Tony if it was not for you and your lifejacket, I would not be sitting here with you, thanks pal!"

That coffee was still hot, it certainly was a lifesaver, and no drink was more appreciated, it certainly revived them both. Tony recognised where they had washed up after a quick look around. They were on the opposite side of the estuary from where we lived, at Haverigg village to be precise, near Millom town. They started to walk towards the shore road to look for a telephone box, they realised they looked a bit of a sight. Two large men wearing bright fishermen's orange smocks, clad in just their underpants, bare legs and feet, at nearly midnight!

Walking along the deserted road towards the village a police car pulled up and asked them what had happened. After hearing the story the policemen put survival blankets around them and drove them to Millom police station. After warm blankets and more hot coffee and refusing to go to hospital, much to the officer's disapproval Tony phoned for a mate to pick them up, and refused to let us know until the next morning. They both did not want any fuss what so ever. The local paper wanted to front page it and the BBC had a program at that time about rescue at sea, and they were asked about participating but politely declined, both wanted to forget the incident.

Their boat was eventually found washed up at the top end of the estuary, and their friends picked up the drifting net. We just thanked God for their miraculous survival.

This mishap did not deter the boys from carrying on fishing, and later on our Tony became a full time fisherman like I used to be. He bought his own small fishing boat, a load of crab/lobster pots and placed them off the Cumbrian coastline. Also they drift netted for bass during the night tides mostly; he had a successful career until the massive wind farms were erected off the coast of Walney Island in the Irish Sea. He gave the fishing up and became skipper of a boat carrying engineers out to the wind farm, our brave son also helped to save a man's life in Walney Channel, the man was hanging at the stern of his boat in the freezing water, Tony and another man rushed to his aid. Shortly afterwards also rescuing a man whose dinghy overturned and was drifting out of the north end of Walney Channel into the Irish Sea in very cold, windy conditions. Tony has proved to be a very brave man and I am proud to be his step father.

CHAPTER TWENTY NINE

BROKEN FOOT

I was alone in the cottage feeling a bit weak after taking a second dose of antibiotics for my stomach ulcer complaint; Pauline had cycled along the perimeter of the golf course to the village for a newspaper. Feeling fed up I went for a walk up to the top of Dunnerholme rock, standing on the lip of the cliff I looked towards the village looking to see if Pauline was on her way back. The sky was a deep pink as the winter sun was dropping late afternoon. The view out to sea was breathtaking; I was feeling a little light headed with all the drugs I had to take.

All I can remember is falling over the edge of the cliff, falling quite a distance, and when I hit the ground below hearing a sharp crack. I looked at my left foot and saw the broken bone trying to poke out of my foot. The pain set in and I thought of the bollocking I was going to get off Pauline, I had promised to stay in the house whilst she cycled to the village. Sitting up I checked over my body for other broken bones, except for massive bruising that I knew would follow, to my surprise my injuries seemed to be light. Cuts, grazing and bruising did not bother me, the broken foot did, and I could not walk at all. Looking up at the cliff face I had fallen over, made me realise that my guardian angel was working overtime again. Of course looking around me I could not see anybody to help me back to the cottage, no walkers, and no bloody golfers when you need one. Mobiles were not around much in those days so I either stayed and waited for Pauline to come and find me, or tried to crawl to the cottage.

Looking back I must have been in shock because of the two routes to choose, I for some obscure reason picked the most difficult one, which meant much more pain to endure. The easier route entailed dragging myself across soft sand dunes and then grass, partly in sight of the golf fairways. The route I chose was one hundred feet of sand, and then up a rough gravel path leading to the rock summit, and an even worse gravel path leading down to our back door, and a good chance of not being seen at this time of day. Now that was a bad decision, crawling on my hands and knees was very painful, I kept stopping for a rest and looking for help, then crawling a few more yards. Finally reaching the top of the rock, I noticed two worn through holes in my trousers, and where my kneecaps were was a bloody mess. What was annoying me the most was the probability that when I finally reached my back door, four golfers would appear around the corner and rush to help me?

Guess what happened, when completely exhausted I reached my door and stood on one leg to open it, no one appeared to help me! Pauline was not even home; crawling into the lounge I collapsed onto my favourite armchair and put my bad foot on a stool. Feeling very sorry for myself and knowing that I would need crutches for quite a while, I craved a glass of water but no way was I going to try and get one.

At last Pauline appeared at the front door, cursing and moaning about peddling against a strong wind, and saying it is the last time she is cycling all the way to the village for a bloody newspaper, for me to moan about the news all evening.

"Have you quite finished your whinge of the day love," I unwisely said.

"You cheeky lazy sod, sitting with your foot on a stool while I cycle miles for your bloody paper, you should show a little appreciation," she said.

Then she spotted the cuts and grazes on my face, and saw my bloodied knees etc.

"Oh my God, look at your ankle it has come up like a football, what have you been up to, you promised to not move off that chair!"

When I told her she went ballistic, after first bathing all my cuts and putting a cold towel on my huge balloon foot. It was obviously broken bones; I refused to go to hospital on the grounds that tomorrow will do. After all if I could crawl all that distance I could wait until the next morning and I might even feel well enough to walk unaided. Of course Pauline played hell with me, wanting to get an ambulance and keep me in hospital for x-rays and observation. Being a stubborn Pascoe I refused, I was a tough guy, ex trawler man, well you get the picture. Also I am a complete dumb arse, spending all night pretending that it did not hurt much, Pauline saying that I was ashen faced and should she call an ambulance. So I stuck the pain out until morning, and was vomiting before attempting a cup of tea for breakfast. My foot was a splendid shade of purple and still swelled up like a balloon. Even I had to admit a quick journey to hospital was probably a bloody good idea. I must have mentioned before that we had about half a mile of unmade track to travel along to reach a tarmac road. The farmer was about due to repair the road so the many potholes were quite deep and numerous, and I think Pauline aimed for the deepest because she liked to hear me scream out in pain, every jolt made the two separate pieces of broken bone touch, and I wished that an ambulance was called yesterday.

When with a relieved smile on her face we reached A&E, she parked right outside the entrance and dashed off to find a wheelchair. Thinking sod that, I will use my dad's old sturdy walking stick and not have to sit in the wheelchair, stubborn to the last. Hobbling through the entrance I staggered to the reception desk, sweat pouring down my face, to register myself in. Just as Pauline arrived pushing the wheelchair, the look on her face seeing I was draped over the desk, standing on one foot, beads of sweat running down my face.

At the top of her voice, "She shouted you bloody stupid man, George's sheep have more sense than you, and I have a good mind to break your other foot, sit in this wheelchair now!"

"Yes dear," I knew when to admit defeat.

The doctor said, "You have not tried to walk on this have you Mr. Pascoe?"

Before I could reply and say no, Pauline said "This idiot of an husband did this yesterday doctor, he fell off a cliff, crawled a quarter of a mile on a gravel track to our cottage and refused to let me call an ambulance, I have bought him here in the car!"

"Remarkable, you are right Mrs. Pascoe your husband is an idiot, any normal person would have passed out with the pain, the two pieces of bone would be grinding together, " said the pleasant and plain speaking doctor.

A plaster cast, a pair of crutches and several weeks of trying to hobble around the cottage followed. The crutches were totally not suitable for the soft sand and grass surrounding our cottage, ensuring lots of times me collapsing in a heap, getting even more annoyed with myself. This was a frustrating and totally avoidable accident and even though Pauline was very patient with me, having to drive me everywhere for various hospital appointments, I must have tried her sense of humour sorely at times. Finally getting the cast removed was a great day for me, the foot was never the same again and arthritic now, but what the hell I could walk again! The worse thing for me was not being able to drive my car for weeks; I am the world's worse backseat driver, and having to watch Pauline opening the level crossing gates in all sorts of inclement weather before driving over, really cheesed me off. What would I have done without her, stuck at a remote cottage for weeks unable to walk around the cottages the ground was too soft to use crutches properly? I really hate relying on people me being so independent but that is what a marriage is all about, being there for each other in good times and bad.

CHAPTER THIRTY

THE GREAT FLOOD

It took longer for my foot to heal than normal because of being male and dozy; I tried to walk too early thinking that I knew best. Eventually walking became possible again without the use of crutches and I could once more drive my car. The medication I was taking seemed to be making me feel a little better, so that was good. I was a little concerned about the weather, the gales were in a constant south westerly direction and the tide seemed to be getting nearer to our back door. The fact that nobody locally could ever remember the cottages ever flooding was reassuring to us.

The wind during the night was horrendous, I had to get up and close our bedroom window, the curtains were blowing horizontally, and the noise of the wind rushing through the trees was keeping me awake. High tide was about seven am, and a ten metre tide at that, I was lying in bed dozing and thinking something was not quite right. Putting my dressing gown on I started to go downstairs and heard our Penny whimpering in fear.

The sight I saw will forever stay in my mind, I could not take in what was happening, and our beloved Penny was swimming for her life in our lounge. A forlorn bundle of fur needing my help quickly, jumping into two feet of water I snatched our little Yorkshire terrier up and carried her upstairs to the bedroom for Pauline to dry and comfort her. A bleary eyed Pauline said, "What the hell is happening Norm, and why is Penny soaking wet on our bed?"

Before I could answer I glanced out of our bedroom window, a bloody seagull was nonchalantly swimming across our lawn. Thinking that this was surreal I said, "Pauline the tide is in our house, we are flooded, there is a bloody seagull swimming on our lawn, take a look downstairs, and leave Penny on the bed." Penny proceeded to burrow under the blankets, which in my opinion was being very sensible, I felt like doing the same thing.

"What is that thumping sound Norm?" Pauline said.

"I assume that is the waves hitting the back door love!" I said.

"What is that loud gurgling noise Norm?" she said.

"That is the sea coming up the downstairs bathroom's plug hole and filling the bath, Pauline stop asking questions I am trying to think about damage limitation, we are both in shock."

Poor Pauline I felt for her, everything she held dear was being ruined, the seawater was brown with the sand and mud churned up in the violent waves. All her cushions were floating about in over two feet of water which seemed to be getting steadily deeper; odd things were floating around in the murky water, books, magazines, clothing, even shoes. The consolation was now I knew why the electric sockets were high up the walls, the electric fuse box near to the ceiling. We both sat on the stairs joined by a shivering Penny. We had no neighbours in the other cottages and would need to inform them later, both were away until weekend, they were both in for a shock.

I suggested getting dressed in warm clothes, then I would wade to our shed and collect our wellingtons, they are on the bench and as it is high water the tide will not come much higher hopefully. Pauline had tears in her eyes saying, "We just had our new fitted carpets laid a month ago, now everything is ruined, the water smells awful, and our lovely suite is soaked too." Pauline grimaced every time a big wave hit the back door jets of water squirted through the gaps.

"These are just material things love, our little dog might have drowned, when the tide turns the water will run back and we can clean up, I will sort it all out please try not to worry."

I had to open the front door to get out, the water was still coming in and my car needed to be moved a few yards to higher ground. Opening the front door allowed a surge of water to rush into the lounge, carrying in a mass of sloppy sheep muck, drowned worms, mice, toads and sundry debris. A howl of protest from Pauline and then I was in the car and just in time. Getting in the car I turned in time to see a flash and hear the crack of my neighbour's ground floor electric box exploding, good job I was not in the vicinity!

The scene that greeted me outside I shall never forget as long as I live, our cottages were surrounded by seawater, and Dunnerholme rock had almost become an island. The marshes were covered; the main railway track leading to the level crossing was flooded, everywhere I looked the scenery was different. Odd pairs of sheep were swimming towards higher ground, rabbits were flushed out of their warrens, and even a lone hare was swimming for its very life. I knew I was looking at a scene that may possibly not ever occur again in my lifetime, I was in total shock and awe. Only the highest gorse bushes were above the water and had several bemused sheep wondering what the hell was happening to their usual grazing areas. Pauline looked a lot better when she realised that the tide was finally receding, and the water level in the cottage was going down quickly, the golf course had several of their fairways covered, our access road did not drain off for at least three hours after the tide left, leaving us cut off.

The wind did not stop howling and the waves on the ebb tide were enormous, the height of the tides were getting less, so we prayed that we would not flood again on the next predicted high water. My canoes had floated away onto the golf course and would have to be collected later. We listened to Cumbria local news and were not at all surprised to hear our entire estuary was caught in a massive storm surge, many sheep had drowned, a farmer had a flounder flapping about in his lounge, and at least he could have it for his supper! The waves stopped the train service for a time the high waves had thrown ballast stones clean over the railway lines! All the people living around the perimeter of the Duddon estuary were affected in some ways.

We both had a coffee and then set to work sweeping the filthy smelly water and mud out of the front and back doors. We knew the carpets were ruined with sewerage and sheep muck and needed to be thrown out. Our neighbours were both rushing home, we knew the top cottage nearer into the cliff would be the least flooded, because all the cottages sloped downwards from the cliff, and ours was the lowest level of all three. The insurance man was calling after dark that very night, he sure was busy in our estuary. We managed to brush most of the water out of our next door neighbour's house because we had a spare key. Three friends, Chris, William, and Dave that were members of the golf club, finally managed to make their way across the debris littered golf course after lunch to help us, they were soaked. We were exhausted by this time and really appreciated their help, between them they took up all the fitted carpets and underlay, cutting it all up into small pieces and dumping it on the front lawn. I lit a roaring fire and the asphalt floor soon dried out, the cottage was beginning to look cheery again.

After our friends had a final brew they left us with our grateful thanks, without their generous help I don't know how we would have managed, they did all the hard work. I walked in the dark to help the insurance assessor across the level crossing; it is a little daunting for somebody crossing for the first time in darkness. His first words were, "Hell it is a little scary driving down here at night Mr. Pascoe, and I don't know how you can stand it."

The howl of the wind rushing around the rock did sound unnerving I must confess. Walking into the cottage and seeing the roaring fire and the place warm and cosy again, he could not believe how quickly we had accomplished it. He assessed us needing a new carpet; all new bottom half of our kitchen units replaced and some electrical appliances. Our furniture was just to be cleaned, so all in all we did not require much help and the insurance company got off lightly.

We did not flood again on the next tide and the gales moderated after that last storm surge in the Irish Sea. We awoke at dawn the next day to see the amazing sight of hundreds of birds of different types, frenziedly feeding on the thousands of drowned worms that lay in heaps all around the greens and fairways on the golf course. Walking around the beach, everything had changed with the stormy wave's erosion, whole sand dune systems had washed away, and mounds of driftwood littered all the beaches. Everything that used to be familiar had changed, it seemed awesome.

We had other great storms lashing the estuary over the coming years and other flooding, but never as bad as the first shocking time. We learned lessons the hard way to make life easier during a flooding situation, we had all the floors sealed and tiled, no fitted carpets, only rugs that could be lifted. The kitchen units lifted higher off the floor, blocks of wood made available to lift our heavy furniture higher. Storm boards that screwed onto the house doors to stop the sea from bursting in, sandbags available, and eventually over the years an early warning system devised by the authorities to phone all house holders in the vulnerable coastal areas to beware of higher than expected tide and river surges. We only had a few inches of sea water ever breached our defences after taking all the new precautions, and when the tide started to ebb it was easy to sweep out of the cottages and dry the house again. There has been several years grace between floods so we found the absolute beauty and privilege of living at Dunnerholme more than outweighed the negatives. Our grand children had so many adventures it was like living 'Famous Five' adventures in real life; they pestered their parents all the time to be dropped off at our cottage with their bags containing a change of clothing.

The children were playing hide and seek in the sand dunes near the cottage when they came across a strange camp. Running quickly back to me shouted "Come and look at this camp granddad."

It certainly was unusual; four empty forty gallon oil drums had been placed in a square, a roof of plywood sheets on top, and sides of tin sheeting and plastic for the inside. We looked in and a figure was apparently asleep inside a grubby looking sleeping bag. Around him were newspapers and plastic shopping bags, and sundry items of clothing. This was intriguing; our neighbours had warned us about a young man in his thirties who was wandering aimlessly about our area for a couple of days. Now we knew where he had been sleeping these past few days, it must have been bloody cold. We left him and told our two neighbours who had already asked the local policeman to check his identity because we had incidents before when escaped prisoners had crossed the estuary in the past from the prison across the bay.

It turned out he was harmless and had mental health issues and just wanted to be left alone. Unfortunately he had picked a bad place to build his camp from the flotsam and jetsam washed up on our beach, the children played all around this area so it was going to be a bit noisy for him. We soon got to know his routine and habits, every morning he walked along the beach to Askam village Co-op store. Here he bought a morning newspaper, large two litre plastic bottle of cola, and several tins of beans. When he walked around the store the assistants had to spray air freshener in his wake. He had no cooking facilities or heating so drank the cold drink and ate cold beans, and this was in January!

George called to see us one frosty morning, and said he was taking his flock of sheep past the shack when he spotted a pair of legs sticking out of the doorway. They were white and covered in a thick layer of frost, George actually thought it was a corpse and kicked the legs to see if there was any reaction, the legs much to Georges surprise moved!

An angry voice said "What the hell do you want?"

George was relieved that it was not a corpse he had to report and said to the shack's occupant, "Look mister this is not the weather to be living outdoors in these freezing conditions, I have a lovely warm barn you can stay in if you promise not to smoke or light fires."

The man told him in no uncertain terms to go away and leave him alone, so George at least felt he had offered to help and went on his way.

You can imagine the pile of rubbish building up around the shack in a few weeks, and it was a site of special interest, the man was living in a tip. We did what we thought was right, once a week when we saw him leaving for the village we took some bin bags and wearing gloves mucked him out. All the dozens of plastic bottles, mounds of soggy newspapers and plastic bags littering our lovely countryside we took to our bins. I think he must have been annoyed but like Pauline commented, which other vagrant could boast of having his very own personal cleaners! One morning the camp was vacated and the strange man gone, it must have been too noisy living near our cottages for him to endure any longer.

The strange man had only moved a half mile down the dune system nearer to the village. He had built another ramshackle camp with various bits of stuff washed up on the tide, obviously he liked the area. We still picked up the rubbish left strewn around his shack; it was not heavy only the usual plastic and bean cans. This routine went on for a while longer until the man decided to move on somewhere else away from our area.

CHAPTER THIRTY ONE

OUR PENNY

Penny seemed to have a new lease of life when we moved to the cottage, she was friends with 'Amos' our neighbours huge black tom cat. When his owner was away working we used to look after Amos and it was a pleasure, in bad weather Penny and Amos cuddled up together in front of our roaring fire. When Amos had enough of being with us he returned home entering through his cat flap, after first going hunting in the dark, catching mice, voles and a host of other creatures that he ran into. When entering the house to feed him every morning you never knew what remains you would find, it could be quite scary at times. One time I opened the front door, Penny and I heard a terrible screech, and quick as a flash a huge black crow flew so close to my head I felt its wings brush my head. I nearly wet myself and Penny ran away as fast as she could move on her tiny legs, Amos must have dragged the terrified bird through the cat flap and the lucky bird escaped, I could see a couple of loose feathers on top of the tall fridge in the kitchen. The crow must have sat there all night waiting for a chance to escape; it gave me and Penny a hell of a fright! This was not the last time this happened, the next bird that was dragged through the cat flap and escaped over my head was a blackbird, but many different corpses told of creatures which did not.

The other friend Penny liked was 'Cuthbert' the black Scotty dog who lived in the end cottage under the rock. All three got on so well, the really special friend of our Penny was 'Flossie' the ewe who called for her bucket of fresh water, no dirty beck water for her, she was class! Flossie featured in a woman's magazine when I sent in a lovely photograph of our granddaughters Victoria and Francesca in their pyjamas giving Flossie her bucket of water at the cottage door. Our Penny was now sixteen years old, and getting slower, her frail little body was covered in small warts and her arthritis was becoming progressively worse. Pauline kept hinting that I needed to prepare myself for her passing away, I knew all this and always hoped like other pet owners that she would make it easy for me and pass away peacefully in her sleep. Now we all know life is not as convenient, and that scenario was not going to happen, when do you know the time that it is in your beloved pet's interest to let go? When Pauline asked if she could buy a pedigree Yorkshire terrier from the award winning breeder who lived next door to us on Walney Island, I said yes thinking it would train to catch rats that raided my hen runs. When a child we had a council rat catcher who peddled around the streets of Barrow catching rats with his six cocky little Yorkshire terriers. His push bike had a box on the handle bars in which sat the two older dogs; the other four ran behind him. I used to see him every day on my way to school and never forgot the sight of four tiny dogs doing their utmost to keep up to the bike going over Greengate Street hill.

Pauline of course picked the runt of the litter, and as a tiny puppy was cute but she never grew bigger than a bag of sugar. We were told by our vet that she was too small to ever risk having puppies, and was always small enough to fit in our pockets. She was always my boss and was clever enough to attach herself to me and not Pauline. Training her was a nightmare, after many sleepless nights of listening to her whining down stairs I relented and Penny slept at the bottom of our bed from then on. Penny actually trained me to give her the way of life she desired, and like a mug I was her servant. I would not ever put her into kennels so she went in holiday cottages, and on canal boat holidays all over the country with us and my mother. Towards the end of her life if we went abroad mother looked after her.

To my utter disappointment Penny would watch the rats pinching food off our hens and ignore the big fine rats that played in my garden. Then just to give me heart failure would run up to huge dogs barking like a maniac and gnashing her tiny teeth. We spent half our lives running to pick her up quickly before Penny was bitten to death by an annoyed Alsatian or bull mastiff, when she had aggressively attacked them. She had used all her nine lives and more in the years we had her, we had heard numerous tales from other yorky owners that big dogs had killed theirs with one bite, or they had accidently slammed a car door on theirs, killing them instantly. I could well believe how easy it was to harm a yorky; we were always tripping over her and suffered many cuts and bruises. One day I shall never forget was when we were driving down the main high street one busy afternoon in Barrow, Penny was yapping as usual on Pauline's knee, this constant noise was infuriating so Pauline gave her a tap on her head. Unfortunately Penny being so light weight shot forward and knocked herself unconscious on the hand brake lever.

Pauline shouted "I have killed Penny; oh by God what have I done, she has stopped breathing Norm!" I acted on reflex jammed the brakes on and stopped in the middle of a busy road, a car crashed into the back of mine and horns were blowing. My one thought was Penny might be dead, grabbing her tiny little body I saw she was not breathing. Pauline was hysterical and sobbing her heart out, telling me to do something and quickly. I started breathing gently into Penny's mouth and giving her gentle heart massage, to my utter amazement she started to breathe again. Leaving Pauline to give the motorist our details I raced to our vets with the dazed cross eyed yorky who probably was suffering with concussion. I dumped the car on double yellow lines and dashed into the vets saying it was an emergency, bypassing the people in the waiting room. Penny had a check up and injection then spent the next day resting and eating chicken and prawns, enjoying the fuss from Pauline's guilty conscience. Of course I received a parking ticket when leaving the vets just to round off the day.

Now I had to face the fact that we were going to lose our dear dog and family pet very soon. Mum was in a care home so would not know about Penny, she did not even remember us. Penny still slept in our bedroom and slept next to the radiator, I would have to get up several times in the night to carry her outside for a piddle. Being a very light sleeper I could hear Penny give a little whine when she needed to go out in the middle of the night, I got straight out of bed and carried her downstairs, our poor dog would not want to do her business in the house. Pauline said it was time to let her go, but I did not mind getting up every night with her and kept making excuses to have her for just one more day. Penny was lying in her basket in the front garden basking in the sun, I sat watching her thinking that sixteen years had flown by and soon she would be gone from our lives. Penny suddenly sat upright, and looking at me seemed to be having some kind of a stroke. Pauline gently said to me "It is time Norm; I will ring our vet and tell him we are coming down now." I was absolutely distraught, sixteen years of loving that utterly spoilt bundle of fur, and I loved the very bones of that dog and was inconsolable. Pet lovers know the feeling of loss and what that entails; I could not talk or stop crying. Pauline bless her, phoned Marian our middle daughter and together they took Penny to the vets to be put to sleep. They knew that if I went I could not go through with it, and would bring her back home. We buried Penny in our cottage garden, in her favourite sunny corner where she liked to sleep amongst the flowers.

CHAPTER THIRTY TWO

VE DAY PHOTOGRAPH

Since having to leave work through ill health I was at a cross roads in my life, I knew nothing about anything but hard graft. Having spent all the previous years working outdoors doing anything connected with boats and the sea, being lucky enough to follow my boyhood dreams. Now all that way of life was finished, everything seemed so boring. When all the grandchildren were at school and nobody was staying with us, we found ourselves waiting for their visits every weekend or school holidays. Pauline suggested I find a hobby but what? What could possibly take the place of skippering a survey or pilot boat I wondered, the small trawler or yacht I had ready for weekends were now sold due to my ill health.

One afternoon Pauline came back from town with a present for me, I unwrapped it and saw it was a compact pocket camera from Argos store, the label on the box said £29.99 plus a free film included. "This is your new hobby Norm give it a go you might like doing it, and if you enjoy it you can upgrade your camera," she said.

Today was VE day and four of the grandchildren arrived for the afternoon, a good time to try out my new camera. Our Laura and her younger sister Victoria wanted to celebrate VE day in some way and decided to make a union jack, the other two children Lee and little sister Sinead decided to go with me on the beach to look for something to use for a flag pole. We left Pauline and the two older girls to make a flag using an old bed sheet, red lipstick and blue paint. On the beach washed up by the tide, Lee found a wooden pole which would be perfect. A couple of hours work and we had produced our union jack on a flag pole, and it looked quite good from a distance.

We all walked onto the sands, the light was perfect, and I took a particularly nicely composed shot with Lee and Sinead holding the flag, with a back drop of the Lakeland hills. Well I hoped they were good photos I had to send the film off first to get processed. We all had a lovely celebration that day and a picnic on the beach, and a good practice with my new camera.

A week later the photographs were dropped through our letter box by our own postman 'Pat' in his little red van. Looking at the pictures they looked pretty good for a first attempt, Lee and Sinead looked so cute holding their flag in the sunshine. Pauline said "That photo is brilliant Norm; I am going to send it into the Sunday Express competition for you!"

"I don't think it is good enough for a national paper competition, they get thousands of entries from all over the world, I think it is a waste of time frankly," I said.

"I am sending it in any way, it is beautiful and our grandchildren will be really pleased to see their photo in the Sunday magazine, and there are runner up prizes too!" she said.

We were going down to the village that afternoon for tea at our Elaine's house in the village, Pauline suddenly realised it was the last post before the Sunday Express deadline for the competition. Don't bother then Pauline, it is not meant to be, we must get a move on our Elaine will think we are not coming for our tea!

"I will borrow Laura's bike and cycle to the post office I will not be long, if I hurry I will catch the last post!" Pauline said.

I had to give Pauline credit when she decided to do something she went through with it, no matter what. After tea Elaine said "What competition are you entering Norm for?"

Pauline said "It is a huge prize of a luxury five star safari photography trip for sixteen days in the best lodges and game reserves in Kenya, all expenses paid, picked up at our door, first class hotels and flights. We would not need a penny, just think of that! Also the winning photo is the front cover of the Sunday Express magazine. Now that is what I call a prize, we would never ever be able to afford to pay for a trip like that." she said.

Our Elaine said "I hope you do win mum, you seem to think you might and you certainly deserve a break, I know you have been worried about Norm's illness and losing his career as well, fingers crossed mum!"

Pauline said "I know Norm laughs about my enthusiasm for his photo but I can see there is something special about it!"

"Well we shall see love, I did not even know what the prize was until now, just do not build your hopes up. I might be to unable to go if I am still ill anyway, but we do not need to speculate, we will not win."

I was sitting on the edge of Dunnerholme rock a couple of weeks afterwards, watching a seal pop it's head out of the water a few yards from me. I always think how much like a Labradors head a seals head looks from a distance, and it was throwing a large salmon up in the air and catching it. Thinking to myself how lucky am I to see a sight like this on my very own doorstep, and nobody else around. A loud shout and a scream bought me back from my daydreaming; running towards me was Pauline waving her arms about like a windmill. I thought somebody in the family must have had an accident, so I started to go towards her, poor lass had tears running down her red face, she tried to tell me something but could not get the words out coherently. After several minutes she managed to blurt out, "You've won, won, won! I told you didn't I, bloody told you, had a feeling about that photograph, it was special, yes, yes, yes, Africa here we come."

I gathered that I had won one of the prizes in the photo competition; Pauline said somebody was going to phone me from London in ten minutes time. I said we might not have won first prize love, I was getting worried that Pauline was getting over excited and would be disappointed, I said wait and see and please calm down. We both sat nervously by the phone waiting with butterflies in our tummies. The phone rang and I grabbed it, dam it was my sister, I quickly said I would ring her back. As soon it was put down it rang again and I grabbed it, hell I was nervous, and Pauline was visibly shaking.

"Mr Pascoe?" a man with a very posh accent said "I have the greatest pleasure to inform you that you have won first prize in our Sunday Express photographic competition. We loved the picture of your two beautiful grandchildren on the beach. It will our full cover picture for Armistice Day issue on November 11th edition, you must feel very proud?"

Was I proud? I was bloody speechless, the thought of my photo on the front cover of a prestigious national magazine supplement that was distributed all over the world was mind-blowing. I was not even bothered about the other prize. The editor said more things, I confess that I could not take in, being in shock, things like this do not happen every day to people like us. The poor man gave up trying to get through to me and I remember him saying details to follow in the post, and his secretary will get in touch with more details. Pauline was sitting sobbing, saying over and over again, that she was going to Africa! That day our adrenalin was sky high, we could not eat, Pauline phoned all our family and friends to tell them our good news.

We could not sleep and the next morning the phone went at nine o'clock a lovely girl told us in great detail what exactly we had won. Taxi to Manchester, flight to London, London to Nairobi, top class hotels, all the top safari lodges to see the 'Top Five' animals and it was a specifically tailored photographic tour, and was very expensive. To sum it up it was the holiday of a lifetime, this young lady was assigned to help us pick the best time of year to go and answer any possible queries we may have. I had the obvious question about my health problems and my doubts about the conditions we may find when we got there. The lady enquired on my behalf and said people will be on hand at all times to assist you in any way, we would be treated like royalty, and to not have any fears about anything.

"Oh by the way the editor suggests you update your compact camera for one more suited to a photographic safari tour," the lovely lady said.

I could only agree with him on that suggestion. Looking around the shops I bought the best I could afford that at least had a changeable telephoto lens, this outfit would not be anywhere near what the other well off tourist would be toting about but needs must, I was now unemployed. My assumptions about all my companions on the tour would prove to be correct. We read up about these top end safari holidays and amazed to find how much lacking in knowledge we had. Me thinking that there would be jungles in Kenya and that all the safari parks were near to each other.

The great day at last arrived; we had been advised to visit Kenya in February the best season, and the temperature being just right. Our taxi picked us up and drove us to Manchester airport to catch a flight to

Heathrow. To say we were excited would be an understatement. Landing in Nairobi another taxi took us to a lovely hotel, where we went to bed to the sound of hundreds of bull frogs croaking all night, they did sound like Natterjack toads calling at Dunnerholme! The next morning a coach waited to take the entire safari guests for a trip to the city's biggest market. Sitting on the bus was an opportunity to meet some of our travelling companions. Our tour guide gave us a safety talk first before setting off, I remember him saying please remove your watches and jewellery before leaving the bus, do not hang your arm out of the bus windows, your rings will be removed from your fingers and possibly your fingers also, the list went on. By the time the bus reached the market there were some very concerned tourist on that vehicle. We stood up to file off the bus and people were asking how long did we have before the bus left, the driver just laughed and said we would be back very soon, he seemed very sure about that.

As soon as our gaggle of nervous tourist disembarked from the bus we were besieged by hoards of locals all talking at once, the women begging for lipsticks, perfume or such like, the men for money. We all grabbed our wife's handbags before they were wrenched from their arms. The tension was palpable and stressful, these people were desperately poor and we must be like manna from the Gods to these unfortunates. We were herding together for mutual support, and reached the market entrance to be joined inside by the stall holders vying for our attention; this was not fun at all. By mutual consent our party herding together like sheep headed back to the bus, the driver had not even bothered to switch off his engine. He laughed when we boarded saying "I said you would not be long!" The driver gave us a bus tour instead around the city, and we realised how dangerous this place was, iron grills over windows, high walls around better class houses and guard dogs.

Our friend who had been to Kenya before, wanted us to post an envelope full of Kenya currency to her friend who lived in a remote village. She asked us to find a post office in Nairobi city because other letter's she had sent containing cash had not arrived at the village. So Pauline and I set off to walk around the area looking for a post office, and worse of all did not tell anybody where we were going. We obviously were acting like stupid naive white tourists, who think everything is always going to be alright. Well we became more and more concerned the further away from our hotel we walked. On every street corner gangs of suspicious looking ragged locals stood around forty gallon oil drums they had cut in half, lit a fire underneath and were roasting corn cobs on, presumably for sale. Nobody would answer our enquiries about the location of any post offices, and a crowd of young men started to follow behind us, most carrying sharp looking machetes.

Pauline whispered to me that we must be the most stupid tourists to ever visit Kenya, I said you are wrong love we are the most stupid tourist to ever leave England's shores, and we better try and find a policeman quick! A stroke of luck, a passing taxi driver pulled alongside of us and without ceremony threw us into his taxi and drove off his tyres screaming. In a lovely cultured accent he said "Excuse me for manhandling you and your lady sir, but I saw you in extreme danger and felt it was my duty to help you both, those men I think were going to do you some harm!"

"Do not apologise mister you came in the nick of time we cannot thank you enough," I said. Of course I gave him a suitable reward.

The next morning after breakfast we assembled for a safety talk, and to divide us into three parties of four to each of the three safari vehicles. With only having four people in the vehicles it meant all four could stand on the seats and look through a large sunroof in the centre of the roof, over which was a sun awning. When travelling at speed along the dusty unmade roads, the sunroof was lowered to keep out the dust.

The convoy of three vehicles were loaded and our driver a local man called 'Ken' led our convoy in the direction of our first road journey approximately 150 miles. This was to Tsavo West to visit the famous Mzima Springs to see the Hippo's and then stay in Kilaguni lodge. The scenery was absolutely stunning around the springs, large trees and bushes gave us cool shade, but the Hippo's were a little camera shy. Travelling to our first lovely lodge we photographed giraffes, zebra's and several types of deer. All the local wildlife would be on the menu in all the lodges we stayed at, bottled water was essential at all times. Our vehicles carried a cool box each day filled with cold soft drinks for our use each day. The temperature was just right we all agreed, because the land being so high above sea level. We were getting to know our travelling companions in our vehicles and grew to like them very much over the coming days, the rest of our group consisted of an ex tea planter owner and his elegant wife who were bought up in Kenya. This very well educated man was old school colonial, and could speak the local dialect, which saved us being exploited by the locals on several occasions. One occasion when we all went out on boats to photograph the Hippo's on Lake Naivasha, I was off the boat first so I thought that it would be nice to pay for our group as a treat for the boat trip, the man helping us off asked for several Kenyan pounds. I paid him and said the bill was settled to our group so not ask for any more money. That night after having our dinner we all sat around having a sun downer, the ex tea planter asked me why I had given the guide that large wad of cash?

"I paid the boats hire for us all as a treat," I said.

When he heard this he disappeared for ten minutes, on his return handed me all my cash back, to my amazement.

"The boat trips were free Norman" he said "I wondered what the local staff were laughing at before, they did not realise that I can speak their dialect, so you can imagine what a surprise they had when I asked for the money back. Do not feel guilty about it Norman they should not be ripping the guests off at all."

We went from here to Amboseli game reserve next passing the beautiful Mount Kilimanjaro, Africa's highest mountain with its crown of snow, looking very dramatic against a blue sky. Staying at the lovely Serena lodge, we went on the afternoon safari and saw wonderful herds of elephants, buffalo, and herds of impala. The plains were green and lush after the rain. We did have a scary moment when two elephants were fighting and one of them who seemed to be coming off worse, spotted us and with a loud trumpet of rage started to charge towards us. Our Kenyon driver Ken, actually turned pale in front of our eyes, and quickly shouted for us to hold on tight we were in extreme danger. Everyone was screaming and I was busy taking close ups of a charging rogue elephant, his ears were enormous, his tusks huge. Ken shouted that he had no room or time to turn our vehicle around; he went in full reverse, clouds of red dust flying into the air, we were in a tangle of arms and legs, thrown together in a heap, all off balance. Our hasty manoeuvres seemed to infuriate our angry elephant even more. Luckily for us the track behind us was not blocked by one of our sister vehicles or we would have been flattened like a pancake.

We saw that Ken was rightly scared out of his wits later on in the trip when he showed us the tangled remains of a rival firm's safari vehicle at the side of the road that had similarly been attacked. I was chuffed the incident afforded me some great elephant shots, and we had a great tale to tell at dinner.

The gangs of cute vervet monkey's and their young hung around our lodge like teenagers up to no good. We were told by our guide to watch out for the monkeys pinching from our rooms and not to leave the veranda doors open. Well it was hot after that long drive so after a shower we lay on the bed relaxing ready for our late afternoon safari. We left the window open to let some air in the room. I awoke sensing something wrong, in my sleepy state when my eyes opened I could see an old wizened man staring at me only inches away from my face, in fact I felt and smelt his terrible breath. Oh my God it wasn't an old man it was a bloody monkey, I nearly wet myself. Sitting bolt upright I looked around the room to see half a dozen more rifling through our belongings, reminding me of a gang of brigands. One cheeky little sod had my sunglasses; another was climbing back out of the window with my camera around his neck dangling from its neck by the lanyard.

Pauline woke up and started to yell "Get out of here you little buggers,"

They all started to head for the window, one carrying a white bra, another with a bunch of bananas from our now empty fruit bowl. Then they were gone like thieves in the night carrying their ill gotten gains.

"We are going to look right idiots when everybody hears about this Pauline, we better see exactly what is missing, before we report it to our guide." We found our tour guide having a cold beer, after saying I told you so, he grabbed a large bunch of grapes and said "Follow me." We suddenly realised these monkeys do it all the time and make a living out of it, the small troupe of vervet thieves were sitting on the patio tables and chairs waiting for us to approach. Our guide quietly approached them and sat down at one of the tables showing them the big bunch of grapes. The biggest monkey let out loud chattering noises as if he was a tribal elder negotiating, which in a way he was. Then my camera, bra, sunglasses, not the bananas though, they had probably been eaten straightaway, they were not obviously open to negotiation. All their swag was placed by them onto one table, when this was done they moved away from the table.

When our tour guide was happy everything bar the bananas was there, he placed the grapes on another table nearby and picked up our somewhat battered and slightly shop soiled items, and gave them back to us. The barter having been successfully concluded, we walked away, the elder monkey started to dish out the grapes to his band of thieves, looking a bit like 'Fagin' in the musical 'Oliver.'

A few times that afternoon our monkeys pulled off other missions with various successes, once only stealing a packet of mints, sundry items of fruit and a ladies handbag. The small troupe of lovable vervets only added to the charm of the lodge, and was something we never forgot. Certainly on this trip there was not a dull moment. When we were sat around the veranda after a sumptuous evening meal, treated like royalty and enjoying hearing about the diverse lives of our new friends, I felt a long way from my humble beginning in 59 Glasgow Street in the industrial shipbuilding town of Barrow-in-Furness. We became good friends of Richard and Trish and seemed to be very comfortable in their company. They said they enjoyed listening to my stories from my fishing trawler days, and stories from around our little cottage at Dunnerholme. Richard seemed to think my tales of the sheep hilarious and wanted to hear more. When I asked what Richard did for a career, he said he was an author and had written several books, had a lovely talented stepson David who was a gifted musician. David was at home looking after their beloved cat.

One night I told Richard that we had won the price of our luxury holiday by sending in a photograph to the Sunday Express magazine, he was amazed when I showed him the photograph I had stowed in my luggage. I thought the photograph deserved to come on holiday with us, looking at it now only made me appreciate even more what had happened because of it. Richard was delighted when I presented the photo to him as a souvenir of our meeting on holiday. Richard only had a camera similar to mine, his wife Trish used a camcorder, but most of the other tourist had top of the range cameras with several different lenses, some telephoto lenses being as big as missiles. In fact the ex tea planter had several bags of various expensive cameras and a lens for every occasion. He was very nice but kept looking at my cheaper camera and trying to persuade me to borrow one of his top of the range models, and Richard could see I was getting a little annoyed about this man being very condescending towards me.

Finally Richard said to the ex tea planter "For God's sake man stop bothering Norm, it is not the price of the equipment you have, but the man taking the picture that counts. Norm is on this holiday because of winning first prize in a national photographic competition using a £29.99 camera from Argos, so I think that proves my point don't you think?"

We visited Lake Naivasha seeing the wonderful sight of so many beautiful flamingos, Lake Baringo and Lake Nakuru. On a small boat trip on Lake Naivasha to see the hippos we were all busy taking photographs of some baby hippos, our boat driver strayed too near to them, just in time he gunned the boat engine to full power as an irate mother hippo came very near to tipping the boat over. This was even scarier than the elephant charging us a couple of days earlier.

Sometimes we had to travel one hundred and fifty miles between our game reserves and this was a great way of seeing the country and how most of the people lived. The roads were always appalling and deep ruts were everywhere. Ken said each tribal area was responsible for their own section of road, but being Africa they could not be bothered. Our vehicles had been specially strengthened to cope with the bad conditions encountered, and remarkably none of our three vehicles even had a puncture. All we encountered on our miles of roads were lorries and buses, all the commerce was carried on these gaily painted lorries. Many shanty towns we passed consisted of ramshackle wooden huts with tin roofs. Some had big signs gaily painted on, saying 'Nairobi Hilton Hotel' or 'Savoy.' A butchers shop with an open front and a counter, had a few pieces of dark coloured meat covered with huge flies hanging on some hooks, outside was one forlorn looking bony sheep tethered to a stake, awaiting its turn. A sign above read 'Joseph' high class butcher. Ken kept up a running commentary for us as we were passing anything of interest. He said that these shanty hotels were used by all the lorry drivers who had to drive long distances, and only slowly along the terrible roads. Ken said prostitutes were on hand to cater to the lorry drivers if required, and it was the only income some of these places had. I missed out on some of the game drives and bird watching expeditions due to severe back pain, even with my pain relievers I found it necessary to spend time lying on my bed whilst Pauline went with the others. The jolting of our vehicles over the deep potholes and the atrocious road conditions exacerbated my spinal condition, but I would not have missed this adventure for all the money in the world.

We took some beautiful photographs of a family of baboons and their babies at Lake Nakuru, and herds of elephants with babies. Magnificent lions, scary crocodiles in the river, and these huge fully grown crocs came right up to the lodge to get fed with chickens by the staff every evening, for the amusement of the tourist. Samburu was good for seeing reticulated giraffe and the blue necked Somali ostriches.

The worst place we stayed at was the world famous 'Treetops,' and only because we had been absolutely spoilt by all the other lovely places we had already visited. Treetop is the first and most famous of all the lodges in Kenya, Princess Elizabeth was staying here when she heard that her father King George V1 had passed away. Since we stayed there many years ago the lodge as been completely renovated, when we stayed there it was very basic, our meals were taken sitting on long wooden benches, and we were crammed in. The top viewing platform on the roof was nice, and wearing soft shoes mandatory plus quiet voices so not to disturb the animals visiting the waterhole. Tourists stop at the Outspan hotel and are transported by coach to Treetops for one night's stay only. A member of staff stays up all night operating a buzzer fixed in the fifty small rooms, each one like a small ship's cabin. One buzz for a leopard, rhino two, elephants four etc. unfortunately our party was plagued by extreme tummy upsets, this caused probably by the lodges washing our salad and fruit in local water. We of course only drank bottled water at all times, even the ex tea planter who said we did not need to buy expensive bottled water succumbed to the tummy bug, we all spent the long night visiting the shared bathroom facilities, kept awake by the annoying buzzers going off all night. After sharing all our 'Diacalm' supply by morning we could embark onto the coach to go back to our lovely hotel. The animals seen that night when we pooled what we had all seen on the way to the bathroom were elephants, bushbucks, waterbucks, hyenas and warthogs.

The Masai Mara national reserve was for us the finest place we visited, and vowed that if we could ever afford it to fly straight here from Nairobi by light aircraft to avoid the rough road trip and stay at the lodge for as long as possible, it's that good. On the road journey to get there we were held up by a huge sand drift blowing across and blocking the road. Big lorries were held up as well as our little convoy. Everybody had to help with a shovel and by pushing each safari vehicle through one by one we got through, it was not easy.

The vast plains provide some of the best game viewing in Kenya. Serengeti and Mara is one massive reserve divided by the Kenya and Tanzania border, and is home to thousands of plains game with their avid following of lion, cheetah, and shy leopard. Game drives were in the early morning and later in the afternoons. I took some spectacular shots of a male lion feasting on a buffalo he had just killed, the female waiting patiently to be allowed to start feasting, the young cubs trying to sneak in before they are allowed. The pecking order was being strictly adhered to by their father. Hyenas were skulking on the perimeter waiting very impatiently for their opportunity, sneaking a little bit too close sometimes and sent packing by the female lion. Waiting in the wings so to speak, on a nearby tree, with their greedy eyes and scraggy necks, ugly looking vultures, row upon row, waiting with hungry anticipation for the free for all they knew would happen when the pride of lions ate their fill and left the kill remains.

We saw so many varieties of wonderful bird life on our long journey around Kenya and colourful species of ornate and brightly coloured lizards. I took reel upon reel of film, and promised to send our new friend Richard and Trish copies. We were treated to some lovely traditional Masai warrior traditional dances before we left our lodge. We had met some lovely people that we knew we would stay in touch with, had the most comprehensive tour of the best lodges in Kenya, and were so sorry to leave it all. The food and service was royalty standard, and I was looking forward to sending the editor of the Sunday Express a short article and some good photographs for them to publish in their daily paper. Two single ladies who shared our vehicle, loved golf so Pauline invited them both to come and stay with us at Dunnerholme cottage, and shortly after did visit us. After a sad last night in Nairobi with the bull frogs croaking, reminding us of our Natterjack toads at home, we left to catch a flight back to dear old England. Our taxi was waiting for us at Manchester, and as we travelled the top road home we caught sight of our beloved Duddon estuary. The tide was flowing in, the golden sands glowing in the afternoon sun, our white painted chocolate box cottage looking beautiful and peaceful. We both held hands thinking we were the two luckiest people to have had so wonderful an experience that we would remember forever. Our best moments in Kenya was of standing looking down into the Rift Valley seeing vast herds crossing a swollen river, this scene reminding us of the Lion King scene. All of us one afternoon standing exactly on the Equator at a place called Nanyuki, one foot on either side of the imaginary line and receiving a certificate each. The opulence of our lodges and the contrast of the way the locals live. The wonderful people we met particularly Richard and Trish who we came to love dearly over the years. If my old dad could see one of his nine children having a whisky with a real live Lord sitting in front of a roaring log fire in Africa, being waited on by several waiters each wearing white gloves, he would wonder what the world was coming too!

I was totally fascinated listening to the different companions we spoke to each night whilst sipping our drinks on the terrace of a beautiful game lodge. The ex tea plantation owner telling us tales of life before Kenya gained independence made history come alive. The elderly famous author who had lived all his life in Kenya and just published another book whilst living full time in the lodge, you could see he was highly thought of by all the staff. Everyone had an interesting story to tell and even my story seemed to be enjoyed by our new friends.

CHAPTER THIRTY THREE

HOME

We could safely say that winning that photographic competition was a life changer for me, it made me realise that I could still achieve something after having to give up my lifetime's obsession with the sea. I started entering every photographic competition that I heard about, having some success seeing my pictures in various magazines and books. The next major competition was having my photo of sheep being cut off by the tide at Dunnerholme being chosen to be in the BBC Country file "Children In Need Calendar." This was fantastic for my confidence and it was lovely to see my photo featured on the television program.

The children were lovely subjects for me when they stayed with us at our cottage, there was not a dull moment and the house always filled with laughter. In one side of the huge mass of Dunnerholme rock, on the seaward side was a small cave hollowed out by the waves, the floor of this little cave was deep sand washed in by the large waves. One of the little ones said to me one day "Is that a pirate cave granddad?" and I said "Yes it was, and sometimes they come in the night to bury some of their treasure in this cave."

"Can we come with our buckets and spades tomorrow granddad and see if they have been, we will get up early before anybody else gets here before us," our Lee said.

Thinking I have started something now, at dawn tomorrow the five visiting grandchildren will be pulling me out of bed to go on a pirate treasure hunting expedition. Before the children woke up the next morning I crept out of the house heading for the pirate cave, scattering all the surprised rabbits grazing around the cottage. Reaching the cave I dug a hole about a foot deep in the sandy floor, and placed a handful of coins in the bottom. Smoothing the sand level and erasing my footprints as I walked backwards, I was feeling pleased with myself and looking forward to seeing the children's reaction. Creeping back into bed Pauline never even noticed that I had even been up. Just as predicted all five excited children were pulling off our blankets saying "Come on granddad we have to hurry, the pirates might have been to the cave in the night and buried something!"

Pauline awoke when the cold air hit her saying "What have you told them now Norm? It is dawn for God's sake, you will have to stop winding them up!"

I winked at her saying we have all got time to get washed and changed and have our breakfast. I explained to an anxious group of children that the pirates would have hidden their treasure well and nobody passing would ever know that treasure had been buried. With great difficulty we managed to get all five fed and watered and kitted out for the beach.

Like ducks and ducklings we headed up the path leading over the top of the rock heading for the cave, every child equipped with a plastic spade. When we reached the beach the children could not contain themselves any longer, they left us behind and raced for the cave, each one wanting to be the first. Of course they all started digging in the wrong place, shouts of disappointment ringing out.

"There is nothing here granddad we told you we should have come here straightaway!"

Then looks of dejection on their faces, I had to explain nobody had been before, that there were no other footprints except ours.

"Well where is the treasure granddad?"

"Maybe you are digging in the wrong place, try over here," I said.

Well they dug down again and a great cry of triumph rang out, coins were being unearthed and happy laughter filled the cave.

Pauline said, "That was lovely Norm, I was worried for a moment thinking that you were playing a joke on them all, they have not even realised that the money is what currency we use every day. Well done, we might get some mileage out of this game and be able to carry on doing it for a while."

The variations of this game were sweets buried and various trinkets, the adventure of the pirate cave carries on to this day with the great grandchildren, and that is the magic of Dunnerholme.

I was always playing practical jokes on the children, sending the girls several Valentine cards each caused mayhem and got them fooled most of the time, until they were all visiting one unforgettable weekend. They must have all got their heads together and voted on the best way of getting their revenge on me. They all got up quietly early one Saturday morning and crept downstairs. Opening the cupboard drawer where nana stored her giant balls of wool; they passed them around each cousin. The instruction from the ring leader Sinead, was to make a dense spider's web of wool around all the rooms downstairs, gradually working their way up the stairs and onto the landing outside our bedroom. Now the amount of wool used was phenomenal, the different balls were huge and all various colours. The remarkable thing was even though the house was full of giggling children; we did not hear a thing. When I awoke needing the use the bathroom down stairs, I tried to open our bedroom door. Thinking it was jammed in some way I heaved on the doorknob with all my strength, after much pulling and tugging I opened it one inch wide so I could peek out.

The sight that I saw was amazing, a complete dense spider's web of wool going off in all directions, from floor to ceiling. The lines of wool wrapped around the bedroom doorknob were impressive alone. Pauline had a look through the gap and gasped in amazement, thinking that all her bloody good wool was ruined, tied in knots around anything that did not move. Then the children started to laugh and say, "Got you back granddad, it has taken us hours to do all this, we got up in the dark and thought you might have woken up and stopped us!"

I thought we would have heard you if we had not been completely exhausted keeping all of you children occupied, all day yesterday and last night. Not to mention feeding you all, you little monsters!

"Right children it was a good joke, and now take it all down so I can use the bathroom, my legs are crossed now," I said.

"We can't do that granddad, we cannot get the knots out, it will take us hours," Sinead said.

"Go down stairs into the kitchen Laura and fetch a sharp knife, I cannot wait any longer, I need a wee!" I said.

"We cannot do that granddad, we are not allowed to touch sharp knives," she said. The children were laughing hysterically, really milking this revenge on granddad episode. I was becoming desperate and Pauline was trying to keep me calm.

"That's it I must get out, I said keep clear of the bedroom door children, I am going to force my way out!" I said.

They made these bloody doors so well I could not even do any damage to it, I jammed a small wooden chair into the gap and used it like a lever, the door handle shot off and the gap widened. I could now get an arm out through the widening gap, to grasp some wool strands. Even Pauline was laughing now at my fevered desperation, the children finding it all hilarious.

Pauline said "It is your fault entirely Norm you wind them up all the time telling those tales of what mischief you and your two brothers and the children's dads used to get up to, they are only copying you!"

I thought my problem of reaching a loo was over once out of my bedroom, it was only beginning, the maze of wool was impossible to break through without a sharp knife, and I was in a hurry. Fighting my way through, over and under any gaps I could find, I got ever nearer to the bathroom, did I make it in time? Nope.

To this day the grandchildren tell their children about the time they took revenge on grand dad Norm and his desperate attempt to cut his way through the maze of wool trying to reach the bathroom. It does take some living down! They all set to with scissors and me with a very sharp knife and spent two hours chopping all Pauline's wool to pieces, and we made the children promise to keep revenge attacks a little less dramatic in the future.

All the children were taught canoeing on the shallow beck that ran past the cottage and into the estuary. We only had one near miss when our Francesca rolled the canoe over and did not come up to the surface again. Pauline and I always stood in the shallow water nearby, keeping a close watch on the three canoes ready to dash to help if needed. When I saw Francesca roll the canoe over I reached her in seconds, she had gone over in the deepest part of the beck which was about three feet, I rolled the canoe upright and she was understandably frightened, and swallowed some water. We took her to the cottage and Pauline calmed her down, and gave her a hot bath. She had opened her eyes underwater and seen a fish close up and this freaked her out. It took a while before she tried canoeing again but soon got over her frightening experience, her preference afterwards was rowing in the dinghy. We had some lovely barbecues on balmy summer nights watching the sun going down over the Blackcombe Mountain that towered over our estuary. Our son Tony fetching fresh mackerel to cook on the charcoal fire was the nights we will always remember.

One day I was grateful that the children were not with me was the day that my guardian angel came to my rescue yet once again, and I think it was a unique experience not many people can say they have had, or would want to have. The wind that morning was really strong and blustery, and howling over the top of the rock. I was taking my customary early morning stroll and walking close under the lee of the rock to keep out of the wind.

The ground was covered in limestone boulders that had over the years fallen off the cliff above me, and I was moving carefully around them. Believe me or not a ewe's body falling from the cliff above actually grazed my head before hitting the rock in front of me with a sickening thud. She landed on a sharp rock and blood poured from her shattered mouth, I could see she was in a bad way. Not only that, I did feel sorry for the sheep but realised she had nearly killed me and missed doing that by a few inches. This was in the days before mobile phones so had to get to our cottage to phone George the farmer who owned the sheep. I went back to the ewe and sat waiting for George to arrive, and saw the blood was still trickling from her mouth, but she was not breathing anymore. This was not a surprise to me considering the height she had fallen. The tractor and trailer arrived, I asked George why a usually sure footed sheep had been so careless so close to the edge?

He said "The ewe had been grazing the lush grass at the very edge and a sudden squall must have unbalanced her, it was just an unfortunate accident, how far were you away when you spotted her falling Norm?"

"Well actually I was nearly hit by her I was that close George; your sheep came very near to killing me as well as herself!"

"Hell Norm there are not many people around that can say they have been nearly killed by a falling sheep is there?"

While I am on the subject of sheep I must tell of another interesting story that happened at Dunnerholme that involves a sheep, a story we kept quiet about for a long time. Shortly after we bought the cottage Pauline was standing outside the back door admiring the view, the high tide that day was fully in and the scenery was breath taking. The tide had stopped only twelve feet away from our cottage door. Pauline shouted to me to bring out our binoculars, she had spotted something odd that was drifting in with the tide. Looking at the object we both agreed it looked like a Second World War mine, complete with those horns that stick out. This was not as unusual as you may think; when I was a trawler man we were always receiving notices about the possibility of ex wartime mines floating or being caught in trawl nets. In fact some fishing boats still get sunk after trawling one up now and again.

Pauline started to panic, thinking that if one of its horns touched the shallow rocks in our bay it may explode and blow the cottages up. She wanted me to not take any chances and phone the police, coast guard and most importantly the bomb disposal squad. Before I did that I wanted to be totally certain it was a dangerous floating mine, so I looked through my binoculars at this floating object from every possible angle. Hell I could even see knobbly ends on the stick like projections, I counted four at least. Pauline was getting excited and wanted to phone now, I was more frightened of getting every emergency department mobilised and making a complete idiot of myself, and the guy's at the docks I worked with would not ever let me live it down.

I was just about to phone when I realised the answer was there in front of me, my canoe. The rowing boat I had to get rid of because of the golfers insisting that I rowed out to save the bloody sheep cut off by the tide. Much to Pauline's utter horror I paddled out to the floating mine, thinking that I need to get my information correct at all cost. Reaching the mine and not without great trepidation I might add, up to the final couple of yards I was convinced it was a dangerous Second World War mine.

I nearly wet myself laughing when I reached it, annoying my wife standing waiting impatiently, nearly having palpitations worried that we were going to be blown to kingdom come. I shouted it is not a mine love, relax it is a bloody stinking, decomposing sheep. The sheep's belly was bloated and was tight as a drum, its four legs and little hoofs looked just like mine projections, and the head was hanging under the water out of sight. Admittedly it did look like a war time mine, and I could not be blamed for calling out the authorities, but was really glad we did not. The stink of the sheep was wafting landwards and the stench became almost unbearable.

Pauline said "You have got to do something if that putrid carcass washes up at the cottages we are not going to live with that smell Norm, and our neighbours will be upset when they return home later."

I had one of my 'eureka' moments, I collected a rope from my shed and thought if I tied it to one of the sheep's legs, then I could tow it out to sea in my canoe, where the ebb tide would take it back out. Sometimes my brilliant ideas astound me, so shortly after I found myself gagging and feeling extremely nauseous tying a rope around this unfortunate beast's leg. I had worked down sewers and not smelt anything like this sheep's smell and certainly needed to get it away from our cottages at all costs. The smell was toxic!

I was pleasantly surprised by the speed I was towing the bloated sheep and making good progress towards the deeper water, where I hoped to cast the carcass off. Just as I gave an extra hard paddle to gain another yard there was a loud whoosh, the carcass exploded. I turned around to see the rope with a leg attached flying backwards hitting me square in my face, closely followed by the green, putrid contents of the sheep's distended belly covering me with indescribable corruption, I vomited. The rest of the carcass disappeared below the waves leaving a trail of huge green gassy bubbles. Paddling glumly towards the shore with stinking gore dripping off me and my canoe, trailing a rope with a leg attached in my wake, I heard a slow hand clapping coming from the shoreline, where a large group of walkers were sitting on a grassy knoll. They must have been delighted at the free cabaret show they had just witnessed; I know I would have been, if having the good fortune to be sitting with them.

Shortly after this incident something else happened but with one of George's ewe's. The daft sheep was running around with my bright yellow plastic water bucket on her head, securely hooked behind her horns.

"This never happens when Flossie drinks water from the bucket Norm," said Pauline after us and five golfers chased the ewe plus bucket all around the bloody golf course causing chaos around the fairways. Nobody came anywhere near to catching the sheep and being a hot day we were all exhausted. One of the golfers had enough of this debacle and decided to phone George from the clubhouse.

"Will you please come straightaway George one of your sheep is running around our golf course with a plastic bucket on her head, the handle is hooked around its horns. Norman and Pauline and a gang of our lads have spent an hour chasing after it but cannot catch it."

George and his trusty sheepdog took quite a while to catch and remove the bright yellow bucket from his ewe, and driving up to the cottage on his quad bike said in an angry voice, "Do you know which idiot left this bucket lying around Norm? It was a good job you noticed; the ewe could not feed or drink with that around its neck."

"No I don't Know George, there are some irresponsible people about but on the plus side you have got yourself a nice new bucket!" I replied.

CHAPTER THIRTY FOUR

BILLY ELLIOT LONDON

It was Pauline's sixty third birthday and the children had bought us tickets for the wonderful new show 'Billy Elliot' showing at the Victoria Palace theatre in London. Not only had we tickets for the best seats but also two nights in a nearby five star hotel, we both love musicals so it was really appreciated. The train journey down to London was even exciting for us, and we were looking forward to seeing our room in the posh hotel. Our taxi dropped us off at the entrance of the hotel where a uniformed man in a top hat quickly dashed to open the door for us, passing our luggage to a porter to carry. "This is getting off to a lovely start darling," Pauline whispered.

"Wow! This is something else" I said when entering our lovely room and seeing all the facilities and luxury fittings. After walking to nearby Buckingham Palace and Hyde Park, we visited Trafalgar Square where it bought back happy memories of feeding the host of pigeons with Francesca and Rebecca; it seemed very strange to see the area devoid of pigeons anymore. They had both won a major photography competition with animal pictures, and had to go to London to receive their prizes off Chris Packham the famous wild life presenter at the Grosvenor Hotel, we took them both down for a couple of days, and saw 'Beauty and the Beast' musical.

I digressed, back to our trip to see Billy Elliot, after sandwiches from Marks and Spencer's eaten in our lovely hotel room we changed into some nice evening clothes for the musical evening. We made our way the short distance to the Victoria Palace, both of us very excited to see the theatre production we had heard so much about. The theatre was packed; we had good seats in the dress circle there were only about ten rows in front of us. The constant worry when visiting the theatre is that when you are short arsed like me, it does not take a particularly tall person to block your view of the stage. Usually I get the only six foot six guy, built like the side of a house sitting in front of me, or the equivalent female with a foot high hair do, that likes eating packets of potato crisps during the performance. Once whilst watching Beauty and the Beast a German couple behind us spent the full performance translating the English into German for his girlfriend, I nearly got arrested for assault and battery! I have bad luck with theatre seating, always have done, sometimes I manage to book front row on the balcony, and this is only rarely achieved by me and puts me in a bloody good mood if it happens. On this happy occasion the people in front were like dwarfs (anybody shorter than me would be classed as a dwarf) and I thanked God for answering my prayers. The price of the theatre tickets for these musicals in London is truly extortionate, so you need to have a good view of the stage. Looking around every seat was taken except for the one next to me, and I was hoping that the person who had booked it was ill or missed their train; selfishly I wanted to use it to store our coats and sweeties on.

Pauline nudged my arm and said "Look at that blond stunner heading your way Norm, it must be her seat next to yours, she has got to be a model she is gorgeous!"

Pauline was right; she was tall, long legged, nicely tanned, a tiny mini skirt, wore a classy top and had a lovely hair style, she just oozed class. I had hit the jackpot on all fronts tonight, anyone would think it was my birthday, I could tell Pauline was jealous. As the dream girl got closer to us Pauline said "I think it is a man Norm, but still stunning all the same!"

Lots of thoughts flew around my head, was this person a deliberate plant, a part of the musical, several people in front were rudely taking photos, maybe they thought or knew it was part of the act. I had to stand up for this lovely creature, with the lovely scent of perfume and let him pass. With a polite, well spoken voice he said gaily "Thank you so much, I am running a little late, the time just flies, don't you think?"

He was so tall and his long tanned legs very shapely, his mini skirt riding right up his thighs, everything about him was quality and nearly everyone was looking at him. There was no way I was going to ignore him, if he was not part of the act, I did not want to offend him if he really was a genuine cross dresser. My nervous opening words were "You have a lovely tan, you look very nice, isn't this a lovely theatre?"

He gave me a lovely smile, showing beautiful white even teeth, and said "Thank you again, you are so kind and yes it is my first time in this theatre, I am really looking forward to the show."

That broke the ice nicely I thought, I introduced us to him and he shook our hands saying his name was Tom and he lived in Essex. He said "You have a nice tan Norm do you have a career outdoors?"

"I have taken early retirement Tom, but have spent my life at sea on trawlers, tugs and suchlike, what about you?"

Well his reply floored me; he claimed that he was a deep sea diver working in the North Sea. After he told me that bit of news we were like long lost buddies, both of us were chatting like fish wives over a garden fence. Pauline said later that we completely ignored her after that, it was all about boats and maritime rubbish has she crudely put it. In fact so engrossed were we that Pauline said we were like a married couple and the people around probably thought the same, and the rude Japanese girls in front were still photographing us.

The lights dimmed, the show began and I resisted putting my hand on his knee, only joking, Pauline was watching me. What a fantastic show and so funny, tears were streaming down my face, I became worried about Tom, and about how would his mascara cope with his tears? That show should be compulsory for all senior school pupils; it had every human emotion played out, we were enthralled by it. The show reminded me about my upbringing and how tough it had been for me and my siblings. At the interval I surprised Tom with an ice-cream and talked about our seagoing careers, Tom had freshened up his makeup whilst I queued up for our ice-creams; I assumed he used the ladies washroom. Tom asked us to go for a drink with him after the show and we said yes. When the show finished to a rightful applause and several encores, we got separated in the crowd when Pauline stopped to buy a Billy Elliot sweat shirt. We never saw Tom again that night and were sorry and disappointed to have missed him.

In bed that night we both agreed that we had met a quite unique character in meeting Tom, and laughed thinking that he was part of the musical. After a lovely full English breakfast we were walking through the very busy reception area, a familiar voice shouted "Hi Norm and Pauline how nice to see you both again!"

Bloody hell it was Tom, you could have heard a pin drop, everyone stopped and looked at us, we looked at Tom, what an amazing sight. He looked a million dollars, tartan mini skirt, fresh white frilly fronted blouse; a white fur stole around his shoulders, and a white fur Cossack style hat sat on his lovely blond hair. Pauline hissed "They are 'Jimmy Choo' shoe's he is wearing, and that is a 'Ralph Lauren' handbag he's toting wow," said with a touch of envy in her voice. He strolled elegantly across the reception area, his highly polished stiletto heels click, clicking across the marble floor, his arms outstretched to give me a hug and a peck on the cheek. I could not help noticing the beautiful 'Rolex Oyster' ladies watch that graced his elegant wrist. Now this does not happen to me very often in our village Co-op, not lately anyway. Pauline got the same treatment of course, but he hugged me for longer, she said afterwards.

Tom was distraught when I said we were checking out of the hotel, fancy meeting him on the next seat in a theatre and being in the same hotel, what are the chances of that happening? Tom tried to get us to extend our stay in London saying he would like to treat us to afternoon tea at the Ritz. We exchanged phone numbers and said our goodbyes, ships that pass in the night. He actually said to me "God bless you Norm, I am so pleased we met," and gave me another hug, Pauline had a tear in her eye as we walked to the subway.

On our way home Pauline said "I think Tom was really taken with you Norm!"

I admired him, he knew perfectly well that he stood out in a crowd and some people rudely stared at him, but he had the balls (literally) to do his own thing, in style with his head held high, and I really liked him.

I said to Pauline "When I saw him this morning I was really embarrassed!"

"Oh Norm that is not a nice thing to say about Tom, I am surprised at you."

"No I was embarrassed that he saw me in the same shirt I was wearing last night in the theatre you said it would do me for another day! After the trouble Tom had obviously taken with his appearance I felt I had let him down, I should have put a fresh shirt on!"

Pauline had the last word on the subject "I do not think our village is quite ready for someone like Tom, do you Norm?"

Actually I did once dress up as a lady several years ago and all because of my eldest stepdaughter Elaine. She and her mum are part of a team involved in running our local village line dancing club, which incidentally have raised over fifty thousand pounds over the years for local charities, and every Christmas party have a friend dressed up as Father Xmas handing out the presents to the members. This routine our Elaine thought was becoming a little boring and predictable, so between her and Pauline hatched up a special Christmas surprise. This particular year a spectacular event would occur involving myself dressed up as 'Hayley Cropper' star of the soap series Coronation Street, and at great expense, my fee being a couple of sausage rolls from the buffet, was going to present the gifts to the club members at the annual Christmas party.

This had to be done in great secrecy and was only being announced on the big party night itself, when they would all be getting ready to moan about the same old routine of Linda dressed as Father Xmas. I was very reluctant to agree but the two girls were very persuasive and it takes a brave man to say no to these two. Pauline assured me that after a couple of hour's makeover I would be mistaken for Hayley Cropper by her own cast members and nobody in our village would know it was me. Pauline bought me a wig from Blackpool and an array of clothes similar to what Hayley wore, including bra, handbag and jewellery. I became worried all this was a step too far and Pauline seemed to be getting a little carried away with my impersonation. The shoes were a problem and Pauline settled for me wearing leather open toed sandals, no 'Jimmy Choo' shoes for me. Pauline shaved my hairy legs below the knees and applied fake tan, what really freaked me out was the large makeup bag that suddenly appeared.

"Jesus is this really necessary Pauline, what if one of the grandchildren calls unexpectedly and sees us; it could mentally scar them for life!" I said.

"Stop your moaning Norm if you want to remain incognito you must have the full makeup, eye shadow, mascara, blusher and lipstick, leave it to me you will look lovely on the night!"

After what seemed to take hours she placed various items of jewellery around my neck, a gold ladies watch replaced my macho divers watch and finally I was informed that the transformation was complete, only a little more padding to be added under my bra. Leading me to a full length mirror I saw what I now looked like, and I said in dismay "I look just like Hayley Cropper Pauline."

"That is exactly who you are suppose to look like you idiot, what seems to be your problem, I think you look fantastic!" she said.

"I rather thought that you would make me more like 'Marilyn Monroe' I look a right plain Jane sort of a girl."

"I cannot make a silk purse out of a sow's ear Norm, so stop the whining, nobody will ever know that it is you in drag!" she said laughing, and crossing her fingers.

The plan was Pauline would get herself ready and go to the party at six pm and sneak out of the club at nine pm and pick me up, I was to wait at the club's emergency exit until Elaine let me inside. This left me three hours at home sitting in full ladies wear praying that nobody would call at the front door, or worse still any of our family who had a door key let themselves in and caught me in drag. The time seemed to crawl by and my nerves were in tatters, I felt as nervous as a turkey at Xmas, the doorbell rang twice but it could have been Jehovah's Witnesses, Mormon's or anybody, I was not going to answer the front door to anyone!

Finally Pauline arrived back home to collect me, I was ready to cancel the night and beginning to realise what a great responsibility I had taken on, how the hell was I going to entertain a room full of women revellers? Walking down our drive to the car the snow had settled a couple of inches deep, Nick our next door neighbour walked past and said "Have a lovely evening ladies, it is snowing heavier now be careful driving, the roads will be treacherous tonight." Pauline loved this and I vowed to never volunteer for a stunt like this ever again. Getting out of the car into the deep snow on the car park made my feet icy cold and numb, I said to Pauline "Tell our Elaine to hurry up and open the door it is bloody freezing out here." I stood nervously swinging my handbag from side to side; amazingly I was beginning to act the part already. It was still snowing and I could see a man smoking a cigarette at the main entrance to the club staring towards me. Oh hell he started to walk over to me, he said "Hello my lovely what are you doing waiting outside on a freezing night like this, you will catch your death of cold!" Knowing who he was, if he realised it was me he would drag all his drinking buddies into the party from the bar to make my life even more miserable tonight than it already was. So I told him in a rather high pitched voice that I was the surprise act from Manchester booked for the Askam line dancer's private party. Thank heavens he did not recognise me without my glasses on, they were safe inside my handbag and the locals would not ever know who I was without me wearing them. The downside was my being blind as a bat without them on.

My new admirer said "I have had a couple of drinks but seem to know your face my lovely, here put my jacket around your shoulders you must feel perished!"

He proceeded to whisper sweet nothings to me and I thought his chat up lines needed to improve urgently if he was ever to succeed with a girl of my high standards! I had to remove his hand a couple of times from my bottom and just before slapping his face, he produced a card with his mobile number on it, telling me to phone him after my show finished.

"We can go on to a nightclub I know in Barrow afterwards darling, I will be in the bar waiting for your call, we can get a taxi," he managed to slur.

Knowing that his wife might have something to say about all this if she found out I just laughed. I was literally saved by the bell; our Elaine appeared at last and took one look at 'Dave' standing with his arm around my waist, his jacket draped around my shoulders and broke down laughing. Handing back his jacket I dashed into the warmth of the club stamping my feet vigorously to get my circulation going again, my legs being blue with the cold. 'Dave' staggered back to the bar no doubt expecting a phone call later.

Our Elaine said "I cannot believe what a good job my mum's done on your make over Norm; nobody is going to guess who it is, hide behind the curtains until I announce you, and be careful of the stage you are blind without your glasses on. Linda will carry the heavy bag of presents for you, hand out one for each person and spend some time at each table telling jokes and making them laugh!"

So not only did she want a female impersonator of a famous soap star but a bloody comedian as well, and I noticed there was bugger all left of the buffet, they must have been like a swarm of locust. I should have done a runner ages ago thinking that my unrehearsed act was going to go down like the proverbial lead balloon. I was announced by Linda as the fabulous "Star of the famous soap series Coronation Street bought to Askam at great expense all the way from Manchester, and already been molested by a local well known local man who shall remain anonymous, unless he buys us all a drink!"

To a thunderous applause Linda who was joining me as a double act announced the beautiful and talented Hayley Cropper! I strolled nervously onto the stage swinging my handbag (which was by now second nature, I would miss it tomorrow) and promptly fell off the edge of the stage. Cries of "She is bloody drunk, this is disgraceful and how much money is this Hayley charging us for appearing in this state?"

Well this bought the house down everyone was in hysterics, Linda was priceless and we did make a brilliant double act. Nobody could guess who I was they had no idea, thanks to Pauline's clever make over, they just thought it was somebody who had a hard life. When all the ladies found out it was me they all wanted a photograph taken with me, to show in the post office and Co-op no doubt, I would have to avoid entering the village for a couple of days. Everybody seemed to have had a great Xmas party and a good laugh which it was all about. I must admit wearing ladies clothing made me feel very uncomfortable, and when asked to do another guest appearance as Hayley Cropper at a local women's institute my answer was not printable!

CHAPTER THIRTY FIVE

THE ROYAL PHOTOGRAPHIC SOCIETY

Looking at my collection of photographs taken in Kenya I thought they looked pretty decent, I wondered if they would be worth sending in to the Royal Photographic Society for assessment. Or would I be seen to be presumptuous and told in no uncertain terms to stop wasting their time, and to please join a camera club. As usual Pauline encouraged me to apply for a Licentiate and send off the fee and apply for tickets to go to their Bath headquarters to be assessed. You needed to send ten enlarged photographs on a white card back ground; and you will be assessed by a distinguished panel of judges. The auditorium held a large gathering of potential critics and if I passed (it would be a miracle I thought) it would entitle me to put LRPS after my name. We decided to travel to the beautiful city of Bath by hiring a canal boat and make it into a week's holiday. Never having visited this wonderful city we were astonished by the fantastic architecture, and the roman bath house, and being able to moor our hire boat right in the centre of Bath. The whole canal journey was through lovely countryside, and the only thing that spoilt our little trip was the thought of my photography skills being laughed at by these eminent judges. I was regretting coming in person after all and wishing I had just posted them, and receiving the comments by post.

Arriving in good time to look around this special centre of photography excellence I was impressed by the atmosphere and the photo museum. Sitting in the cafe listening to other excited people wondering if their particular photo displays were going to pass muster, I again questioned myself of the arrogance I was showing by thinking my photo's were good enough to be shown here in this world famous home of photography. I said to Pauline "This is not a good idea, I feel more comfortable in a storm at sea, and my hands are shaking."

Then it was time to file into the hall and not surprisingly every seat was taken except the two left for us. Having not ever visited the world famous Royal Photographic Society before we were looking forward to seeing what exactly happens on these assessment days. When it is your turn to be judged the photo's are arranged on a special stand, ten in my case for a 'Licentiate' these are respectfully placed in order, by an assistant wearing white gloves. The afternoon was passing very slowly I thought, some people passed and some did not. The judge gave honest criticism for each applicant I thought, if he judged that the applicant needed to go away and start afresh, he said so. One or two took his advice badly I thought, and the ones who passed sometimes got an ovation. Of course not everyone who sent in photo's managed to be there on the big day, and would be notified by post in due course, which is what I should have done.

As the afternoon wore on, my nerves were going into overdrive, I kept whispering to Pauline different scenarios of why my photos were not being shown. They went from maybe they have been lost in the post, to the judges keeping them until last to show as an example of how stupid people are by not joining a proper photography club.

The judging was coming to a close, mine must be the last one's to be shown, I was having a bit of a panic attack, and Pauline looked really worried. My hands were sweating and I felt like leaving the room, before I was verbally torn to shreds. I recognised my enlargements being carried onto the well lit stage, first the full head shot of a zebra, and then male lion lying across a dusty track, two elephants fighting, they all certainly looked presentable from a distance. The main judge said "Last but not least! A selection of animal pictures from Norman Pascoe taken in Kenya, he informs me that he is entirely self taught and never joined any clubs," he said laughing.

"That is sometimes a good thing in my opinion, and in Norman Pascoe's case I find that his selection of photographs far exceeds the standard required for a 'Licentiate' congratulations Norman, and I would ask for a round of applause for this man".

Well you could have knocked me down with a feather, Pauline had tears in her eyes and I needed to get back to the boat to have a lie down, I was in shock. A humble lad from Glasgow Street who left school with no qualifications had finally received something to be proud of, and to think I learned the trade by trial and error, thus enabling me to put LRPS after my name. This trip to RPS at Bath gave me the confidence to enter more competitions, and my photograph of three sheep crossing over a stone bridge in snow, was picked by our local hospice to be on their Christmas card and sold many copies. This charity was very dear to me and I know how hard it is to keep it going financially.

We sent our new friends Richard and Trish copies of all our safari photos and he said he loved them. Richard phoned us one night saying that he had bought us tickets for 'Beauty and the Beast' showing at the west end in London, saying it was to repay us for our kindness with the photos. He said for us to meet them at a small family owned classy hotel in Baker Street in London. We travelled from Cumbria by train and took a taxi to our hotel, where we found Richard had already booked us in. Afternoon tea awaited us and we had a lovely catch up before a taxi picked us up for the theatre. The show was fantastic, and we did not tell Richard that this was the fourth time we had seen the show in London. We had to take all the grandchildren in three batches because of the price; we had to save up between trips to pay for it. We wanted to pay for the best seats so that the children had the best views after travelling all that distance, also to encourage them to enjoy live theatre for the first time. Sitting in this very posh hotel lounge later that night talking about this and that, Richard had some photos in his wallet most were of his beautiful cat but one showed him alone in the middle of a swimming pool. So straightaway I said he must have been on holiday out of season?

"Why do you say that Norm?" he said.

"The pool is empty except for you Richard."

"I am sorry Norm I do not understand what you mean."

"You must be on holiday at a quiet time in the season Richard, the bloody pool is empty."

He roared with laughter and finally said "I am so sorry you must think I am being rude, I am laughing at myself, how silly I am not to understand what you were meaning. It is my fault I should explain; the pool belongs to me and is in my house, you must come and visit us very soon, you are funny Norm!"

"Well in my world Richard, the only pool we had when I was a child growing up in Glasgow Street was a zinc one, it hung on a nail in our back yard and once a week on a Sunday night, nine of us queued up to use it," I replied. The evening meal we had in this lovely hotel that night amazed me; two of us had Dover sole the other two had Bass. Looking at the tiny portion each on our plates, I could not help saying to Richard that in my freezer at home it is packed with Dover sole, Bass, Salmon and rather large lobsters that our Tony keeps bringing home. When Richard next visited us at our house he would be served the full fresh fish and not disguised with a load of sauce. We visited our friends later on and had a wonderful time at their lovely home, taking them some fresh fish of course. In Richards library was a shelf of over sixty books he had written over the years, he had told me that he was a retired author, and I did not realise that he was such a prolific author. They both visited us and were driven to our house by their two American friends who were on vacation from their home in Florida. They absolutely loved our beautiful little cottage and its secluded location. I took them all out on the sands picking cockles and showing them all the different species of sea life in the rock pools, also trips into our beautiful Lake District. Richard persuaded us to travel to Florida to stay with their American friend's for a month; they lived near Disney World and chauffeured us around for the full month visiting everywhere in Florida. All the many Americans we met were utterly charming people and so friendly and welcoming towards us. Back in the United Kingdom staying at Richard's house before the long drive home to Cumbria, I found out by accident that we had been on holiday with a Lord and Lady after seeing a newspaper clipping of their wedding day, which was attended by some very high profile dignitaries. I asked him why he had not mentioned about being a Lord and he said "It is not anything that I am particularly proud of Norm." And that was the end of it. We cherished our friendship with Richard and Trish and loved to listen about all his wonderful experiences he had, when travelling all over the world. When Richard passed away he left a great hole in our lives, but we were privileged to have met one of life's truly great gentlemen.

CHAPTER THIRTY SIX

ENDANGERED NATTERJACK TOADS

We were lucky to live on a site of Special Scientific Interest and a prime stronghold of the endangered natterjack toads, their scrapes in the marsh and dune areas around Dunnerholme were used to lay their strings of eggs. The mating call can be heard on a still night for a mile or so distance, it was a lovely sound to hear from our cottage door. Leaving the cottage doors open could give you a shock, whilst watching television on several occasions and seeing an adult natterjack toad running across our lounge carpet, they do not hop like frogs but can run quite fast. We found them wandering inside the house, and the gardens, we had to be very careful walking outside in the dark to fetch a bucket of coal into the house. We had to shine the torch on the path in front of us at all times. Nobody is allowed to touch them without a special licence, of which we were supplied having to pick them up to remove from our cottage and garden, the penalties for harming them are severe.

We involved the grandchildren in recording sightings and counting the strings they lay each year in the different scrapes and ponds. The toads are in severe danger and becoming rarer each year, they seem to have all the odds stacked against their survival. Common toads and frogs take over their ponds, and natterjacks breed later so if the rainfall comes a bit late the ponds may already have dried out, leaving their masses of tadpoles to dry out. Their scrapes sometimes have so little water in them that, black birds, crows, magpies, and herons feast on them when they are congregated in thick swarms of tadpoles in the shallow puddles left. The grandchildren loved to carry a bucket of water from a deep pond with no toads in, and trickle the water in gently to save the tadpoles drying out and dying. Sometimes one bucket of water was enough to save a full scrape full of tadpoles until the rain came again to top them up again. This gave the children a good feeling knowing that they made some difference to the Dunnerholme natterjack population in a small way. They filled in an official record of how many were calling on every day, and counted the strings, the first calls came usually at the start of April. They noted which scrapes were used each year, temperature and rainfall. At the end of the season sent the report in to the Herbilogical Society in Bournemouth. Many natterjacks must get drowned in the occasional storm surges that inundate our estuary and marshland.

The children's lives were enriched at Dunnerholme, they were learning about all the sea life and varied bird life, the animal species, picking berries and mushrooms, learning conservation, and having the adventures they would never forget. That was the magic of Dunnerholme always something different happening. The time came when I had little choice but to part with my beloved cottage. One morning Pauline fell ill with severe breathing difficulties, I called a doctor and he called out an ambulance straight away. The ambulance arrived and placed Pauline in the back of the vehicle with an oxygen mask on to help her breathing, the paramedic said it was a heart problem. They went as fast as possible along our rutted road, and when we reached Furness General hospital the ambulance driver advised me to move house, our rough track had just about wrecked his vehicle, and the paramedic said that he had a terrible job keeping the oxygen mask on Pauline's face.

That settled things for me and thinking that it could happen again I reluctantly put the house on the market, I already felt guilty about calling doctors out to such a remote place for me. All the children were upset but understood that their nana's needs came first. We had lots of viewings and even an offer from the estate agent wanting to use it for renting to holiday makers. None of the people wanting to buy seemed to suit our cottage, and I thought too much of my two lovely neighbours to let it go to anyone. Something told me that the perfect people would come along. One beautiful sunny morning the estate agent phoned and said could this couple call straightaway for a viewing, we said of course. This lovely couple called at the open front door and when they stepped in, a lone swallow swept inches above their head, turned around in the lounge and flew out again. The lady was called Gleny's and her husband Dave, she was enchanted with the cottage I could tell straightaway that she was going to buy the cottage, it seemed to suit her. They told us over fresh scones and coffee that they lived on the outskirts of Manchester and were searching for a holiday home. They said they had looked at a hell of a lot of properties and were particular about the type of cottage they required. Dave said they would go away and think about it, then shook hands and left, promising to let us know their decision soon.

I knew that lone swallow was a good omen, ten minutes later an excited Gleny's was entering the cottage and telling us she was having it; she had fallen in love with our cottage. We left just about everything in the cottage for them, furniture and horse brasses so they could start using it straightaway as their holiday home, like the kind people before us did. We bought a bungalow in the nearby Ireleth village near to where all our children lived; we could still see our beloved cottage from our conservatory window. Dave and Gleny's appreciated how much I missed our cottage and would not let me give my key back saying you can always pop in and make yourself a drink whenever you like. I keep an eye on the place on the rare occasions when they cannot be there. They have become our best friends and the fitting owners of Dunnerholme cottage, and have as much fun as we did, with their grandchildren and the magical pirate cave.

Life of course has changed again in very many ways after leaving our cottage and luckily I was shown a fisherman's website, this is dedicated to all things maritime, and it is free to join. If anybody has photographs old or new to post they are shared enthusiastically by people all over the world. It has taken me a few years to download over seven thousand of my photos onto this site, but well worth it, up to date I have had nearly four million hits on my photos alone! This hugely popular site is called 'trawler photos' and is about anything concerned with the sea, sea creatures, birds, coastal scenery, and of course boats, and it is free. My wife pointed out that it is a safe place to put them because after I pass over the bar they might have been thrown away into the bin. I still do the odd photograph competition, but mostly spend my free time writing or having the great grandchildren visiting.

I wrote a book called 'A Boy from Glasgow Street' which is the first part of my story and the proceeds go to our local Duddon Inshore Rescue lifeboat, this boat is totally funded by local people and as saved many lives since being started in 1969. The first edition sold out and a reprint had to be ordered from York Publishers, the book featured in the Evening Mail, Westmorland Gazette, and Cumbria Radio invited me onto their 'My Life' daily program for two weeks of talk about my life, very scary but rewarding. The best selling 'Fishing News' kindly did a brilliant article, the world famous 'FAFB' site gave me valuable free advertising space for one full year. Also the book featured on our very own 'trawler photos' web site, so you can see how kind people have been to me. Our local village post office is run by a lovely man called 'Pav', who stocked my book, and nearly everybody in our village has read it, we all support each other. I hope you have enjoyed reading this final book of my life story, I certainly enjoyed writing it. We will always miss our adventures at Dunnerholme a truly magical place, I still have my key to the cottage and can still take our great grandchildren down to visit accompanied by their parents. Lots of the fine characters that were our neighbours have passed on but the place stays the same, the cycle continues, the children take over the farms.

This book to be published this summer 2015 is the second part of my autobiography, it has taken two books to fit it all in. The first book is about growing up in a large poor family in a tiny Victorian terrace in the ship building town of Barrow-in-Furness in the 1950's. Life was extremely hard and we children always hungry, but we had an enormous adventure playground on our very own doorstep. Miles of beaches and estuary's where an abundance of cockles, mussels, winkles, crabs and fish could be harvested. Sprawling docks where other gangs of children roamed freely, totally unsupervised by adults. I grew up to buy my own boats to fish the deadly waters of Morecambe bay and the Irish Sea, all the adventures I had, salvaging a sunken trawler, rescuing the crew of a stricken coaster in a howling gale, and many other tales are in my first book.

Both books are for sale on Amazon Kindle/paperback www.ypdbooks. com and Waterstones Barrow, Heaths and Barrow Dock Museum and in all good bookshops. A donation from each of my books goes to our village lifeboat so thanks again for your support.

I hope you have enjoyed reading this final book of my life story and have had a few chuckles. I have enjoyed writing both books immensely, and particularly loved being contacted by so many interesting people from my past and strangers from all over the world; I have been well and truly blessed in so many ways.